THE LOCAVORE'S DILEMMA

THE
LOCAVORE'S
DILEMMA

IN PRAISE OF THE 10,000-MILE DIET

Pierre
DESROCHERS

Hiroko
SHIMIZU

PUBLICAFFAIRS

New York

PublicAffairs books are available at special discounts for bulk purchases in
the U.S. by corporations, institutions, and other organizations. For more
information, please contact the Special Markets Department at the Perseus
Books Group, 2300 Chestnut Street, Suite 200, Philadelphia, PA 19103, call
(800) 810-4145, ext. 5000, or e-mail special.markets@perseusbooks.com.

Library of Congress Cataloging-in-Publication Data
Desrochers, Pierre, 1969-
    The locavore's dilemma : in praise of the 10,000-mile diet /
Pierre Desrochers and Hiroko Shimizu. — 1st ed.
        p.   cm.
    Includes bibliographical references and index.
    ISBN 978-1-58648-940-3 (hardcover) —
ISBN 978-1-58648-941-0 (e-book))
    1. Produce trade.   2. Local foods.   3. Food supply—Economic
aspects.   4. Food supply—Social aspects.   5. Food—Transportation.
6. Transportation—Environmental aspects.   I. Shimizu, Hiroko, 1965-
II. Title.
    HD9000.5.D446 2012
    338.1'9—dc23

                                                    2012001263

First Edition
10 9 8 7 6 5 4 3 2 1

To Ferenc ("Ferko") Csillag (1955–2005),
dear friend and mentor.
You are sorely missed.

[T]he time has arrived . . . when the various portions of the earth will each give forth their products for the use of each and of all; that the over-abundance of one country will make up for the deficiency of another; the superabundance of the year of plenty serving for the scant harvests of its successor . . . Climate, seasons, plenty, scarcity, distance, will all shake hands, and out of the commingling will come enough for all . . . God provides enough and to spare for every creature He sends into the world; but the conditions are often not in accord. Where the food is, the people are not; and where the people are, the food is not. It is, however . . . within the power of man to adjust these things . . .

—THOMAS SUTCLIFFE MORT, Speech delivered on September 2, 1875, Lithgow Valley Works (Australia). Quoted in "Mort, Thomas Sutcliffe (1816–1878)" in David Blair. 1881. *Cyclopaedia of Australasia.* Fergusson and Moore, Printers and Publishers, pp. 245–247, p. 247.

Experience keeps constantly adding to our knowledge of the special advantages of each locality, and every free movement of trade and industry increases the sum of their usefulness to the human race. Scarcity of food can no longer exist among nations that have kept abreast of this economical revolution . . . Those who doubt the advantages of this universal, world-wide intercourse and exchange are bound in consistency to advocate the reversion of society not merely to any earlier stage in its development, but to that state of things which preceded its initiation—that is, to pure and simple cannibal-ism; for an argument that is good against one step in this march of progress is equally good against another.

—J. J. MENZIES. 1890. "The Localization of Industries." *The Popular Science Monthly* 36 (February): 454–460, p. 455.

CONTENTS

ACKNOWLEDGMENTS

—————

Best-selling nonfiction books typically discuss the lives of interesting people, relationships, sex, soul searching, societal and environmental collapse, babies, cats, and food. While this book does address the last of these topics, we fell short in terms of providing memorable recipes, miracle weight loss cures, and shocking exposés of mad scientists playing God with our groceries. Even worse, we did our best to slaughter as many sacred cows in the food activists' intellectual herd as we could. And, perhaps worst of all, we are reasonably optimistic about the future! Our first thanks must therefore go to our publisher, PublicAffairs, for taking a chance on two unknown authors during troubled economic times and for giving us the opportunity to work with a seasoned editor, Mindy Werner.

As we explain in our preface, the chain of events that ultimately resulted in this book was somewhat fortuitous. Truth be told, we would have been more hesitant to write our first policy paper on the local food movement without the assurance that we would benefit from the advice and support of our good friend Andrew Reed, who worked for a few decades and in various capacities in the agri-business sector. Andrew once again read the whole manuscript of this book and provided much valuable feedback. Other individuals who shared their knowledge of agriculture with us include, most prominently, Dennis Avery, Gary Blumenthal, E. C. Pasour, and P. J. Hill. Thanks also to Blake Hurst for not only writing the foreword to our book, but for the chuckles he gave us through his other writings. Of course, none of them should be held accountable for errors and omissions in our manuscript.

Work on this project began at Duke University's Center for the History of Political Economy where we were both hosted for a semester by Professor Bruce Caldwell. Feedback on various portions of our draft was then provided by some of Pierre's colleagues in the department of geography at the University of Toronto Mississauga, namely Tom McIlwraith, Joseph Leydon, Monika Havelka, and François Ndayizigiye. None of them should be held accountable for the fact that we did not always heed their advice. Pierre's department is not only an intellectually diverse environment, but also one that truly lives up to the academic ideal, in no small part because of the man who was most influential in shaping it, the late Ferenc Csillag, to whom this book is dedicated.

FOREWORD

Pierre Desrochers and Hiroko Shimizu should not have had to write this book. In a more rational world, their defense of what is so clearly true would not be needed. History, theory, common sense, and the most cursory observation and thought about the subject of food and how and where we grow and buy it would lead most of us to the conclusions drawn by the authors. However, our world is not rational, and most of what passes for thinking about food is as full of air as an elegant French pastry. Hence, the need for this valuable contribution.

Desrochers and Shimizu take the idea of local food to the back of the barn and beat the holy livin' tar out of it. The idea of food miles will never again rear its ugly head in polite company, nor should we have to hear about how far farmers are from their consumers. Now, I've no doubt that food miles will continue to be mentioned, and farmers at farmers' markets will still have those little signs measuring how far their wares have traveled, but everybody will know it's just horse manure, in the same way that we know we won't get to take the prettiest girl home if we drink Bud Light. We Missouri farmers will still drink Bud Light, and I have no doubt that people will continue to patronize the Ferry Market in San Francisco, but one can hope those programmers and executives in Northern California will never again take local food marketing claims seriously. That's how important this book is.

According to surveys I've seen, only about 5% of the consuming public will pay more for local, organic, or sustainably grown food. That

statistic is no surprise to my wife and me. We grow vegetable starts and
flowers at our small greenhouse in rural Missouri. Our customers are
extremely price sensitive: the fact that we are local and employ local
people matters not a whit to our typical buyer. We survive by offering
the newest varieties of flowers at competitive prices. We've tried to carry
a line of heirloom tomatoes as well, but we've yet to have a repeat buyer.
People will read an article trumpeting the wonderful taste of German
Johnson or Brandywine tomatoes, buy a few, and lose them all to blight.
The next year, they ask for hybrids with blight resistance.

Now, other growers have had better experiences branding themselves
as local and selling traditional varieties. After all, our part of Missouri is
notably short on upscale, trendy consumers. We live in a farming community, where people are careful with their dollars. They typically grow
the latest and most technologically advanced hybrids on their farms,
and the thought of paying extra for a tomato variety that is more susceptible to disease and yields less strikes them as crazy.

If local food is just a lifestyle choice made by people with money
aplenty, and if the adherence to local food is the latest example of the
human need to preen, why should a book like this one need to be written? Why, indeed, should we care what Michael Pollan eats for lunch?

We should care because ideas have consequences. Many, many more
people will pledge allegiance to the local food movement than will actually pay a premium in price or inconvenience for local food. They'll
support politicians who pay fealty to the latest trends and complain
about conventional food to pollsters. Consumers and voters are willing
to show support for local food while letting others pay the bill for their
good intentions. The notions that the past was better, local is important,
technology should be feared, and trade is bad are powerful, and extremely dangerous.

After the January, 2010 earthquake in Haiti, the biotech company
Monsanto donated 475 tons of seed to Haitian farmers. Monsanto is
not known for being nimble in its relations with the public, but the
company made sure that none of the donated seed was genetically al-

tered. That gesture wasn't enough; protests quickly erupted all over Haiti and the U.S. You would have thought Monsanto was passing out free cigarettes to teenagers. "Peasant groups" in Haiti marched under banners of "Down with GMO and hybrid seeds." Hybridization has been around since Gregor Mendel experimented with peas in the 1850s. Hybrid crops have saved the lives of billions of hungry people. Farmers in the U.S. began adopting hybrid seeds in the 1920s, and hybrids have increased yields for every crop that lends itself to hybridization. Donating hybrid seeds is not exactly pushing the envelope of food or farming technology, but breeding and producing hybrid seed is a complicated process typically done by large firms and never by individual farmers. That was enough to set off the protests.

The Organic Consumers of America sent 10,000 emails damning Monsanto. Doudou Pierre, the "grassroots" National Coordinating Committee Member of the National Haitian Network for Food Sovereignty and Food Security, said: "We're for seeds that have never been touched by multinationals."[1] U.S. writer Beverly Bell explains: "The Haitian social movement's concern is not just about the dangers of chemicals and the possibility of future GMO imports. They claim that the future of Haiti depends on local production with local food for consumption, in what is called food sovereignty."[2] Church groups in the U.S. donated some 13,300 machetes and 9,200 hoes to, I guess, encourage traditional agriculture in Haiti. It's worth noting that defenders of "traditional agriculture" are usually several generations removed from its practice. The romance of swinging a hoe or a machete is largely lost on people who've actually spent some time on the business end of those "traditional" technologies.

One in four Haitians was hungry before the earthquake: local food for local people was and is sentencing Haitians to a life of misery, disease, and all too often death. The position of the groups protesting Monsanto's donation is that brown people should starve rather than plant seeds touched by the hands of multinationals. Desrochers and Shimizu write not because it matters what the residents of Berkeley or

the Hamptons eat, but because it matters that the residents of Haiti
don't eat. It is the worst kind of cultural imperialism for wealthy and
well-fed Americans to sentence their neighbors to a life of hunger and
machete swinging. Bad ideas can have terrible consequences, and hopefully this book will help to put some of those bad ideas to rest.

Only three countries in Africa allow the use of biotechnology because of the reluctance of international organizations to approve the
technology and the fact that the European Union will not buy most genetically modified products. While U.S. yields are increasing at 2% a
year and Asian yields have quadrupled over the past 50 years, African
yields haven't increased at all. There are many reasons for Africa's lagging
yields, but the refusal of most of the continent to adopt biotechnology
explains much of the disparity.

On my farm in Missouri, we use genetically modified seeds that control insects. African farmers have not had the opportunity to plant similar
genetically modified varieties, and can't afford insecticides. Consequently,
each year African farmers lose a large portion of their crops to insects.

Rice varieties genetically modified to prevent blindness have been
tied up in the regulatory equivalent of purgatory for 13 long years. The
Swiss biologist who invented the technology is furious, as well he should
be. The delay, according to him, has been "responsible for the death and
blindness of thousands of children and young mothers."[3]

African farmers are aware of what is happening to them, and they
aren't happy. Matthew Ridley, writing in the *Wall Street Journal:* "In
Uganda, where people often eat three times their body weight in bananas a year, a GM banana that is resistant to a bacterial wilt disease,
which causes $500 million in annual losses and cannot be treated with
pesticides, is being tested behind high security fences. The fences are
there not to keep out anti-GM protesters, as in the West, but to keep
out local farmers keen to grow the new crop."[4]

It's clear that something more than a debate about health and science
is going on here. The EU recently allowed the planting of a genetically
modified potato, and even though this tuber was intended for paper pro-

duction and not for human consumption, the Italian Agriculture minister protested, vowing to "defend and safeguard traditional agriculture and citizen's health." It is no coincidence that the mention of "traditional agriculture" was given precedence in the Minister's statement. The reluctance of much of the world to adopt biotechnology is not about the safety of the seed, but rather the preservation of "traditional agriculture" and what the Haitian protesters called food sovereignty. In large parts of the world, local trumps science, and people suffer as a result.

The Obama administration has had much to say about local food. The First Lady has planted a garden, organic, of course, and the Department of Agriculture is spending 50 million or so on a program called Know Your Farmer. The effort is likely to disappoint: in fact, a suburban housewife determined to know this corn farmer is likely to be mortified by my looks, the way I smell, and my opinions. I can't imagine why any resident of Manhattan would want to know me, and, trust me, some of my neighbors are even worse.

This is all right with us. There's a certain comfort that comes from never having to make a sales call. I raise #2 yellow corn, and it's worth no more or no less than any other farmer's corn. As a producer of commodity corn and soybeans, the fact that I'm wearing bib overalls and am the antithesis of charming doesn't affect my success at all. One of the assumptions implicit in all this local food stuff is that we farmers are dying to make a connection with our customers. In many cases, nothing could be further from the truth. All we want is to sell corn and be left alone.

Political leaders are telling farmers to grow and sell local, traditional, and even organic foods, and the culture and the intelligentsia are telling us much the same. As the authors point out, Michael Pollan is a rock star, and Oprah Winfrey spent a lot of time criticizing our present food system. Food Inc. was nominated for an Academy Award and has become part of the curriculum for an untold number of college courses. Everybody that matters advises me to find a farmers' market and set up a stall. I should concentrate on marketing directly to consumers, including computing the food miles I have to travel to reach that market.

Perhaps Community Supported Agriculture (CSA) would be just the thing—I'll arrive on your front porch once a month, with corn, soybeans, and maybe even a geranium or two.

There is a problem with this plan. "Think local" may be what the culture prescribes, but the market is sending a markedly different message. Farm income was up 28% in 2010, topping 100 billion dollars for the first time. There's no better way to make a farmer mad than to accuse him of making a profit, so please don't quote me, but many "industrial" farmers are thriving. Corn and soybean exports are booming; beef and pork exports are at record highs. It is a very good time to be a monoculture growing industrial farmer using genetically modified seeds. Come to find out, the world desperately needs what we industrial farmers produce, and doesn't seem to care very much how we raise it.

This is exactly the opposite of so much of what we read about farming. One of the mainstays of the literature on the corruption of our present food system is that we farmers are mere grit in the gears of the industrial food system, ground to nothing by the ring gear of corporate greed and the pinion gear of concentrated markets, ruthless advertisers, and a political system controlled by Big Food. Michael Pollan spends a few days with an Iowa corn farmer in one of the early chapters of *The Omnivore's Dilemma*. By the end of the chapter, I felt like sending the farmer a bus ticket to the nearest homeless shelter. The combination of monopolistic purchasers of his products, price gouging suppliers, and the general tendency of everyone in our economy to stick it to the small farmer made Pollan's aggie quite a sympathetic character. Except the book gives just enough information for me to estimate his income in the past year, and if he didn't make $150k in 2011, I'll eat my hat.

The long-term trend for food demand is up. The U.N estimates that we'll have to increase food production by about 70% by the year 2050 in order to keep pace with the expected worldwide growth in population and income. Increases in food production will undoubtedly occur where it's most efficient to produce that food, which is often not where the hungry people live. International trade will have to grow and grow rapidly. Food is destined to become less local, not more. This book makes the important and irrefutable case for why all these things are so, and marshals fact, quotation, and anecdote in a relentless march toward that inescapable conclusion.

The following beautifully written excerpt from Rod Dreher's book, *Crunchy Cons*, perfectly illustrates the idealized, romantic vision of farming that has captured the imagination of so many well-educated, high-income consumers:

> When you've seen the face of the woman who planted it, and shaken the hand of the man who harvested it, you become aware of the intimate human connection between you, the farmer, and the earth. To do so is to become aware of the radical giftedness of our lives… Learning the names of the small farmers, and coming to appreciate what they do is to reverse the sweeping process of alienation from the earth and from each other that the industrialized agriculture and mass production of foodstuffs has wrought.

It's almost impossible to read this passage without breaking into laughter if you've ever actually had to grow food, and deal with "the earth" in anything more than a metaphorical sense. Thanks to Pierre Desrochers and Hiroko Shimizu for helping bring some hard truths to the conversation about food. I hope their book is read far and wide.

–Blake Hurst
Tarkio, Missouri

Blake Hurst farms in Northwest Missouri with his family on a four-generation family farm. He and his wife Julie also own and operate a greenhouse business selling flowers in four states (Hurst Greenery http://www.hurstgreenery.com/). He is currently President of the Missouri Farm Bureau. His essays have appeared in *The American*, the *Wall Street Journal*, *Readers Digest*, *PERC Reports*, *The Wilson Quarterly*, and several other national and regional publications.

PREFACE

———

A few years ago, we attended a lecture by a distinguished environmental studies professor that was in large part a hymn to "locavorism." By producing an ever-increasing portion of our food supply closer to where we live, he argued, we would simultaneously heal the planet, create jobs, ensure a more reliable and nutritious food supply, and improve physical, spiritual, and societal health. Strangely, though, he did not address why the globalized food supply chain had developed the way it did in the first place, an omission that we—economic policy analysts who know a little bit about the history of famines and the economic rationale for international trade—found rather myopic.

Had the speaker limited his talk to questionable generalizations about food production and availability, we would have likely not felt the urge to issue a detailed rebuttal. At one point during his speech, however, he opined that Japan was the most "parasitical" society on Earth because of its unparalleled dependence on food imports. Suddenly, the discussion was getting personal, as one of us was born and raised near Tokyo. True, her people made their home on a few crowded islands whose limited agricultural potential is periodically subjected to natural disasters and therefore had no choice but to rely on others to help them obtain a decent diet. Were they to revert back to the insular self-sufficiency of their ancestors, present-day Japanese citizens would have to get by with minute quantities of rice, potatoes, sweet potatoes, buckwheat, and vegetables, and would periodically struggle with malnutrition, hunger and starvation.[1]

Fortunately, the Japanese people have had the opportunity in the relatively recent past to specialize in other types of economic activities and to trade whatever they produced for food grown elsewhere. As a result, they developed new technologies and products that increased living standards the world over and enjoyed a much more abundant, diverse, and affordable diet in the process. What was wrong with that? Should the Japanese people have instead committed hara-kiri on a societal scale because nature had denied them the prime agricultural land that Americans, Brazilians, New Zealanders, and Frenchmen have in abundance? Or perhaps the distinguished professor would rather deal with the military backlash that might ensue if Japan had its access to foreign resources curtailed? After all, in the early 20th century the proponents of Japan's imperialistic drive often justified their actions, such as taking over Manchuria in order to grow soybeans, by invoking the risks of relying on foreign food producers and the unwillingness of other nations to open up their markets to Japanese goods. As the old saying goes, if a man misses his meals one day, he will lie. If he misses his meals two days, he will steal. If he misses his meals three days, he will kill.

So, admittedly inspired by having been insulted, we took a closer look at locavorism. We learned that its main critics were, by and large, scholars based in engineering schools who had painstakingly documented why the movement's key concept of "food miles"—the distance food travels from the location where it is grown to the location where it is consumed—was a worthless measure by which to assess the environmental impact of agricultural production. Among other findings, they reported that transportation accounts for only approximately 2% of total American energy use. Moving things from farms to distant retail stores, it turns out, was only one-twentieth as significant in terms of overall environmental impact than other stages of food production, such as preparing the ground and planting seeds; mining, manufacturing and spraying fertilizers and pesticides; irrigating fields; harvesting, drying and preserving crops; and powering the necessary machinery. Producing food in the most suitable locations and then delivering it over long distances, especially by highly energy-efficient container ships, these scholars argued, made more environmental sense than growing vegetables or manufacturing dairy products in nearby locations that required energy-guzzling heated greenhouses, massive amounts of irrigation water, and large volumes of animal feed to make up for pastureland of poor quality.[2] More food for less money and reduced environmental impact—what wasn't to like about international trade?

Unable to counter the facts regarding food miles, committed "locavores" instead claimed broader economic, health, and security benefits for their prescription, but these struck us as old biological myths and economic and political fallacies. Yet, no one had systematically challenged the locavores' expanded rhetoric. With Japanese pride at stake, we set other projects aside and got to work on what we originally planned to be a brief policy memo on the subject.

Like everybody else, we came to the subject with a few preconceived opinions, such as a conviction that small subsistence farmers the world over should be given the opportunity to pursue whatever aspirations they might have, especially if these go beyond mere survival and back-breaking labor. Another was that in a system as complex as our modern economy, the law of unintended consequences often rears its ugly head and even derails the most well-intentioned interventions. We also had a few nagging questions, such as: Why had countless individuals worked so hard and for so long to create our globalized food supply chain if things were so great when most food was produced and consumed locally? And why did earlier generations of consumers so readily purchase items produced far from them? Looking for answers, we quickly realized that there was little in the policy agenda of the present generation of food activists that hadn't already been argued over, tried, and convincingly disproved many times.

Our short memo quickly turned into a more substantial piece of work that was published in the fall of 2008 by the Mercatus Center, a public policy think tank based at George Mason University in the Virginia suburbs of Washington, DC, where some researchers study the African agricultural exporters who have become the main victims of locavorism.[3] To our knowledge, it was the first, and remains the only, policy primer that succinctly addressed *all* the main arguments put forward by local food activists in recent years.[4] Because locavores roam over very large intellectual pastures, however, neither our supporting evidence nor our arguments were as broad and detailed as we wished them to be, but we thought our key facts and conclusions unassailable. Locavorism, we argued, is "at best, a marketing fad that frequently and severely distorts the environmental impacts of agricultural production." At worst, it constitutes "a dangerous distraction from the very real and serious issues that affect energy consumption, the environmental impact of modern food production, and the affordability of food." If pursued on a large scale, it would result in greater environmental damage, reduced economic growth, and significantly more food insecurity than is now the case. The road to agricultural, economic, environmental, and food safety and security hell, we concluded, was paved with allegedly fresher and more nutritious local meals.

To our delight, the piece received much attention in the Canadian media as well as press coverage in the United States, Latin America, and Europe. In time it would also be referred to in a number of policy papers and government reports. Even more amazing, much of this coverage was positive! Clearly, we weren't the only people who felt that locavorism was too simplistic a concept and that it created unnecessary anguish among grocery shoppers.

Our publication, in turn, led to numerous debates with local food activists. These experiences confirmed our prior impression that locavorism couldn't be dissociated from romantic beliefs about nature, food, rural life, and self-sufficiency that had been coupled with a profound disdain for the anonymity and profit-driven nature of long-distance trade and large corporations. Most locavores we encountered were quite taken aback that anyone might sincerely challenge their convictions that nature is inherently wholesome and that tampering with it can only result in catastrophe; that "happy peasants" should forever remain restricted to subsistence farming; that using vast amounts of synthetic pesticides and fertilizers for quick profit will kill the fertility of the land; that the nutrient-depleted and cancer/heart attack/diabetes/obesity-causing offerings of agribusiness kill more people every year than the shortage of synthetic fertilizer in sub-Saharan Africa;[5] that everything "local" by definition implies greater care and community benefits; that a shortage of usable energy resources is just around the corner; and that local soil (wherever it might be) has the surprisingly universal quality of being uniquely beneficial. Several locavores further argued that their physical and mental health had improved significantly after their adoption of a chemical-free/organic/vegan/local diet that supported nearby producers who had also become good friends. How dare we be opposed to all these good things and efforts to promote them?

Trained as economic policy analysts, we brought up statistics, contemporary case studies, historical parallels, discussions of standard research protocols, and some personal anecdotes. Especially frustrating was how quickly many activists resorted to challenging our motives rather than our arguments. We were told that we were in the remunerated service of agribusiness, Big Oil, the logistics industry, and even the New Zealand government. (Strangely, though, our mortgage debt is still significant.) Based on the volume of hateful correspondence sent our way, we sometimes felt that questioning the existence of God at a revival meeting would have elicited more measured and polite responses.

While we were pleased with our original policy paper, we felt the need to spell out our case in more detail in order to counter the broader intellectual underpinnings of locavorism; hence, this book. Although our discussion is anchored in one particular controversy, we cannot avoid taking sides in the current culture war over modern farming. As the late agricultural economist Bruce Gardner summed it up, the basic facts about American agriculture over the past century are not really in question, but they have paved the way to two bitterly opposed sets of interpretations by equally well-meaning individuals. In the left corner, the farm sector is viewed as "a chronically troubled place, with farmers typically hard pressed to survive economically and continually decreasing in number." Modern farming technologies are "environmentally suspect," farm laborers "exploited" and the wealth farming generates "increasingly concentrated on relatively few large farms" that benefit from "billions of dollars taxed from the general public." More optimistic analysts emphasize instead "the increased acreage and output of the average farm," the "sustained growth of agricultural productivity," and the "substantial improvements in income and wealth of commercial farmers, the predominant role of the United States in world commodity markets, and American leadership in supplying both technological innovation and food aid for the developing world."[6] In the international development arena, a similarly bitter divide exists between individuals who advocate large-scale commercial agriculture and the phasing out of smallholder farming as the only practical way to escape the poverty trap in which many countries are mired, and the anti-globalization activists who view all large-scale agriculture as a source of social inequality, a threat to the peasant way of life, and subordinating human needs to the profit motive.

Because our emphasis is on long-term trends rather than current difficulties and imperfect practices, our overall stance on most controversial issues is typically of the "glass half-full" type. We do not deny the severity of many agricultural and social problems, most importantly that, according to official statistics, around one billion individuals are still malnourished and therefore less productive and more prone to disease, poor health, stunting, and wasting than they would otherwise be.[7] This being said, the available evidence convincingly demonstrates that long distance trade and modern technologies have resulted in much greater food availability, lower prices, improved health, and reduced environmental damage than if they had never materialized. Indeed, more trade and ever improving technologies remain to this day the only *proven* ways to lift large numbers of people out of rural poverty and malnutrition. To revert to former practices can only deliver the world of yesterday, exemplified in the poorest sections of our planet today with its attendant widespread misery, malnutrition, hunger, and famine.

To tell you a little bit about ourselves: One of us was born in the greater Tokyo area and spent most of her life in other big cities, including Zhengzhou (China), Kyoto and Osaka (Japan), Baltimore (United States), and Montreal and Toronto (Canada). Trained in history, economics, and public policy, she has visited about a third of our planet for both professional and personal reasons. She is also "wise" enough to remember a time when bananas were expensive in Japan (and something that you would only be given when you were sick) and shrimp was a luxury item that would mainly be consumed in a special New Year's Eve dish called *osechi*. She eventually married a French Canadian and spent the better part of the last decade in the Greater Toronto Area (GTA), one of the world's most cosmopolitan urban agglomerations. To this day, her favorite thing about the GTA is the true cornucopia of culinary opportunities it offers, from Portuguese bakeries and Polish meat shops to vegetarian Indian restaurants and giant Chinese supermarkets. Living close to the Niagara peninsula, she also enjoys the local farmers' markets for a short period of time each year, but never quite understood why she should be made to feel guilty about being an unabashed "globavore" and having the opportunity to enjoy the best our planet has to offer.

The other member of this writing duo is a French-Canadian raised in a rural village in the Saint Lawrence Valley, an agricultural area of Quebec characterized by fertile soils and abundant water, but also a rather harsh climate. He held a number of low-level agricultural jobs in his youth (including a short stint working for the Quebec Farmers' Union), formally studied agricultural trade barriers and is now gainfully employed as an economic geographer, a small academic sub-discipline whose practitioners are given incredible latitude to consider subjects such as business location decisions, transportation and energy systems, regional economic growth, and a range of related topics. A few years ago he was convinced that the remainder of his career would be devoted to studying urban and industrial problems—but then he never planned to marry a Japanese city girl either . . .

Our goal in writing this book was to redress the one-sidedness of current discussions on locavorism. We make no bones about the fact that what we present is our personal take on several complex issues. To the open-minded locavores who are still with us, be assured that our conclusion that a balanced diet includes a healthy portion of foods grown far away from your favorite farmers' market is entirely derived from our research and best judgment. By all means, let us know where you think we went wrong in matters of economic logic and factual arguments. We look forward to answering your challenge.

Kampai!
À votre santé!
Rockwood, Ontario

INTRODUCTION

SOLE Food

Again and again I hear leading men of our state condemning now the unfruitfulness of the soil, now the inclemency of the climate for some seasons past, as harmful to crops; and some I hear reconciling the aforesaid complaints, as if on well-founded reasoning, on the ground that, in their opinion, the soil was worn out and exhausted by the overproduction of earlier days and can no longer furnish sustenance to mortals with its old time benevolence.

—LUCIUS JUNIUS MODERATUS COLUMELLA
De Re Rustica (On Agriculture), approximately 65 AD.[1]

In the early 1970s, a young New York City chef enrolled in the French Literature Ph.D. program of Columbia University, in the hope of eventually moving into the more respectable halls of academia. Things turned sour when he suggested a rather unusual dissertation topic: the history of French food as revealed through the writings of some of the country's literary giants, such as Ronsard, Proust, Voltaire, Zola, and Balzac. His would-be adviser shot down the proposal on the grounds that food was too trivial a subject to serve as the basis of a dissertation. Fortunately for America, Jacques Pépin had by then already decided to give up on academia and return to the kitchen.[2]

What a difference a few decades make! Food history, production, and policy are now the bread and butter of numerous professors of social and cultural studies and rapidly expanding cohorts of graduate students. Policy analysts and essayists write reams on food security and sustainability, and some prominent practitioners of this genre, the premier example being journalism professor Michael Pollan,[3] have become intellectual rock stars.

In an age where in the United States both lawyers and prison inmates outnumber full-time farmers, working to familiarize urbanites with some of the intricacies of modern food production and politics is a valuable endeavor.[4] Unfortunately, a lot of recent scholarship and the smorgasbord of television reports, magazine cover stories, popular books, and shock documentaries it has inspired are largely built on older and more questionable muckraking, populist, protectionist, pastoral nostalgia, "small is beautiful" and "vitalist"[5] traditions. The result is a one-sided narrative that decries our industrial food system as being rotten to the core without acknowledging some of its very tangible benefits when compared to older practices. To give but one illustration, a professor at a well-respected American university proudly states that his course "Food: A Critical Geography" does "not attempt to provide 'both sides' of the food system story" as his students are allegedly being "inundated" with the corporate perspective on a daily basis, often "without being aware of it." Those who would like to hear or feel something different can simply "turn on the TV, go to the supermarket, or eat at McDonald's!"[6]

Sure, Pollan and his disciples grudgingly admit, thanks to large firms and technical advances "edible foodlike substances" and "nutritional simulacra" are now more abundant, consistent, convenient, and (much) cheaper than ever before. But look at the downside. Food, "something that nourishes people and provides them with secure livelihoods," has been transformed into a "commodity for speculation and bargaining."[7]

"Hungry for profit" agribusiness has created a "globesity pandemic" because "stuffed but starved" children of the corn and their fossil-fuel fed parents ingest chemical residue-ridden processed meat, grains, fruits, and vegetables that have the taste, consistency, and nutritional value of cardboard. Dangerously unstable monocultures (the practice of growing a single crop over a large area) created through carpet bombing the soil with harsh chemicals and the depletion of aquifers are triggering massive erosion while drastically reducing biodiversity. Animals pumped full of antibiotics are raised in cramped quarters that breed super bacteria. Migrant farm workers are paid slave wages to toil in a chemical stew that freely seeps into nature where it triggers all kinds of dangerous mutations. And, unlike supermarkets, which only care about making money, local family farmers feed local people first. Then there are the concerns about bovine spongiform encephalopathy (BSE), salmonella, *E. coli*, mercury, superweeds and superbugs, terminator genes, soaring cancer rates, food safety crises, foreign oil dependence, increased greenhouse gas emissions, declining rural communities, marine dead zones, and neo-colonial land grabs in poor countries. . . . As activists see it, our modern-day genetically-modified "corn-utopia" is soaking up a rapidly vanishing petroleum pool while delivering junk food, rural poverty, and agricultural pollution.

The path out of this agricultural wasteland, we are told, boils down to consumers paying more and eating less, a wholesale rethinking of the way everything is done from "plough to plate," and promoting regional food economies both in America and around the world.[8] Crucial steps in this respect involve a carbon-fuel detoxification diet and a radical reduction, if not an outright ban, on the consumption of meat products and foreign food. Ultimately, corporate agriculture must be put to death by thousands of sustainable, organic, local, and ethical (SOLE)[9] food initiatives whereby increasingly self-reliant communities escape from the grips of the "Monsatans" of this world through their support of small-scale rural operations and the conversion of suburban crabgrass wasteland and urban rooftops into edible bounty. While this "Delicious

Revolution" may add a few digits to our collective grocery bill, more sustainable practices, increased quality and safety of food, healthier bodies, and improved spiritual well-being make it worthwhile.[10]

From our perspective, the most fascinating aspect of the SOLE narrative is how quickly it displaced once widespread fears about the imminent detonation of the (over)population bomb. After all, it was less than five decades ago that Harry Harrison published his dystopian novel *Make Room! Make Room!* (the inspiration behind the 1973 movie *Soylent Green*), in which food shortages were addressed through covert cannibalism. In a world where no good deed goes unpunished, the individuals who actually defused the P-bomb[11]—from large scale farmers, professional plant breeders, and manufacturers of synthetic pesticides and fertilizers to agricultural equipment and packaging manufacturers, commodity traders, and logistics industry workers—became increasingly demonized as poor stewards of the Earth and public health threats. The nature of the foodstuffs being supplied, rather than their potential shortages, became the new focus for food activism in advanced economies.

Of the four SOLE components, "local"[12]—the idea that an ever-growing portion of our food supply should be produced in close physical proximity to the consumers who will eat it—has made the greatest gain in popularity in the last two decades and is now, not surprisingly, being endorsed by influential political figures such as the U.S. Secretary of Agriculture, Tom Vilsack, who stated:

> In a perfect world, everything that was sold, everything that was purchased and consumed would be local, so the economy would receive the benefit of that. But sometimes that stresses the capacity: the production capacity or the distribution capacity. Especially since we don't have yet a very sophisticated distribution system for locally grown food. One thing we can do is work on strategies to make that happen. It can be grant programs, loan programs, it can be technical assistance.[13]

In December 2010, President Obama signed into law the Healthy, Hunger-Free Kids Act, which contained a provision to bolster farm-to-school programs through the government-subsidized National School Lunch, School Breakfast, Special Milk, Child and Adult Care, Fresh Fruit and Vegetable, and Summer Food Service programs. As a follow-up on this legislation, in April 2011, the United States Department of Agriculture (USDA) announced that it had introduced a new rule that will give preference in contract bidding for school meals to local farm products.[14] In November of that year, Senator Sherrod Brown and Congresswoman Chellie Pingree introduced the Local Farms, Food, and Jobs Act, a series of measures to support local farm programs worth approximately $200 million, intended to "increas[e] access to fresh, local foods" while "creating jobs and strengthening [local] econom[ies]. . . . Making it easier for farmers to sell food locally and easier for consumers to buy it translates directly into a more healthy economy and more jobs in our communities," Pingree said, adding that consumers "want to be able to buy fresh, healthy food that doesn't have to travel halfway around the world to get to them."[15]

There is, however, still no agreement on the true meaning of "local food" (or "foodshed" or "regional food system") among its various proponents. While apparently nobody thinks of it in terms of a single household or farm, is it (or should it be) limited to within a few miles of one's residence, as was often the case for most of human history? Within 100 miles (160 kilometers) from consumers in our car-dominated era? Within the larger confines of a modern metropolitan area and its surrounding countryside? Perhaps even a day's drive from a locavore's home or a distribution warehouse? Or even "less than 400 miles from its origin, or within the State in which it is produced," as stated in the 2008 U.S. Farm Act?

Adding to this confusion are a few other issues. For instance, what about food grown or caught near its final point of purchase but then trucked, shipped, or flown over significant distances in order to be processed in a large manufacturing operation or inspected in a central distribution hub, before being shipped back to a store near its production site? (For instance, squids caught on the California coast are now reportedly sent to China in order to be cleaned and frozen before being shipped back to California.[16]) Should one also care about the geographical origins of the electricity, gasoline, diesel, packaging material, computers, fertilizers, pesticides, and even the seeds and embryos used by "local" producers?

Another paradox is that, as a result of thousands of years of agricultural diffusion and adaptation, "local" agriculture has long been based for the most part on nonnative species while all "national" culinary traditions rely to a large extent on once foreign ideas and commodities, ranging from grilling, baking, and confectionary techniques to sugar, coffee, chocolate, chili pepper, citrus fruits, and tomatoes. For instance, Indian curries, Hungarian paprika, and Korean kimchee did not exist before the introduction of the American chili pepper. Staple American crops such as soybean, corn, and wheat are native to China, Mexico, and the Middle East, respectively. In fact, if modern-day activists were to cling to any consistent notion of "local" food, a truly "made in the USA" agricultural diet would be limited to turkeys, some farmed native fish and shellfish (including Atlantic salmon and Brook trout), sunflowers, blueberries, cranberries, Jerusalem artichokes, and some varieties of squash.

Leaving aside the complexities of properly defining the term "local," the case put forward by local food activists can be divided into five broad arguments.[17] To summarize:

- *Social*: The globalized food supply chain and big box retailers have eroded the community ties that once existed between geographically proximate food producers and consumers. Unlike the impersonal nature of large stores and shopping malls, farmers' markets promote camaraderie, informal conversation, and good will, thus helping to foster relationships, neighborhood ties, and vibrant local communities. Eating locally connects consumers to a larger, though circumscribed, social world.

- *Economic*: Local food purchases improve the economic circumstances of mostly small-scale farmers (especially those not using vast quantities of synthetic chemicals and mammoth machinery for mass production) who otherwise struggle in the face of international competition, along with the fortunes of independent stores who cannot access the international food market as easily as large retailers. Money spent locally moves through fewer hands, thereby ensuring that more of it ends up in local producers' pockets than when it is sent out to the distant headquarters of monopolistic large retail chains, shipping companies, and mega corporate farms. Local producers are also more likely to pay their staff a living wage and be attuned to social justice concerns than large corporate entities that exploit workers both at home and abroad.

- *Environmental*: Because locally produced food travels fewer miles, it generates less greenhouse gas emissions than items brought in from more distant areas. Local food production systems that serve a broad array of needs are also more diverse than large, export-oriented systems where only one or a few varieties of crops are planted. Increased farming biodiversity is not only desirable from an ecological perspective, but also more aesthetically pleasing than factory farming. In addition, large-scale producers are much less likely to be held accountable by distant consumers for the damage they cause to ecosystems. Promoting local food production also encourages land conservation for agricultural purposes and is an indirect way to fight urban sprawl. Unlike imported food, locally grown produce is often sold without packaging that then gets thrown away.

- *Security*: Populations fed by local producers can always count on them in times of crisis such as during wars or with sudden price hikes on imported food items. By their very nature, international food markets only cater to the highest bidders and are not concerned with the fate of marginal populations. Diversified local agricultural offerings are also less likely to succumb to diseases than

monocultures and will still be around when our petroleum supply
is gone and we have no choice but to revert to local production.

- *Taste, Nutrition, and Safety*: All other things being equal, locally
grown food is fresher than that which has traveled over long distances on cargo ships, railroads, and trucks. Such food not only tastes
better but also is more nutritious as it has spent less time in various
forms of storage and is more likely to have been picked at its peak of
freshness. Food produced in countries with lower overall health,
safety, and environmental standards is also, by the very nature of the
methods and lack of care involved, going to be more harmful to consumers. And unlike the food contamination that takes place in central processing facilities where vast quantities of food from diverse
geographical origins commingle and are exposed to undesirable elements such as salmonella, the small scale of local food production
ensures that any such problems remain localized and are easily traced.

While superficially compelling, SOLE has drawn fire from a number of critics, such as Missouri conventional farmer Blake Hurst;[18] journalists Joe Pompeo,[19] Stephen Budiansky,[20] and Ronald Bailey;[21] writers
Dave Lowry[22] and Greg Critser;[23] academic economists Thomas R. De-
Gregori,[24] Art Carden,[25] Steven Landsburg,[26] Steven Saxton,[27] Edward
L. Glaeser,[28] and Jayson L. Lusk, and F. Bailey Northwood;[29] political
scientist Robert Paarlberg;[30] and private sector agricultural policy analyst Gary Blumenthal.[31]

As these and other critics see things, locavores belong to an environmentalist sect that makes a moral issue out of where your food is
grown and are satisfied with the appearance of green behavior rather
than facts and effective results. Oblivious to what life is really like when
most food is organic and locally produced, they promote a dire lifestyle
now limited to our planet's most destitute locations.

If you want to embrace locally produced organic and nonprocessed
food, the political scientist Robert Paarlberg points out, you could move
to sub-Saharan rural Africa, where SOLE is a daily reality. There, about

60% of the population is engaged in either farming or herding from dawn to dusk. In addition, because these farmers can't afford modern technologies, they must rely on traditional organic methods, and only about 4% of their cropland is irrigated, *de facto* protecting precious local watersheds and underground aquifers. Because approximately 70% of households live more than a 30 minute walk from the nearest all-weather road, residents must purchase and sell most of their food locally while their primitive cooking technologies and lack of access to processed food ensures that they must devote much time to food preparation. What is the reality of this SOLE dream? Average cereal crop yields that are at best one-fifth as high as in advanced economies, and life as our ancestors pretty much knew it, with average incomes hovering around $1 a day and an approximately one in three probability of being malnourished.[32]

In the end, critics tell us, SOLE is essentially a fad promoted by bi-coastal urban "agri-intellectuals" whose knowledge of and practical experience with food production are typically limited to the world of hobby gardening and a once-in-a-lifetime foray into hunting or killing a backyard animal. Among other problems, these fans of the local uncritically champion a few "alternative" operations, such as Joel Salatin's *Polyface* farm, a "family owned, multi-generational, pasture-based, beyond organic, local-market farm, and informational outreach in Virginia's Shenandoah Valley" that is in the business of "healing the land, healing the food, healing the economy, and healing the culture." Yet, they rarely mention Poly-face's low productivity, high prices for common "industrial" livestock breeds, arguably greater health risks in light of their livestock's management practices, and dependence on both conventional producers for livestock and apprenticeship programs for cheap labor. Furthermore, Salatin derives substantial revenues from his numerous (and often distant) engagements as both a speaker and consultant to supplement his farming income, something which could obviously never be duplicated by producers who would adopt his holistic organic farming model.[33]

Too busy denouncing some imaginary ills of modern farming, agri-intellectuals and proponents of locavorism do not ask why large-scale agricultural producers—who alone can feed large numbers of people at affordable prices—raise crops and care for livestock the way they do. Enthralled by romantic notions of rural life, they care little about the damage inflicted on unprotected crops by pests and weather, don't consider the real-world consequences of food shortages, and brush aside concerns about the large-scale deforestation that would inevitably ensue from the much less productive methods they promote.

To food writer Dave Lowry, the largely upper middle-class followers of SOLE principles are often "foodiots," who, already saddled with "anti-capitalist sensitivities," too much income, and unsubstantiated fears about conventional food quality, further live "in constant fear of being identified with the McRib-gobbling proletariat."[34] Another "benefit" of the SOLE fad, according to health writer Greg Critser, is that it helps reconfirm the elite status of professional chefs and food critics threatened by the ever-increasing abundance and affordability of once scarce and expensive ingredients.[35] Farmers' markets have in the meantime evolved into a combination of premium boutiques and environmentalist temples whose main offering is "feel good" value at premium prices. In the end, the real magic of locavorism, Lowry tells us, is that it allows some individuals to achieve the non-negligible feat of being simultaneously snobs and "one of the folks."[36] Locavorism, according to food policy analyst Gary Blumenthal, essentially boils down to "social affinity, a sense of sympathy for David and antagonism toward Goliath due to concerns about tribe, equity, and greed."[37]

While one can always find some committed practitioners of the SOLE lifestyle who do make significant economic and personal sacrifices to live up to their ideals, it remains by and large the province of an elite customer base that can afford a residence near a prime and diversified agricultural area in a temperate climatic zone; higher food prices; much spare time devoted to cooking and preserving food; a large and fully equipped kitchen, a second freezer, and significant storage space for canned goods. As acknowledged by Clara Jeffrey and Monika Bauerlein, editors at *Mother Jones*, "by focusing on consumer choices—always more available to the affluent—the foodie movement has . . . perpetuated a two-class system: pesticide-laden, processed, packaged, irradiated slop for the many, artisanal sheep's milk cheese for a few."[38] Echoing this sentiment, on April 27, 2010, Republican senators John McCain, Saxby Chambliss, and Pat Roberts wrote a letter to the U.S. Department of Agriculture requesting information on the "Know your Farmer, Know your Food" program, in which they opined that this $65 million initiative to promote urban farmers' markets was mostly catering to "small, hobbyist, and organic producers whose customers generally consist of affluent patrons." These "feel-good measures which are completely detached from the realities of production agriculture," they added, were depriving suffering rural communities from much needed assistance in order to favor urban consumers who had no real need for it.[39]

Many committed locavores are also long-time activists who, once organic and fair trade commodities became widely available at Wal-Mart and other large retail stores (often through the good services of food manufacturing giants like PepsiCo), went looking for other ways to stick it to large polluting and profiteering corporations. As the organic farm certifier David Gould put it: "Know your farmer, that was one of the keys of the organic mission that has been lost."[40] For Gould and like-minded individuals, "organic agriculture" should not be simply about the way food is produced, but just as (and perhaps even more) important, about an alternative economic, social, and ecological paradigm that reconnects urban consumers to the land, or at least to small-scale organic producers, and teaches the value of a simpler and less consumption-based lifestyle. But as the leitmotif of for-profit business has long been "when there is a demand, there is a way," many large chains have in recent years increased their "local food" offering.[41]

In our view, food activists have yet to answer satisfactorily four fundamental questions:

If our modern food system is so bad for us, why do we now enjoy dramatically longer and healthier lives than our ancestors?

How can less efficient alternatives to current food production methods provide adequate and affordable nutrition to the soon-to-be nine billion human beings, approximately 85% of whom will be living in developing countries, and who, in the coming decades, will need more food than was eaten in the last ten thousand years?

How many million acres of wildlife habitat should be sacrificed to implement local and organic farming methods that, while deemed more sustainable by activists, gobble up a lot more land to produce the same amount of food as more technologically advanced ones?[42]

If local food production in earlier eras was so great, why did consumers increasingly favor items from ever more remote locations?

The first three issues have already been capably addressed in much detail by other authors, and we will consequently deal with them on an as-needed basis only. The last one, however, is where we hope to make a significant contribution.[43]

What Is Our Beef With?

Food production and distribution is a complex business, so let us begin by making the obvious point that not all "local" food is created equal and that some of it is perfectly fine with us. For instance, New Hampshire maple syrup, California strawberries, Alaskan salmon and crabs, Washington apples, Florida oranges, Michigan cherries, and Iowa corn are among the best and most affordable in the world and, as a result, have long been enjoyed by nearby and distant consumers alike. Competitively priced, high-quality seasonal local fruits and vegetables have also long been sought after by nearby grocers and restaurateurs alike. "Hobby" gardening is its own psychic reward and should not be judged by economic criteria. In isolated rural areas where land is cheap, game animals abundant, and economic opportunities limited, it often makes perfect sense to cultivate large vegetable gardens along with fruit and nut trees; to keep animal coops while having a few grass-fed ruminants roam over the surrounding pastureland; and to supply one's pantry, root cellar, and freezer with the results of hunting, fishing, and harvesting wild food of various kinds. Local food items that might not be the most delicious or economical might also have other redeeming qualities, such as an orchard that survives on "pick-your-own" family outings or an otherwise average vineyard to which a gourmet restaurant has been added. Some overpriced local food might also be sold for charitable purposes.

"Local when sensible" is obviously not our concern, nor do we believe that most committed locavores sincerely promote the cultivation of pineapples or bananas in the American snowbelt; in our experience, they would rather have local residents get by without them. We don't even disagree with their belief that "eating locally means eating seasonally," which, in turn, results in "deprivation lead[ing] to greater appreciation."[44] In our view, food masochism should be left to the realm of personal preferences. Rather, we draw the line where local food is deemed desirable simply *because of its geographical origin* and is not more affordable, nutritious, safer, or better tasting than alternatives produced further away.

Locavores and people otherwise indifferent to the movement might interject that life is not only about turning a profit and what people do on their own time and with their own dime is their business. Besides, if the current obsessions with small organic homesteads, urban gardens, green roofs, and backyard poultry are nothing but the latest in a long line of pointless food fads, why argue over the issue? The problem is that local food activists are spreading environmental misconceptions, increasingly picking our pockets, and threatening our food security. "Vote with your fork and your consumer dollar!" might be their unofficial slogan, but their campaign material so frequently and so severely distorts the true impact of uncompetitive local agriculture that they could be held liable to prosecution under false advertising statutes. On top of that, many activists have been hard at work to mandate the purchase of pricier local food by public institutions (most prominently government agencies, school boards, hospitals, prisons, universities, and military bases), prevent the redevelopment of abandoned marginal agricultural land for other useful purposes, prohibit modern agricultural practices, and ultimately close national doors to foreign products.[45] For reasons that we will discuss in more detail later on, the outcomes of such initiatives range from bad to utterly disastrous.

To sum up our basic argument: If widely adopted, either voluntarily or through political mandates, *locavorism can only result in higher costs and increased poverty, greater food insecurity, less food safety, and much more significant environmental damage* than is presently the case. Policies should be judged by their results, not their intentions. Consumers who bought into locavorism because they sincerely cared about making our food supply ever more secure, safe, affordable, and sustainable while supporting their local community should reexamine whether the supposed means actually lead to the desired ends.

As we will illustrate in the remainder of this book, our modern food system is an underappreciated wonder that is the culmination of thousands of years of advances in plant cultivation and animal breeding; harvesting, storing, transporting, and processing food; and retailing and home cooking techniques. Only through greater technological advances, economies of scale and international trade can we achieve the locavores' worthy goals of improving nutrition while diminishing the environmental impact of agricultural production.

Our text is structured as follows. We begin with a brief look at the emergence and development of the globalized food supply chain, along with a short discussion of the backlash against it that has ensued at every step of the way. We then offer an in-depth analysis of the five key arguments espoused by locavores and discuss why, if implemented as proposed, such a food system can only ever deliver increased social and economic misery, environmental degradation, greater food insecurity, and poorer nutrition. In the final chapter, we further discuss additional policy steps that would be required to make locavorism a reality and explain why they would again fail to meet their objectives. Our main conclusion is that the best way to achieve the outcomes desired by locavores is paradoxically to globalize our food supply chain even more than it is at the moment. It is our hope that readers come away from this book with an understanding that buying or abstaining from buying local food should be a *shopping* decision, not a *moral* or *political* one.

Writing in 1923, the British professor of agriculture Thomas Hudson Middleton observed that his compatriots were "chiefly fed upon imported food, and are interested in the quality and price of their foodstuffs rather than in its origins, the ordinary consumer takes little interest in the well-being of agriculture."[46] (Most of his compatriots did not even care whether or not foodstuffs were produced in the British Empire, thus prompting the creation of an "Empire Marketing Board" in 1926.) Despite the fact that they have been conditioned to provide SOLE answers when formally quizzed on their shopping habits, today's British consumers are apparently still behaving like previous generations.[47] This, we will argue, is the right path for all consumers to pursue. Getting the most for your hard-earned dollar is not only enlightened self-interest, but also the best way to create a better world.

1

The Globalization of the Food Supply Chain and Its Discontents

The railroad, the steamship, the telephone, and the telegraph have opened to us a world market and world commerce. The novelty of these opportunities has caused them to be used to excess. Man may be said to have gone on a transportation spree, a very orgy of transportation. We have unduly separated man's home space from his sustenance space, to the detriment of both sustenance and home . . . Mr. Ross [Department of Food Supply, Committee of Public Safety of Pennsylvania] worked out a plan which should some day be applied to every community in every civilized country if modern society improves as we have reason to expect it to do. The plan is to study the local food needs and the possibilities of local food production, and so far as is feasible to make the locality feed itself.

—JOSEPH RUSSELL SMITH. 1919.
The World's Food Resources.
H. Holt & Company, pp. 566 and 568[1]

In the words of urbanists Branden Born and Mark Purcell, the "local trap" is the "tendency of food activists and researchers to assume something inherent about the local scale" in terms of the values they hold dear, from democracy, social justice, and food security to ecological sustainability, better nutrition, freshness, and quality.[2] A logical outcome of this stance is to consider large multinational corporations inherently bad and "foreign" goods suspect. According to some evolutionary psychologists, our natural propensity to favor members of our community over distant people[3] owes much to our foraging heritage because, for countless generations, human beings were group and territory-based creatures. The fact that these instincts are still very much with us today can be observed at any meaningful sporting event involving rival teams. Nonetheless, all economically prosperous episodes in human history have been characterized to one degree or another by the expansion of a community's food provisioning.

A Short History of the Global Food Supply Chain[4]

With the exception of nomadic groups, most of the food supply of our hunter and gatherer ancestors came from within a rather limited territory. At some point, though, humans developed what the economist Adam Smith described in 1776 as the propensity "to truck, barter, and exchange one thing for another," a capacity which proved so advantageous in evolutionary terms that it became "common to all men."[5] Although much debate still surrounds the origins of trade (for instance, did it first occur within or between groups?), no one disputes that it is substantially older than the development of agriculture and many suggest that from its beginning it probably entailed interactions between and beyond "local" communities. Until time travel is developed, however, the study of the ancient long distance trade in food will remain difficult as, unlike stones and bones, perishable items left very little trace in the archeological record. More recent evidence nonetheless suggests that it might have been significant in some locations. For instance, before European contact, the native inhabitants of a portion of northern British Columbia, who lived in three different yet adjacent climatic and biotic zones (the Pacific coast, the boreal forest, and the interior plateau), traded goods such as dried seaweed, edible candlefish grease, and dried salmon for items such as moose hides and caribou and other meat. As stated by some of their descendants: "No one community existed in economic isolation, and the use or value of resources was not limited to its place of harvesting . . . [the regional economy] was never isolationist [and] combined elements of domestic production and consumption with an elaborate complex of trading networks."[6]

For approximately 90% of their existence, anatomically modern humans managed to survive without practicing what we now call agriculture.[7] In time, though, some wild plant and animal species were domesticated, meaning that they were brought under human control and gradually modified, at first through selection, breeding, hybridization, and grafting to which would later be added exposure to potent chemicals and irradiation,[8] and rDNA technologies. As a result, plants and livestock were progressively given features better suited to human ends, from larger seeds and simultaneous ripening to a greater capacity to convert biomass into meat and less aggressive behavior.[9] Significant and rapid advances in this respect preceded the advent of modern agribusiness. As the economic historians Alan L. Olmstead and Paul W. Rhode observe in their 2008 survey of American agricultural history, the varieties of corn, wheat, fruits, cotton, and tobacco grown at the beginning of the 20th century were dramatically different from the varieties grown one hundred years earlier, while 1940s farm animals such as swine, sheep, and cattle bore little resemblance to those of 1800.[10] Of course, along the way innovative farmers adopted and adapted domesticated plants and animals that had been developed in distant lands, such as in the "Columbian exchange" that followed the incorporation of the Americas into the world economy more than 500 years ago. Native American contributions included edible crops like the tomato, potato, sweet potato, chili pepper, cocoa, pineapples, beans, cassava, and corn, as well as tobacco and some varieties of cotton. Many products refined in the Old World, from wheat, rice, and soybeans to onions and peaches and virtually all of its domestic animals, traveled west and significantly altered the American landscape.

Along with the rise of agriculture, permanent human settlements gradually increased in size, numbers, and economic diversity. Indeed, regardless of the location or time period, economic growth has never occurred without the development of cities. There are several reasons for this. In short, the geographical agglomeration of diverse economic activities makes possible the profitable operation of a transportation hub through which firms can better serve a broad range of activities (both in local and more distant markets) while facilitating the lucrative transformation of production residuals, such as when a manufacturer of wood alcohol uses as its main input the sawdust created by a nearby sawmill.[11] Being located next door to suppliers, customers and creative people in general facilitate the diffusion and development of a broader range of skills and the launching of new innovative businesses. Urban labor markets are also much larger and diversified than those of rural areas and smaller towns, thus making it considerably easier for entrepreneurs and managers to find the specialized or temporary workers they need and for individuals to invest in the acquisition of ever more refined skills.

A compelling description of some of these unique features of large cities was penned more than two millennia ago by the Greek historian and philosopher Xenophon:

> In a small city, the same man must make beds and chairs and ploughs and tables, and often build houses as well; and, indeed, he will be only too glad if he can find enough employers in all trades to keep him. Now, it is impossible that a single man working at a dozen crafts can do them all well; but in the great cities, owing to the wide demand for each particular thing, a single craft will suffice for a means of livelihood, and often enough, even a single department of

that; there are shoemakers who will only make sandals for men and others only for women. Or one artisan will get his living merely by stitching shoes, another by cutting them out, a third by shaping the upper leathers, and a fourth will do nothing but fit the parts together. Necessarily, the man who spends all his time and trouble on the smallest task will do that task the best.[12]

In the end, the crucial differences between urban and rural folks is not that the former are inherently harder working and more creative, but rather that they have access to more opportunities to specialize and act on their insights and vision, and to turn them into economic realities.

In the words of economist Edward Glaeser, there is "a near-perfect correlation between urbanization and prosperity across nations." This is now as obvious as ever as the per capita income in countries with a majority of people living in cities is nearly four times higher than in countries where a majority of people still live in rural areas.[13] And despite long-standing predictions that recent advances in transportation and communication technologies (going back to the development of the railroad and the telegraph) will reverse this trend, it shows no sign of abating.[14] To give but a few numbers, the proportion of the world's population living in cities remained below 5% for most of history and even in the most advanced societies of past periods, from the Roman Empire to Ming Dynasty China, probably never exceeded 10%. In 1800, less than 10% of the U.S. population lived in urban areas while between 70 and 80% of the working population in the richest economies of the time was still engaged in agriculture. Back then, only two cities—London and Beijing—had populations exceeding one million individuals. By 2000, there were 378. The average size of the world's 100 largest cities was 0.7 million inhabitants in 1900, 2 million in 1950 and 6.3 million in 2000. In 1900, one could count 6.7 rural dwellers to each urban dweller worldwide. In 2008, for the first time in history, the world's urban population exceeded its rural population, and, at more than 3 billion people, was actually larger than the world's total population in 1960. According to recent UN projections, by 2025 there will be at least three urban to two rural dwellers. By 2050, approximately 70% of the world's population will be living in cities.[15]

Urban agglomerations have always proved essential for agricultural advances, be it in terms of providing the best setting for technological innovations, by offering large and concentrated markets for rural goods, and in generating the capital required to invest in rural development. As the urban theorist Jane Jacobs observed in 1969, agriculture "is not even tolerably productive unless it incorporates many goods and services produced in cities or transplanted from cities. The most thoroughly rural countries exhibit the most unproductive agriculture. The most thoroughly urbanized countries, on the other hand, are precisely those that produce food most abundantly."[16] Of course, many past agricultural advances can be traced back to the work of specialists such as livestock and crop breeders, geneticists, nutritionists, chemical and mechanical engineers, veterinarians, plant pathologists, and soil scientists who were sometimes (but often not) based in more rural regions. Yet, these people typically benefited from other advances first developed in urban contexts.

The key point for our discussion, however, is that urbanization has long been impossible without substantial food imports from distant locations. As some of Plato's characters in his *Republic* observed so long ago, to find a city "where nothing need be imported" was already then "impossible."[17] Some of these included grazing and foraging livestock (such as beef, goats, and sheep) that could transport itself over some distance on land despite the poor state of road transportation at the time. Items that could be shipped by boat covered much more distance. In the Ancient Mediterranean era, these included grain, wine, olive oil, fish sauce and paste, salt, and, to a lesser extent, honey, and spices (some of which came from as far away as India and China).

Over time, the development of ever better means of transportation (improved sailing ships, canals, and barges; coal, gasoline, diesel, residual fuel oil and kerosene-powered rail locomotives, boats, ships, trucks, and cargo planes; and intermodal shipping containers) and improvements in old ways of preserving food and the development of new ones (from fermenting, drying, smoking, salting, and pickling to canning, juicing, chilling, freezing, and irradiation) provided urban consumers first—and rural consumers later—an ever broader range of commodities that had traveled over long distances, from pickled herrings, salted and dried cods, sugar, coffee, tea, and cocoa to canned fruits, frozen meat and eventually fresh produce, meat, fish, seafood, dairy products, and eggs.[18] Apart from increased diversity and volume of supply, advances in transportation also equalized prices between locations. For instance, between 1820 and 1830, the development of steamboats helped reduce the price differential between Cincinnati and New Orleans by 19% for wheat, 68% for mess pork, 84% for coffee, and 74% for sugar.[19] In the trans-Atlantic trade, the advent of ever better performing steel hull steamships reduced the cost of transporting a bushel of wheat from Chicago to Liverpool from approximately 37 cents in 1869 to approximately 10 cents in 1905.[20]

Until slightly more than a century ago, much food production for the urban population of the world's most advanced economies still took place within or in close proximity to city limits, especially in the case of items such as produce, animals, and animal products (mostly milk and eggs) that did not travel or keep well, or else could turn urban organic refuse of all kind into edible calories. To give a few less than idyllic illustrations, in Korea and China, "privy pigs" were kept to convert human excrement into meat (in technical terms, these pigs were "scatovores"). Walking through the streets of Manchester, England, in the early 1840s, Friedrich Engels blamed much of the filthy conditions on the Irish workers' "multitude of pigs walking about in all the alleys, rooting into the offal heaps, or kept imprisoned in small pens." Urban poultry in 19th century London was fed maggots raised on the carcasses of dead urban work horses.[21] Dairy cows converted much swill and brewery by-products into milk. Urban work horses and dairy cows not only gave cities like London a "distinctly agricultural whiff,"[22] but also generated valuable manure that was turned to good uses by local produce growers.

Perhaps the most celebrated past local "urban farmers" were the Parisian *maraîchers* who, through the use of about one sixth of the city's area, supporting technologies (from greenhouses to cloches) and very long hours,[23] grew more than 100,000 tons of produce annually in the late 19th century.[24] Unlike today's locavores, however, not only did Parisian truck farmers do their best to defy the seasons (they were already producing green asparagus year-round in the 1820s[25] and a few decades later had managed to grow significant amounts of pineapples profitably), but they also exported their crops to distant urban markets including London. Interestingly, as two Parisian producers observed in 1845, it was their profession's ability to defeat seasonality that had significantly enhanced its prestige among the rest of the population while the greatest ambition of all *maraîchers* was to find ways to be the first to deliver a specific produce to the market in any given year.[26]

Residents of the world's most advanced cities have thus always relied on both distant and local sources of food. For instance, in 1856, the English historian George Dodd listed the geographical origins of the main food commodities sold in London (see opposite page).

Today, in the largest cities of less advanced economies, approximately 200 million producers and perhaps as many as 800 million consumers rely at least partly on local urban agriculture for their survival.[27] In all rapidly developing economies, however, the unmistakable trend has long been the displacement of urban food producers by more distant and suitably located firms. Apart from the development of better transportation and food preservation technologies, this process was also driven by increases in urban land value that mandated their conversion to more profitable activities; better economic opportunities for urban and peri-urban agricultural workers; the advent of the automobile, which drastically curtailed the local availability of urban horse manure; and epidemic diseases that could be traced back to or affected urban livestock.

TABLE 1

Meat	Livestock (general): England, Scotland, Wales, Ireland, Denmark Bacon & salt meat: Ireland Hams: England (Yorkshire), Germany, Spain Games: England (Northern Counties), Scandinavia Rabbits: England (Southern Counties), Belgium (Ostend) Poultry: England (half the counties)
Eggs	Ireland, France
Fish	All the seas around and between the British Islands
Bread (grain)	Western Europe, Eastern Europe (Prussia), Russia (Odessa and Tagarong), USA, Moldavia
Cheese	England (over a dozen counties), Holland, America
Butter	England (over a dozen counties), Ireland, USA
Milk	Within thirty miles of London
Produce	Gardening belt surrounding London, many European countries
Tea	China
Coffee	Ceylon (Sri Lanka), Arabia, Brazil, West Indies
Cocoa	West Indies, South America
Sugar	East Indies, West Indies, Brazil, other tropical countries
Salt	150 miles from London
Spices and condiments	One half of the circumference of the globe
Alcohol	Brandy: France
	Wine: France, Italy, Spain, Portugal, Germany (Rhineland), Hungary
	Whiskey: Scotland, Ireland

Source: Adapted from George Dodd. 1856. *The Food of London: A sketch of the chief varieties, sources of supply, probable quantities, modes of arrival, processes of manufacture, suspected adulteration, and machinery of distribution, of the food for a community of two and a half million.* Longman, Brown, Green and Longmans, pp. 102–103. http://books.google.ca/books?id=wlUZAAAAYAAJ&source=gbs_navlinks_s

Along with long distance trade and rapid urbanization came an unmistakable trend towards large-scale monocultures and regional specialization. As the American agricultural economist Lorian P. Jefferson observed in 1926, while a few decades before "most communities produced many or all the products they required," the U.S. agricultural landscape was by then thoroughly dominated by great geographic specialization and few sections of the country could now "supply all their own food needs. Areas of production are generally devoted largely to those products for which they are peculiarly adapted by soil and climate" and deficits in local production had to be "made up from distant sources." Overall, though, improved facilities for transportation and storage had "made available for nearly all markets the products of the entire country in fairly uniform supply, and the variety of our foods has been greatly increased."[28]

Reflecting upon the changes he had witnessed during his lifetime, the *San Francisco Chronicle* editorialist Edward F. Adams wrote in 1899 that the quasi-subsistence lifestyle of his youth was no longer possible nor agreeable to the American farmer because "it would involve a distinct lowering of our present standard of comfort, which, with all our complaint, is far higher than formerly, and would not result in the same content and consequent survival which the same conditions formerly induced. The impossibility of the life will be seen by any farmer who will trace out what would happen should he attempt it."[29]

The results of these advances was that, as the French agronomist Henri Hitier observed in 1901, for the inhabitants of the world's most prosperous economies, "the steam engine had eradicated seasonality"[30] and that the quality, price, and geographical origins of their food bore little resemblance to the offerings available to previous generations. The geography textbook writers of the time were also fond of describing the increasingly globalized nature of the meals served on American tables. To give but one illustration, one Jacques Redway not only observed in 1907 that there was "scarcely a country in the world that does not yield something or other to civilized peoples... scarcely a household whose furnishings and contents do not represent an aggregate journey of several times around the earth," but also that a typical middle class New York family would partake for breakfast "of bread made of wheat from Minnesota, and meat from Texas prepared in a range made in St. Louis; coffee grown in Sumatra or Java, or tea from China . . . served in cups made in Japan, sweetened with sugar from Cuba [and food seasoned with] spices from Africa, South America, and Asia."[31]

Interestingly, the distant origins of many food items were often marketed as providing some assurance of superior quality. For instance, in the 1930s, the candy, chocolate, and restaurant chain Schrafft's advertised that the fresh grapefruits, oranges, and strawberries in its fruit cocktails had cumulatively traveled 7,800 miles to its New York City locations while the components of its vegetable salad had racked up more than 22,250 miles.[32] As Redway had observed a few years earlier: "An old saying, 'All the world feeds the rest of the world,' is fast coming true."[33]

In the last few decades, the extension of seasonal production using alternative methods such as large-scale greenhouses; the diversification of production locations; transportation advances and deregulation; product-capacity expansion; a growing awareness of the nutritional benefits associated with fresh produce; and the establishment of large-scale temperature-controlled logistic systems built around refrigerated containers and cold-storage facilities have again dramatically expanded the range, quality, volume, and reliability of traded varieties. At the same time, their prices dropped, especially for exotic fruits and vegetables (such as lychees, passion fruits, and Chinese cabbages), salad greens (such as arugula and chicory), and baby vegetables. These changes also brought significant benefits to less developed countries, whose exports of fresh produce have risen significantly in the last few decades—fruits and vegetables now account for more than 20% of their exports—and have not only considerably enriched our daily diet, but also the wallets of previously much poorer agricultural workers in less advanced economies.[34]

Of course, the globalization of the food supply chain was not limited to final products such as grains, spices, meat, and produce. Over time, an increasingly wider range and volume of inputs came to be manufactured by specialized producers in comparatively few locations and traded over long distances. For instance, animal producers have long relied on "nonlocal" frozen semen and embryos, animal feed and feed supplements, veterinary products and building structures, plastic products of all kinds, cages, fences, and ventilation, feeding and breeding equipment. For their part, crop producers have come to rely on a wide range of nonlocal seeds, fertilizers, pesticides, fungicides, herbicides, rodenticides, desiccants, tractors, combines, sprayers, crop dusting airplanes, plastic sheeting, irrigation systems, global positioning satellite data, and drying, storage and refrigeration systems. For example, for more than two centuries seeds of all kinds have been profitably marketed by private producers, both in order to export domestic surplus and to import foreign material of greater quality. By specializing in one type of crop, seed producers were able to develop higher yielding and more resistant plant material along with various ways to address funga and bacterial diseases. Especially significant in the context of this book is that these firms are typically active in more remote regions or confined environments where diseases often endemic to large-scale production zones are, ideally, entirely absent, where maintaining varietal purity can be more easily achieved, and where more numerous cropping cycles can be realized in shorter periods of time (such as in tropical locations for non-tropical plants). Among other advances, because of their ability to work in both the northern and southern hemispheres, the best seed companies have been able to halve the period of time required to develop new seeds.[35]

Food manufacturers have long relied on distant suppliers for additives that affect not only color and flavor, but also extend shelf life while often reducing production costs. People afflicted by diabetes, obesity, and dental decay have benefited from non-nutritive sweeteners such as saccharin, aspartame, and acesulfame K, used in everything from soft drinks and chewing gum to mouthwash. The application of fumigants keeps worms away from grain products such as flour and spices, a problem that was once significant. The fortification of staples such as flour, milk, sugar, and salt with the likes of iron, vitamins, and iodine also had important benefits including eradicating blindness (vitamin A), beriberi (vitamin B_1), ariboflavinosis (vitamin B_2), pellagra (vitamin B_3), anemia (vitamins B_6 and B_{12}, iron), scurvy (vitamin C), rickets or insufficiently calcified bones (vitamin D), birth defects (folic acids), and weak immune system and growth (zinc). As with other manufacturing processes where economies of scale are significant, the production of food additives now takes place in a few large plants, some of which are located in India and China.

To summarize, over a period of a few thousand years, humanity transitioned from foraging, a mode of subsistence that required about 1000 hectares of land to support an individual, to a globalized food supply chain characterized by regionally specialized and extremely productive monocultures, a relatively small number of producers, and a large supporting infrastructure that can feed an individual on perhaps as little as one-tenth of an hectare.[36] Much innovation and tampering with nature was required, but long-distance trade also drastically changed the character of our food supply and its availability. In past eras, fresh fruits and vegetables could only be consumed at harvest time, fresh meat only immediately after slaughter and in the winter months, anything ingested had to have been dried, smoked, or steeped in brine. In the last two centuries, however, consumers went from shopping in "dry good" stores to the "permanent summertime" produce sections of progressively larger supermarkets whose ever expanding range of offerings have become only safer, healthier, and considerably more affordable.[37]

Perhaps most remarkable, however, has been humanity's capacity to nearly defeat famine and hunger. As late as 1950, at least 1 billion people out of about 2.5 billion were thought to be going hungry every day. Today the number is below 1 billion out of about 7 billion people. In other words, in about six decades the percentage of the human population that suffered from hunger and malnutrition went from nearly 40% to less than 15% while the absolute number of people who were provided an adequate diet rose from about 1.5 to 6 billion—an accomplishment even more remarkable given that, if 1950s technologies had been used in later decades, an additional land area equivalent to South America would have needed to be ploughed under in the process.[38]

The Call of the Local

While greater reliance on long-distance trade delivered ever more abundant and affordable goods to consumers and significantly improved overall standards of living, it drew the ire of uncompetitive local producers and of a wide range of people uncomfortable with the social changes brought about by urbanization, the seemingly ever widening disconnect between urban and rural populations, and the perceived over-reliance on foreigners for something as crucial as food. Tapping into these sentiments, countless political leaders throughout history did their best to keep foreign supplies at bay and to increase domestic food production.

This mindset characterized a dominant segment of the Athenian elite more than two millennia ago when they made economic self-sufficiency (*autarkeia*) one of their main goals. Autarky, they argued, would make their compatriots freer by *minimizing* their dependence on international trade. Because all geographical territories, even the largest ones, suffer from resource shortcomings of some kind, this stance inexorably led to the creation of an "Athenian empire" to access vital commodities that were in short supply locally. In later centuries, classical Roman agricultural writers such as Cato the elder, Pliny the Elder, and Varro all praised self-sufficiency, and autarkic instincts undoubtedly played their part in shaping the course of Roman imperial history.[39]

Closer to us, a century ago in Japan, the push for greater autarky became ever stronger after agricultural protectionists politically defeated industrialists (and their workers) and managed to block rice imports in

1904. Even though this policy stance resulted in domestic prices that were 30% above world prices during World War I and, later, shortages that caused food riots, the Japanese government went ever further down that road by embarking on an imperialistic drive with the avowed goal of producing all of their own rice, mostly by developing production in its Korean and Taiwanese colonies. One result of the "fortress Japan" pursuit was that, by the late 1930s, Nippon rice prices were 60% above the international rate. Despite having been crushed soon afterwards, Japanese authorities never changed course in this respect and decided by the end of the Second World War to expand this tariff protection to a wider range of agricultural products, thus essentially taxing over 99% of the population to support a few uncompetitive agricultural producers.[40]

Historically, the push for greater agricultural self-sufficiency was never limited to political and military leaders bent on imperialistic pursuits, but also often included a fair number of romantic ideologues, politically connected nationalists, supporters of "good old" and "small is beautiful" ways, and farmers who had no qualms about using the latest technologies but insisted on keeping out the products of their foreign competitors. By and large, past initiatives reminiscent of today's locavore movement were motivated either by economic recessions (to boost regional economic activity or as a form of protection against price inflation), wars or their threat (to increase local food security), romantic impulses during relatively prosperous times (as a way to live in greater harmony with nature and as a form of dissent from market-oriented society), a deep-seated belief that modern transportation systems were inherently inefficient and wasteful (compared to direct links between producers and final consumers), and a profound dislike of allegedly redundant (if not outright parasitical) profit-seeking intermediaries. A brief discussion of some past American initiatives to promote increased community food reliance will now set the stage for a broader discussion of the inherent flaws of locavorism.

As should be expected, the American pioneers of what could be termed the "romantic" wing of the local food movement originated from some of the wealthiest and most economically advanced regions of the country. After all, "moving back to the land" implies that you have other opportunities available, something that was obviously not the case for subsistence farmers. Best known are the New England Transcendentalists, who rejected science and objective experience as a basis for developing knowledge in favor of intuitive thought processes that transcended the physical and empirical world. Their creed included the dismissal of "urban life in favor of nature in all its wildness." Their best known representative was Henry David Thoreau, whose classic 1854 work, *Walden; or, Life in the Woods,* criticized the division of labor on the grounds that it removed people from a sense of connectedness with society and with the world at large and nature in particular.[41]

There were other attempts by New Englanders of the era to experiment with various alternative lifestyles, including efforts to rebuild community spirit around small-scale and self-sufficient farming communities. One was Brook Farm (also known as the *Brook Farm Institute of Agriculture and Education*), a socialist cooperative of the early 1840s where each member could select the work he or she found most appealing and where all would be paid equally, regardless of gender or the task performed. Revenues for the community were to be based on farming and from selling handmade products (especially clothing), through fees from paying visitors, and from tuition fees for the school located on the premises.

Another was Fruitlands, whose founders wished to pursue the ideals of simplicity, sincerity, and brotherly love. This would be best achieved, they thought, by withdrawing from the market economy, which the leader of the experiment, Bronson Alcott (the father of Louisa May Alcott of *Little Women* fame), described as having selfishness as its roots, property as its trunk, and gold as its fruit. Its members would forego trade and strive for self-sufficiency by growing their own food, holding all property communally, and keeping material possessions to a minimum. While residents were expected to subsist on farming, they were forbidden to use animal labor and to eat or use any animal substance, including milk, honey, eggs, and wool (in modern parlance, they were ethical vegans). Other peculiar rules included interdictions to drink anything other than water (this rule specifically targeted stimulants such as tea and coffee), to use artificial light, and to heat water for bathing.

Not surprisingly, if Brook Farm managed to last a few years, Fruitlands was abandoned after less than one.[42]

Similar sentiments would later be echoed by a wide range of Americans, from the so-called American Dutch Utopia painters at the turn of the 20th century who created visions of Holland that celebrated a preindustrial lifestyle,[43] to the Southern Agrarian writers of the 1920s and 1930s who opposed the urbanization, industrialization, and internationalization of their country. And then there were the hippies of the 1960s and 1970s. Perhaps as many as a million of them temporarily moved "back to the land" and attempted to live from it before most eventually abandoned rural bliss and returned to the trappings of civilization.

There is also a long history of politically-driven attempts to promote local food production in urban settings in times of economic depression. Much like the rise of agrarian romanticism, it was a reaction—in this case to the fact that much old-fashioned urban food production had vanished. One such initiative was the "Urban Potato Patches" launched in Detroit during the depression of the 1890s, in which municipal authorities asked owners of vacant lots to allow unemployed individuals to grow vegetables on their land. The measure was soon copied by mayors of other large cities at the time, while urban gardening as something of a social welfare policy would reappear in various forms and labels ("Garden City Plots," "Depression Relief Gardens," "Welfare Garden Plots," and "Community Gardens," among others) over the next century.[44]

Many readers will no doubt be familiar with the "Liberty Gardens" and "Victory Gardens" of the First and Second World Wars. Among the most interesting sources on the topic is a collection of wartime local food posters now available on the U.S. Department of Agriculture (USDA)

Source: USDA 1917: War Era Food Posters http://www.good-potato.com/beans_are
_bullets/chapter2/ch2gallery6.html

website.[45] With little tweaks in language, design, and content, some of these, such as the one found in the figure on the opposite page produced in 1917, would not seem out of place in today's farmers markets.

The spirit behind such efforts during World War I was well captured by Charles Lathrop Pack, the President of the National Emergency Food Garden Commission, who observed that it was

> conservative to state that by the planting of gardens where none grew before the nation's food supply has been increased to the extent of more than $350,000,000. The canning and drying movement has brought back to thousands of American households an art almost forgotten since our grandmothers' days. This particularly applies to the drying of vegetables and fruits which this year, in addition to canning, is being done by good housewives far beyond any anticipation.[46]

These results, he later added, were especially remarkable in light of the fact that this food was raised where none had "been produced in peacetime, with labor not engaged in agricultural work and not taken from any other industry, and in places where it made no demand upon the railroad already overwhelmed with transportation burdens."[47]

Less well-remembered than wartime gardening policies are the Franklin Delano Roosevelt Administration's promotion during the 1930s of "subsistence homesteads"—the best known being Arthurdale in West Virginia—into which impoverished laborers and coal miners could relocate and revert back to the land. From their beginnings, however, these experiments proved to be money-losing propositions that only lasted as long as their government funding.[48]

Sophisticated critiques of the modern food supply chain and proposals remarkably similar to those now put forward by locavores also have a long history. For instance, in 1918, Morris Llewellyn Cooke, then a former Director of Public Works of the City of Philadelphia, asked why do strawberries go from Selbyville, Delaware [the largest strawberry-shipping point in the United States at the time], to Philadelphia, 104 miles distant, to be resold and go back again over the same route as far as Wilmington, Delaware, 27 miles away, to be hauled to the storage house of the commission man, again sold, and hauled by huckster's team fourteen miles to reach the consumer at Kennett Square, Pennsylvania? ... Any quality left in the berries after the last leg of this roundabout journey is due rather to the providence of God than to the wisdom of men.[49]

Cooke added that the berries lost between 25 to 35% of their value during the trip, a "relatively simple and obvious example of the want of organization in the marketing of our local products." To his amazement, however, the railroad managers of the time "ridiculed all proposals to effect any advantageous changes in the cities' food supply through the encouragement of local shipments and the local consumption of locally grown foods."[50]

In another study published in 1913, Clyde Lyndon King, a political scientist at the Wharton School of the University of Pennsylvania, argued that perhaps as much as a third of the price of foodstuffs in northeastern American cities could be traced back to "cartage and delivery costs" and "retailers' profits," a share he deemed excessive.[51] In 1916, Henry W. Collingwood, editor of the *Rural New Yorker*, described the distribution system of his time as "so costly, cumbersome, and complicated that it is little short of robbery of both producer and consumer."[52] The future American President, Herbert Hoover, similarly attributed the high cost of food in cities at the time to "faulty transportation" and the multiplicity of "wholesaler, transportation agent, commission man, cold-storage warehouse, food manufacturer [and] retailer," that each needed to make a separate profit on their investment."[53] (More recently, Michael Pollan apparently hit upon the same line of thought when he suggested that the USDA "should make grants to rebuild local distribution networks in order to minimize the amount of energy used to move produce within local food sheds."[54])

Early 20th century American local food activists were given an opportunity to test their ideas during the First World War when the Hoover-run U.S. Food Administration promoted a "policy of local consumption of the vicinity-grown produce."[55] King believed that wartime conditions would make it possible to demonstrate that "to clear the way from the farm to the city and from the city to the farm" would "decrease the farmer's transportation costs and the amount of time spent in marketing his goods; . . . enhance the facilities through which the stores in the small towns can handle more economically both their incoming and outgoing freight;" and "extend the bounds of social life in each agricultural district." Efficient trolley freight service to outlying areas, he added, would "give to the retail stores a smaller transportation charge; give to Philadelphia's manufacturing establishments and stores increased facilities for sales; and give to Philadelphia's consumers fresher produce at better prices."[56]

Meanwhile, a Pennsylvania agricultural extension employee by the name of A. B. Ross proposed a "point of origin plan for marketing" whose key objective was to "reduce transportation to a minimum." This, in turn, would allow

> the feeding of each community, as far as possible, with food from within its own natural trading area, and the laying by of dried, canned, and stored reserves of food from local sources; the keeping of community money within the community area, and using it for community development; the making of each community a self-contained, self-sustaining, compact trading unit; the development of the smaller community centers into exporters of food to the larger cities, reversing the present system whereby natural food-producing areas are importing food.[57]

Ross argued that this plan had been built upon "ten years of patient study, labor, and experimental marketing carried on jointly by farmers and myself" and had met "with the instant, unqualified, and enthusiastic endorsement of the great mass of farmers to whom it has been submitted, and who joined the ranks of nonproducers of city food because they could not make production profitable." His most detailed case study had been conducted in Altoona, then a railroad hub of 58,000 inhabitants. According to his 1915 food survey, of a total annual food bill of $4,200,000, "not less than $1,680,000 [had been spent] for a riot of transportation and retransportation, handling and rehandling, commissioning, jobbing, and the allowance for waste which the retailer must make knowing the condition of the produce when it reaches him."[58]

Commenting on Ross's proposal, the economic geographer Joseph Russell Smith added that approximately 80% of the city's perishable goods were delivered by train, "often [from] long distances" and were therefore chiefly "stale and therefore tasteless, unappetizing and partially inedible vegetables." This situation was actually "typical not only of the small town, but also of the great city" and helped "explain why the way of the vegetarian [was] hard" to follow and why Americans farmers were keen to convert most of their crops into animal meat.[59] If replicated on a large scale, the geographer argued, Ross's plan would allow

5,000 little towns each [to be fed] with good fresh, home-made vegetable food from its own local plant. It would eliminate the waste of vegetables so common in farmers' gardens, for the farmer is not in a position to handle small surpluses. It would eliminate waste of labor by greatly reducing railroad freightage; it would reduce waste of work and lumber by saving the making of thousands of packages. It would reduce waste of labor and money, for middlemen's work and profits would not need to be paid. It would reduce the price of meat, because people would have more abundant and satisfying supplies of substitute foods. By giving to the farmers around every population center the local market for twelve months in a year, it would aid greatly in the intensification of our agriculture and in its fine adjustment to need. We are at the present time a nation that is freight car crazy. We are also crazed by freight car shortage. Next year it will be worse. Here is a way out. Such a point-of-origin standardized plant would give the small town its natural and proper advantage of a lower cost of living than any great city could rival.[60]

In subsequent years, a number of grants were made available to agricultural economists to study local food markets and assess the sensibility of these earlier "eat local" proposals.[61] In recent decades, too, numerous governmental and activist-based initiatives have promoted local food production in contexts ranging from American inner cities to Native American reservations.[62]

Clearly, much historical and recent material can be brought to bear on the current "local food" rhetoric—and we haven't even said anything about the history of similar attempts in Europe.[63] As we will now argue, all the available evidence suggests that locavorism is a fundamentally futile and counterproductive endeavor that repeatedly failed because of sound reasons and not because of conspiracies involving big agricultural interests. Locavores might wax poetic about wartime gardening and other past initiatives, but the fact remains that none of them lasted once most people had other options available to them. As the social reformer Frederic Clemson Howe observed nearly a century ago:

> To many people the city is an evil that exacts so terrible a tribute of misery that they would have us "return to the land." They dream of an age of rural simplicity in which wealth and want no longer stare each other in the face. They would stem the tide to the city and turn back the movements of a century and re-establish the conditions of our fathers. To them the city is not the hope, it is the despair of civilization. But the tide will never turn. Back to the land is an idle

dream. We can no more restore the pastoral age than we can go back to the spindle and the loom.[64]

We will now begin our detailed critique of the locavore rhetoric and policy agenda with the seemingly innocuous claim that getting farmers and end consumers to know each other directly improves a community's social capital.

2

Myth #1: Locavorism Nurtures Social Capital

When each village was a virtually self-sufficing economic
unit, some sense that he was helping to feed his neighbor
must have accompanied the work of the husbandman who
tilled the soil; but the Dakota farmer, whose wheat will
pass into an elevator in Chicago and after long travel will
go to feed some unknown family in Glasgow or in Ham-
burg can hardly be expected to have the same feeling for
the social end which his tilling serves.

—JOHN ATKINSON HOBSON. 1910.
The Industrial System: An Inquiry into Earned and Unearned Income.
Longmans, Green & Co, p. 320

From the beginning of markets and civilization, intermediaries have
been engaged in the assembling, grading, packaging, processing,
storing, transporting, financing, distributing, and advertising of goods
and services of all kinds. As a result of their activities, primary producers and final consumers quickly lost track of each other. Writing
more than two millennia ago, Plato described in his *Republic* a class of

41

"retailers" who "sit in the market-place [and] engaged in buying and selling." These individuals proved especially useful when a farmer brought "some production to market . . . at a time when there is no one to exchange with him."[1] Closer to us, in an economic fable written in the 1840s, the economist Frédéric Bastiat described a French shoemaker who could not identify the countries of origins for the wheat that fed him, the coal that kept him warm, and the leather, nails, and hammer that he used in his trade.[2] In *Tess of the d'Ubervilles*, Thomas Hardy's 1891 novel, two protagonists talk about the milk they have just loaded onto a train in the following way:

> "Londoners will drink it at their breakfasts to-morrow, won't they?" she asked. "Strange people that we have never seen."
>
> "Yes—I suppose they will. Though not as we send it. When its strength has been lowered, so that it may not get up into their heads."
>
> "Noble men and noble women, ambassadors and centurions, ladies and tradeswomen, and babies who have never seen a cow."
>
> "Well, yes; perhaps; particularly centurions."
>
> "Who don't know anything of us, and where it comes from; or think how we two drove miles across the moor to-night in the rain that it might reach 'em in time?"[3]

By the early 1920s, the geographer Ray Hughes Whitbeck documented how "one or more railway companies, several truckmen, a wholesale dealer or two, a retail dealer and his clerks, a delivery boy, and perhaps several other persons or corporations" along with perhaps even "one or more brokers" stood between a grapefruit grower and his laborers and his final consumer in a northern American city.[4]

Not surprisingly, these activities have long been decried as superfluous and parasitical by critics who, as Bastiat observed in 1848, "would willingly eliminate the capitalist, the banker, the speculator, the entrepreneur, the businessman, and the merchant, accusing them of interposing themselves between producer and consumer in order to fleece them both, without giving them anything of value."[5] Antipathy against intermediaries was always heightened during food crises. Writing in the early years of the Napoleonic wars, a time of rapid price increases, the political economist Robert Thomas Malthus observed that the general indignation of common people had fallen upon "monopolizers, fore-stallers, and regraters—words, that are . . . applied indiscriminately to all middle men whatever, to every kind of trader that goes between the grower of the commodity and the consumer . . ."[6]

Today's locavores are but the latest activists to echo this sentiment with their contention that direct relationships between producers and consumers will improve a community's social capital while putting more money directly into farmers' (as opposed to intermediaries') pockets. Another frequent claim is that the prying eyes of nearby consumers will drastically accelerate the adoption of more sustainable farming practices than if food is sourced from distant producers subject to impersonal competitive pressures. To quote activist Jill Richardson:

> At its heart, the [local food] movement is about relationships. When you buy food at the store, your purchasing decision rests mainly on marketing claims. But when I pick up my weekly box of produce from Farmer Phil, I know exactly how and where he grew my food, and that his values are consistent with mine. Organic certification alone does not certify anything other than a minimum bar of stan-dards; by buying from farmers who are part of my community, whose farms I've visited, I am contributing to my local economy, supporting my friends' businesses, and getting great, fresh food. And the farmers from whom I buy are taking care of the land right near where I live.[7]

Despite its appeal, the locavores' well-meaning longings for direct relationships will prove inherently expensive and wasteful—and, as such, unlikely to promote the creation of much social capital. Our point here is not that all intermediaries necessarily add value; rather, what we challenge is the belief that the elimination of intermediaries will in itself benefit both producers and consumers.[8] In order to make our case, though, a few words are warranted on some underappreciated mechanisms and institutions that underpin modern market transactions.

Grades, Standards, and Brands

Consumers can typically learn about the variety, quality, and countries of origins of the fruits, vegetables, meat, and farm-raised fish and seafood they purchase on a regular basis, but not necessarily the name of specific producers.[9] So why do we buy specific grades of different types of apples rather than the offerings of farmer McDonald? Simply put, because the advantages of such a system were too great for both consumers and the most efficient producers to be ignored. Think of it this way. While most apples in retail stores have become "undifferentiated" as far as their appearance and quality are concerned, not all apples - even if grown on the same tree—are treated the same. In our country, they are classified according to quality and consistency: Canada Extra Fancy, Canada Fancy, Canada Commercial, Canada Hailed, Canada Commercial Cookers, Canada No. 1 Peelers, and Canada No. 2 Peelers. Depending on their grade, apples will be sold directly to consumers or to food manufacturers who need "good enough" apples for making juice, pie and pastry fillings, jelly and other products rather than the perfect apples sold directly to consumers.

Grades and standards help to ensure that producers of quality output obtain maximum value; that buyers of all kinds of agricultural commodities know exactly what they are getting without having to inspect every shipment; that handling (regular size and shape are essential for most efficient and secure packaging) and transportation can be done more effectively by combining the production of similar goods from different producers; and that commodities not deemed suitable for human consumption are nonetheless put to other appropriate uses (from animal feed to industrial grade alcohol). This system had many pioneers, but Danish pig producers were once among the most celebrated. As the geographer Joseph Russell Smith wrote admiringly in 1917, the "marvelous [standardized Danish pig] is a certain cross of breeds being grown by thousands of farmers, fed in approximately the same way, slaughtered at the uniform size of maximum efficiency for food consumption, cut up and cured in the prescribed way so that a piece of Danish bacon is a piece of Danish bacon, and you can buy it with your eyes shut."[10]

One often-highlighted advantage of product standardization in its early days was that it significantly reduced food waste. Manufacturers were able "to pack the produce of a hundred gardens from a hundred nearby farms or backyards, freely commingling them if need be, and put up standardized packages of peas, beans and beets of the same variety, picked in the same degree of ripeness and thus acceptable in any market to which they could be easily sent."[11] By facilitating sales in a wide variety of markets, grades and standards ensured that orders could be made in advance and perishable produce shipped around most efficiently where there was an effective demand.[12]

Predictably, the geographical origins of standardized commodities became increasingly distant from their points of sale. In 1925, the Deputy Secretary of Agriculture of Pennsylvania observed that, despite the initiatives of local food activists described in chapter 1, chain stores had from their beginning been "more inclined to buy in carload lots from the large producing centers, where they can get a standard grade of product which will run more uniform than the seasonal output of local producers." Nonetheless, local producers who could supply a "substantial quantity of graded, dependable products" were able to thrive. He further added that through modern methods "the number of intermediate handlings are reduced very greatly and transportation charges are at a minimum with the result that both producer and consumer find the outcome satisfactory."[13] However, as could be expected of all public officials whose support relied to some extent on local farmers threatened by "outside" competition (in this case, mostly from Virginia, Delaware, and Maryland), he insisted that a "better balance between local production and consumption is in the interest of society as a whole" and that it would "seem desirable from many standpoints for our population to spread out in more moderate-sized centers, within easy reach of extensive food production areas, rather than to further congest in large cities."[14] As we now know, none of this happened in following decades as customers typically insisted on maximum value for their dollars rather than giving priority to geographical origins.

Greater quality, convenience, affordability, and reduced waste are not the only tangible benefits of modern retail food practices. Through the development of brands for mass-produced commodities and products (brand-name reputations for luxury products go back at least to Antiquity), consumers were able to economize on the time that would have otherwise been required to establish the trustworthiness of multiple suppliers. Of course, marketers rarely refrained from simultaneously using both technological novelty and pastoral nostalgia or to stretch or bend the truth as much as possible in order to promote their products. For instance, the Quaker Oats man came to symbolize a firm with no connections to the Society of Friends, but whose founders liked the values associated with the group. Nonetheless, individuals who purchased Quaker Oats products could be assured of their quality, uniformity, and reliability. Large businesses that claimed too much for their products were always kept in check by trial lawyers and competitors on the lookout for deep pockets that strayed too far from truth-in-advertising. Some readers might remember the case of the *Papa John's* chain, which got into legal trouble in the late 1990s because of its slogan "Better Ingredients. Better Pizza!" something the firm obviously couldn't prove. Small firms and fly-by-night operations, on the other hand, rarely if ever face such constraints as they are not worth their competitors' and trial lawyers' time and resources.

Interestingly, 19th century food activists were forever denouncing the shady dealings of *local* businesspeople whom they accused of adulterating food in various ways, be it by adding water to milk, wine and beer; roasted chicory roots, peas, beans, and other grains to coffee; poppy seed oil to olive oil; leaves of all kinds to tea; floor sweepings of pepper houses into pepper; alum, chalk, white clay, bone ashes, field beans, and copper sulphate (to mask its spoiled character) to flour; rice powder and arrow roots to cream; crushed olive stones in pepper; starch to sausages; spurred rye to bread; glucose, sorghum, corn, and boiled brown sugar to maple syrup; and of artificially inflating the weight of wheat by keeping it in humid conditions; feeding salt to cattle in order to get them to drink plenty of water and artificially increase their weight, and tampering with weighing devices, among others.[15] A classic 1820 treatment of the issue is entitled *Treatise on the Adulteration of Foods, and Culinary Poisons, Exhibiting the Fraudulent Sophistications of Bread, Beer, Wine, Spirituous Liquors, Tea, Coffee, Cream, Confectionery, Vinegar, Mustard, Pepper, Cheese, Olive Oil, Pickles, and Other Articles Employed in Domestic Economy, and Methods of Detecting Them.*[16]

Not surprisingly, such accusations were always easier to direct at foreign than local producers. For instance, a French Inspector General at the Paris Customs, Jacques Savary des Brûlons, observed in the late 18th century that Irish producers had "no scruples about adding all matter of substances to increase the weight [of goods] such as… tallow in butter, pebbles in tallow and the horns and feet of cattle in barrels of salted meat."[17] Of course, it is probably worth keeping in mind that because of the inherently protectionist bent of the French administration at the time, Savary des Brûlons might have had a vested interest in denigrating foreign goods or keeping silent about the fact that French merchants might have been just as bad in this respect. Be that as it may, as the author of the 1911 *Encyclopedia Britannica* entry on "adulteration" observed, the practice was "as old as commerce itself."[18]

Lest we convey the mistaken impression that most agricultural producers, intermediaries, and merchants are inherently dishonest and have no interest in building repeat business, the fact remains that not everyone who welcomes customers with broad smiles and open arms at farmers' market might be telling you the truth. Indeed, the determination of local food activists to purchase as much as possible "beyond the barcode" rather than from "brand bullies" greatly facilitates the shady or unprofessional dealings of unscrupulous and inefficient producers and retailers.

The Pitfalls of Farmers' Markets and CSAs

Farmers' markets—while often limited in terms of convenience (from out-of-the-way locations and poor parking conditions to restricted hours and a lack of protection from the elements) and typically offering slim pickings at the beginning and end of growing seasons—often provide enjoyable shopping experiences. If busy and tired farmers (as they often are when their produce is in season) can muster the energy to engage in long conversations with inquisitive customers, then so much the better.

One recurring problem at these markets, though, is that some merchants are actually resellers peddling nonlocal products under false pretenses.[19] Sometimes, as we observed on a couple of occasions at a Mississauga, Ontario, farmers' market, the brand-named boxes in the back of their trucks will give them away. Of course, other dishonest sellers are regrettably cleverer in this respect, but some investigative actions can nonetheless expose them. For example, in 2010, an NBC News team in Los Angeles paid a visit to the farms where vendors claimed the food at their stalls had been grown. In some cases, the investigators found "fields full of weeds or dry, empty fields. The vendors were selling vegetables and fruits they had bought wholesale, and were selling it at premium prices at local farmer's markets, claiming it was locally grown and organic." Several "organic" and "pesticide-free" items tested positive for chemicals at a level that could not be accounted for by pesticide "drift" from nearby farms. Commenting on such occurrences, a food activist who acknowledges that similar problems are "happening all over the country" makes the following recommendations:

- *Research, research, research.* Try to get to know a few vendors really well. Ask where their farm is located, how long they've been farming, how they handle pest and disease issues. See if they're listed on sites such as Local Harvest—not all farmers are, but it doesn't hurt to check. Ask them the specific variety of whatever produce they're selling. If they really grew it, they should be able to tell you that those are 'Emerite' filet beans, not just "green beans."

- *Look over the display.* Really look . . . Are all of the tomatoes the exact same shape and size? Do the apples have that waxy supermarket look? Are the cucumbers all perfectly uniform? Are they selling "local" watermelon in Detroit during the first week of May? If so, they probably went to the warehouse club and bought produce to sell at a premium at the farmer's market. Steer clear.

- *Know what's in season!* If you see watermelon in April or peppers in December in Minnesota or Michigan, chances are good that they have not been grown locally. While some farmers have large heated greenhouses to grow produce year-round, not all do, and it pays to ask questions if the vendor is displaying a lot of out-of-season produce.[20]

Good advice, if you can spare the time and are really passionate about local agriculture and farmers . . . Yet, it can be problematic on a few levels. A food policy analyst acquaintance of ours was thus told by some farmers that they now send their worst produce to farmers' markets because customers think that imperfections and blemishes are an indicator of authenticity. According to Linda Crago, a Niagara peninsula organic producer, local farmers will not always give truthful answers to customers. Besides, even a local certified organic producer who knows what he is talking about might have resorted to using other technologies to address a recurring pest problem or simply to increase his yields and profits. This problem is made even worse by the fact that certified North American organic farms are never field-tested, let alone randomly tested. Ms. Crago personally witnessed her vegetables listed on the menus of restaurants she had never sold to, even sometimes in May when the produce is a long way from being ripe. She had been invited "to appear at events in restaurants so there is the appearance of a close relationship with a chef. Sometimes there is no relationship . . . only for the event, but not before or after."[21]

While alternative producer Joel Salatin is fond of saying that "you can't legislate integrity,"[22] the fact remains that small operators have much less at stake than bigger ones in this regard as they have small pockets and are not worth suing. And unlike full-time buyers and food safety inspectors employed by large corporations, locavores can only ask superficial questions, rarely if ever spare the time to inspect agriculture operations and virtually none of them could recognize *Salmonella* under a microscope. Can the old-fashioned locavore's way ever deliver greater honesty than brand names and legal actions? If this were the case, there would have been no need to develop brand names in the first place.

Small local farmers, like large commercial ones, may also select the most lucrative path above the ethos of locavorism. The issue was given some prominence a few years ago at the renowned Santa Monica Farmers' Market in southern California when home cooks began to complain that purchasers employed by local high-end restaurants would show up at the crack of dawn and quickly whisk away the best of the most exotic produce. Soon after, produce companies did the local chefs one better by ordering items in advance and selling them to high-end restaurants and markets across the country.[23]

Even more problematic are community-supported agriculture (CSA) initiatives.[24] In such schemes, farmers who grow food and a group of individuals who decide to support them agree on advanced purchases of items such as vegetables, fruits, meat, eggs, cheese, honey, and frozen produce off-season. Depending on the nature of the arrangement and prices paid, the participating farmer will offer a selection of seasonal items at regular intervals (typically once a week) and either deliver them to consumers' doors or arrange for pickup at a central location or at the farm (sometimes with additional work being done by the purchaser).

The key features of CSAs are that deliveries vary greatly from week to week depending on the available crops (leafy greens one week, blueberries another) and that participants "share the risk" with the farmer they support. In other words, if a farmer experiences a good growing season, the weekly haul may be larger than expected, but the reverse is also true. The main benefits touted by CSA promoters include getting to know the people who produce your food, cutting out intermediaries, the possibility of directly supporting socially conscious farmers who rely on organic methods and pay their workers a living wage, and fresher and healthier products. And yet, as promoters and supporters themselves have been forced to acknowledge, these schemes are full of difficulties.

According to Atlanta-based journalist, blogger, and former CSA member Patti Ghezzi, "inconvenient drop-off locations or contracts that require more time or money than you can afford" are a major hurdle. She also had to face a "sudden onslaught of produce" that required the acquisition of significant cooking skills and equipment along with a serious time commitment for food preparation. When time was in short supply, the outcome was the "composting [of] a lot of produce." Production problems on the farm, be they weather, pest, or equipment-related, also forced her to buy produce at the grocery store that at the end of the season proved to be a "budget buster." Turning random and little-known produce into edible meals was often too challenging. As she put it: "Some greens are tricky to prepare. I never could figure out what to do with parsnips and some of the funny-looking squash I received. And the pumpkin I got in November? It rotted on my porch."[25]

Another freelance writer and blogger, Lynda Altman, complained that "shared risk" often "meant receiving produce with major insect damage. In particular, one delivery of apples was full of worms and could not be used. Other times, the produce was beautiful, but I expected that there would have been more." She further found out that the delivery time was not as convenient as she had first expected in light of her own hectic schedule. Planning each delivery according to family requirements was extremely challenging (for instance, what if the kids are gone for a few days or if you're hosting extra guests?) and resulted in much more waste than if the food had been purchased at the supermarket. Indeed, she learned that "wasted produce is the most common reason for people not to continue with a CSA program."[26]

Even CSA proponents recognize that products will typically "vary in size and appearance and do not follow the rules of systematic grocery store perfection," that "unfavorable weather and field conditions may occasionally cause crop shortages, resulting in less-than-perfect quality of one or more types of vegetable for a while, or even their complete absence," that the "same vegetable or fruit may show up in your shares for several weeks in a row," that participants "receive what the farmer gives [them and] cannot pick and choose [their] produce," and that "other than items that can be stored, such as onions, potatoes or dried beans, [participants] receive produce that is in season." For some participants who are expected to pick their share from the fields, it must be done "every week on a specific day during a specific time period," and if they don't, it is donated to charity.[27]

Problems such as these could have been easily anticipated by individuals more familiar with the valuable role played by intermediaries in the food trade sector and are a useful reminder of why our modern food supply chain evolved as it did. Gathering, inspecting, sorting, packaging, and delivering food items where and when they are sought after is no mean feat. In our assessment, what CSA promoters are truly achieving by eliminating middlemen is to shift the risks inherent to food production from growers and intermediaries onto consumers. As the agricultural policy analyst Gary Blumenthal observes, the real importance of the "small, local, and organic" movement is that it has "enabled some farmers to avoid the cost and risk of innovation by instead extracting greater income from consumers by utilizing psychological manipulation."[28] Attempts to rebuild social capital through such one-sided relationships are not worth supporting.

Mom-and-Pops vs. Megastores

Another recurring complaint related to vanishing social capital is that megastores and international chains are rapidly eradicating "mom-and-pop" operations. Such a stance, however, ignores the fact that consumers ultimately determine the outlook of the retail landscape through their decisions on where they spend their money (including online shopping). As such, one can hardly deny that they have long favored the greater variety and lower prices of large retail stores over their alleged special relationships with smaller outlets.[29] True, the world is becoming more homogenized as each city or town increasingly features the same stores and restaurant chains.[30] This reality hurts the sensibilities of well-off tourists, cultural critics, and activists who would rather have each location be more "authentic"—except typically for the one where they personally reside, which must readily offer the best of everything. Yet, national and international retail chains still ultimately get the bulk of their business from physical stores located in specific communities where local inhabitants are free to patronize them, their large competitors, or smaller outlets. As such, they add value to the lives of their customers as long as they remain profitable, for consumers ultimately express their appreciation with their shopping dollars. Besides, many local retail outlets of "national" corporations sponsor local activities. By providing more convenient and affordable shopping experiences, they also leave otherwise busy people more time and money to volunteer or donate to various causes and activities. Nurturing social capital is not a small business monopoly.

Shantytowns and Social Capital

Many locavores bemoan the dislocation or obliteration of traditional lifestyles in the pursuit of greater material wealth. In their opinion, more abundant consumer offerings are poor substitutes for friendly smiles, ready laughter, and communal bliss. This romantic longing for a way of life from the distant past is probably as old as urbanization and the existence of wealthy individuals—from aristocrats to the progeny of prosperous urban merchants and professionals—who could afford to see urbanization, long-distance trade, and new technologies as fundamentally incompatible with the "natural" order of things. This attitude goes back at least to Roman antiquity[31] as exemplified in Virgil's *Eclogues* (or *Bucolics*, poems written in a classical style on a rural subject)[32] and Horace's references to big city life as a "bit of Hell" and his observation that "the whole choir of poets loves woods, and hates the city."[33] In England and the United States, a long line of activists, writers, poets, craftspeople, visual artists, and documentary filmmakers have expressed such pastoral and anti-urban feelings.[34]

Yet the fact remains that, throughout history, significant migratory movements of populations have taken place from the countryside to the cities and not the other way around—in fact, some ancestors of today's most fervent urban and suburban locavores must have been part of this movement. From the perspective of individuals caught in the urban rat race, small-scale farming and the promise of a simpler life often looks appealing. But the harsh reality is that agricultural production has never been all that enjoyable, as working outside not only meant fresh air but also burning sun, rain, insects, snakes, large dangerous animals, mud, and dust—all for a typically meager and uncertain return. As one African rural migrant observes: "My mother still sleeps in a mud house, drinks from polluted streams, and walks for long distances carrying heavy loads of cocoa... This is not because it is idyllic to do so, and neither is it because it is part of her culture; it is because she has no choice!"[35]

Wasn't it also Adam who, upon being chased out of the Garden of Eden, was condemned to a life of agricultural toil and unrelenting drudgery after he had eaten the forbidden fruit? Whatever else they may have gotten wrong about the origins of life and pre-agricultural societies, the authors of the book of Genesis knew firsthand the reality of primitive agriculture when they wrote that "Cursed is the ground . . . through painful toil you will eat of it all the days of your life. It will produce thorns and thistles for you . . . By the sweat of your brow you will eat your food until you return to the ground . . ."[36] Also cursed, observed Thoreau in *Walden*, were the young men living in the vicinity of Concord, Massachusetts, "whose misfortune it is to have inherited farms, houses, barns, cattle, and farming tools; for these are more easily acquired than got rid of. Better if they had been born in the open pasture and suckled by a wolf, that they might have seen with clearer eyes what field they were called to labor in."[37]

From the real-world perspective of a subsistence farmer or farm laborer, the lure of city lights is easily understood. As the Marxist theorist Karl Kautsky observed over a century ago, "towns offer wage-labourers quite different opportunities for employment than rural areas, much more opportunity for establishing a household, more freedom and more culture. The larger the town, the more these advantages grow, and the greater its drawing power."[38] The same process has also occurred more recently and for the same reasons in less advanced economies, as observed by the Canadian regional economist Mario Polèse:

> Surveys carried out in third world cities have time and time again arrived at the same conclusions: in almost all cases, individuals who had left the countryside for the city stated that their condition had improved. This conclusion is perhaps difficult to accept, but in the end the prevailing conditions in the countryside determine the relative attractiveness of [a] city. By almost any measure (health, employment opportunities, sanitation, educational facilities, etc.) conditions are generally far worse in rural areas... People move to where the opportunities are, even if such opportunities may appear terribly inadequate to today's western observer. People move because they believe they and their children will be better off. Were they worse off in the city, they would move back to the countryside.[39]

Polèse also observes that it "should thus come as no surprise that attempts to slow down or to stop urbanization have failed miserably" and that in places like China where political authorities were able to do so temporarily, the result was "even greater rural-urban income disparities and an explosion of urbanization once the measures [were] lifted."[40] People should be given the alternatives that only large and prosperous, if chaotic and unsettling, cities can offer. As the economist Edward Glaeser observes: "Megacities are not too big. Limiting their growth would cause significantly more hardship than gain, and urban growth is a great way to reduce rural poverty."[41] And reducing rural poverty, we suggest, is a great way to improve social capital.

Higher Food Prices and Humanistic Pursuits

The greatest social blow delivered by locavorism, however, is ultimately much reduced food diversity (for no location can produce more than a fraction of the world's offering) and higher food prices that will either force people to cut down on overall consumption or switch to less interesting alternatives. Michael Pollan's mantra to "pay more, eat less" may seem eminently sensible to upper middle class consumers who can always cut back on the cappuccinos in order to spend eight dollars for a dozen eggs and $3.90 for a pound of Frog Hollow peaches.[42] Yet, we somehow doubt that most folks who do their best to stretch their food budget—not to mention malnourished people the world over—will become more likely to contribute to a thriving community life as a result once they leave the cash register.

The basic contention of local food activists that their initiatives promote the acquaintance of food producers and consumers is unassailable. Yet, because something is true does not make it significant or worth pursuing at all costs. In the end, as the agricultural policy analyst Gary Blumenthal reminds us, "while 70 percent of the world's poor may be farmers, 100 percent are consumers and the fastest way to elevate the well-being of poor consumers is to reduce their share of income spent on food."[43] Providing the basic necessities of life at ever more affordable prices should be the starting point of all discussions on local social capital. Locavorism should at least do as well as our modern food system in this respect. To underline this point, let's start with a current benchmark: In 2010, American families and individuals spent 9.4% of their disposable income on food compared to more than 23% in 1929; in terms of home food consumption expenditures, Americans only spent 6.4% of their disposable income compared to about 15% in Japan and European Union countries, and more than 40% in some African countries.[44] As we will explain in the next chapter, the real price tag of locavorism would be much closer to that higher figure.

3

Myth #2: Locavorism Delivers a Free Economic Lunch

Message to the Shopping Public—British First! Buying Empire goods means buying the produce of your own Country and of the Empire Overseas, instead of the produce of foreign countries . . . Support your own Best Customers. Last year the Nations of the Empire Overseas spent the enormous sum of nearly £335,000,000 on goods produced in the United Kingdom. Man for man, they are your best customers. And that is a sound practical reason for "shopping within the Empire" yourself. Every time you buy Canadian salmon, Australian fruit, New Zealand lamb, South African wine, Indian tea, you are dealing with the very people who go out of the way to spend money on the goods made in your own country, and so to create employment, pay wages and increase prosperity here. Buy Empire Goods. Ask—Is it British?

—EMPIRE MARKETING BOARD,
proposed advertisement for British newspapers, 1926[1]

Perhaps the most appealing claim of locavores is that diverting consumer dollars once spent on "distant" food items towards others produced nearby will boost local employment. But as with all protectionist schemes that keep more affordable foreign products out of a local economy and undermine the production of things in the locations where they make the most economic sense, locavorism can only deliver poorly paid jobs and massive wealth destruction.

The Broken Window Fallacy

Apart from encouraging consumers to spend more of their own money on local food, a key belief of locavores is that a greater percentage of governmental food purchases for school lunches, prisons, military bases, hospitals, and other agencies and bureaucracies spent "within 100 miles [will] revive local agriculture… create more jobs on farms [and promote] rural redevelopment."[2] Channeling "even a small portion of institutional food purchasing to local food," Michael Pollan argues, "would vastly expand regional agriculture and improve the diet of the millions of people these institutions feed."[3] The reasoning underlying such proposals was spelled out more explicitly by the writer and communication consultant Leah Bloom:

> [When] you buy local, a large percentage of the money stays in your community. The farmer can afford to have the local mechanic fix his truck, the mechanic can afford to hire a local accountant to do his taxes, and the accountant can afford dinner out at a local restaurant. The wait staff makes decent tips, and the restaurant can afford to buy more fresh, local food to serve. Money also trickles into the local infrastructure—improvements to the public park, funding for academic enrichment, and so on. Everyone wins.[4]

The fundamental problem with this argument was perhaps best addressed by the economist Frédéric Bastiat in his classic 1848 essay, *What*

Is Seen and What Is Not Seen, in which he states that a good economist will take "into account both the effect that can be seen and those effects that must be *foreseen*." This difference is crucial, "for it almost always happens that when the immediate consequence is favorable, the later consequences are disastrous, and vice versa." A bad economist, Bastiat wrote, will pursue a "small present good that will be followed by a great evil to come." A good one, on the other hand, will pursue instead a "great good to come, at the risk of a small present evil."[5]

Bastiat illustrated this insight by imagining an all too typical reaction from an onlooker reflecting on the accidental breaking of a store window. "Everybody has to make a living," he observes. Besides, what "would become of the glaziers if no one ever broke a window?" Fair enough. But the passerby then observes that "it is good to break windows" because "it helps to circulate money," something which benefits the economy in general. Well then, the economist interjects, don't you see that "since our citizen has spent six francs for one thing, he will not be able to spend them for another?" If the windowpane was still in one piece, the store owner would have spent his money on something else, perhaps a new pair of shoes or a book. What is true for this citizen is also true for industry in general. "If the window had not been broken, the shoe industry (or some other) would have received six francs' worth of encouragement; *that is what is not seen*." In one case you have an economy in which a window has been broken and replaced. In another, you have an economy that has a perfectly good window *plus something else*. Despite the recurring nonsense emanating from the media in the wake of wars and natural catastrophes, no economic blessings stem from destruction.

The basic logic of what Bastiat enthusiasts have dubbed the "broken window fallacy" similarly applies to the short-sighted reasoning of local food protectionists. By forcing people to buy more expensive local food, locavorism impoverishes consumers who will then have less money to spend on other things, including other locally produced goods and services. For instance, a few years ago, one (admittedly, industry funded) food analyst observed that for $12.25 he could purchase at a nearby supermarket items comparable to the 7 ears of corn, 7 jumbo apples, 6 tomatoes, and loaf of multigrain bread he had bought for $29 at a Washington, D.C. farmers market.[6] In the original "100-mile diet" experiment,[7] in 2005 a couple based in southwest British Columbia had to spend significantly more money on purchasing locally grown products (both organic and conventional) than if they had bought comparable substitutes at their local supermarkets. For example, a locally grown organic salad mix cost $17.99 a pound compared to about $7.00 a pound for a conventional salad mix and honey, $11 a kilo instead of $2.59 for a kilo of sugar. (Of course, a beekeeper friend of ours insists that these are really not substitutes, but bear with us…) In addition, the time spent acquiring and preparing food (for both immediate and later consumption) was comparable to holding a part-time job.

Truth be told, however, the higher prices paid by the British Columbia couple were only a small fraction of what they would have been if the other local people they bought various goods and services from had also engaged in their experiment. This is because the extra time and money these other merchants and farmers would have had to devote to local food purchases and preparation would have forced them either to increase the costs of the services they provided or cut down on their capacity to offer them. Furthermore, because locavores will buy less from foreigners, the latter will have fewer resources available to purchase other goods and services made wholly or partly in the locavores' community, thus destroying a number of "local" jobs in the process.

Although this should go without saying, higher consumer prices always and everywhere mean greater poverty and a lower standard of living for all. True wealth and job creation do not flow from consumers paying more to obtain less, but rather from innovative developments that deliver better products at lower prices, in the process allowing individuals to increase consumption and to invest in the creation of new ways of doing things and of new useful things to do.

In the realm of food production, significant advances in the volume, quality, and affordability of items created would have been impossible without the development of long distance trade, regional specialization, and economies of scale. In the long run, these not only improved the living standard of consumers, but also of agricultural workers who remained in this sector and those who left it for better opportunities. Unfortunately, locavores typically misconstrue the real economic impact of each of these factors, as we will now illustrate.

Physical Geography and Agricultural Specialization

As with all economic activities, a range of factors affects the profitability of agricultural endeavors, from the costs of various inputs (from diesel to insurance) and tax policies to consumers' shifting demands and producers' marketing abilities. More than any other sector, however, the success or failure of agricultural productions depends on where they take place. True, innovative behavior can sometimes overcome the shortcomings inherent to poorer, rockier, or less leveled soils; unsuitable climate for certain crops; less abundant water; or the poor quality of pastureland. Yet, as Adam Smith observed over two centuries ago, in many cases the "natural advantages which one country has over another in producing particular commodities are sometimes so great, that it is acknowledged by all the world to be in vain to struggle with them." For instance, with the help of the greenhouse technologies of his day, Smith observed, decent grapes could be grown in Scotland from which a very good wine could be made—but "at about 30 times the expense for which at least equally good can be brought from foreign countries." He then asked rhetorically if it would be reasonable to adopt a law "to prohibit the importation of all foreign wines, merely to encourage the making of claret and burgundy in Scotland?" Doing so, he points out, "would be a manifest absurdity" inasmuch as Scottish people would have to use thirty times as many resources than if they were to import wine from Southern Europe, resources which would then be no longer available to create wealth in other activities more suited to local conditions.[8]

Smith's example was deliberately extreme in order to make his point, but many significant productivity differences between locations are often not obvious to nonspecialists. For example, fruit and vegetable producers located in more humid regions typically face more serious fungus problems than those located in drier ones. Some apple varieties are less resistant to cold weather than others. Dairy farmers whose pastureland is chock full of clover and high quality grass have less need to buy additional feed for their cows than competitors whose animals graze on poorer vegetation. Producers who benefit from a substantially longer growing season can justify massive investments in the development of new plant varieties that yield more berries over longer periods of time.

Whether obvious or more subtle, however, the most glaring shortcoming of the locavores' economic rhetoric is that it ignores productivity differentials—and therefore production costs—between agricultural locations. As all of agricultural history illustrates, trade between regions that specialize in products for which they have significant advantages (say, wine or wheat) delivers more food for less money than if producers in both regions tried to grow a range of crops unsuitable to their soil and climate. Though this is a basic fact of agricultural life, a growing number of local food activists argue that present-day regional specialization is largely the result of agricultural subsidies that benefit a few select crops such as corn. Get rid of these "comparative advantage mirages," they argue, and the economic profitability of monocultures will quickly be overtaken by those of polycultures—plots of land on which multiple and complementary plants and animals are produced.[9] These arguments, however, do not stand up in light of the available historical evidence.

First, large-scale monocultures long predate modern subsidies and are as ancient as urbanization and maritime transportation—as is attested by, among other evidence, the large grain and olive-oil trade of Mediterranean antiquity. For instance, during Ancient Athens' peak period, its soft bread wheat supply was imported by ships from production zones located in what is now southern Russia, the Aegean islands, and the Greek mainland. Because of their poorer soil and drier climate, producers in Athens' hinterland could not compete with these foreigners and instead focused their efforts on growing barley (mostly for local consumption) and replanted lands formerly devoted to grain production with vineyards and olive and fig orchards, the output of which was both consumed domestically and exported over long distances.[10]

The case made by food activists on behalf of polycultures is similarly weak. In short, polycultures—thanks to the supposed positive effects of the interactions of their attendant species—are said to deliver large amounts of food from little more than "soil, water, and sunlight."[11] To bolster their case, proponents of alternative agricultural systems often point to the Japanese farmer Takao Furuno who, on his seven-acre Kyushu farm, produces enough rice, vegetables, duck meat and eggs, fish, and vegetables to feed 100 local families.[12] How this approach fundamentally differs from old-fashioned subsistence agriculture—now often labeled "globally-important ingenious agricultural heritage systems" (GIAHS) by activists and sustainable development theorists[13]— isn't clear to us. After all, subsistence agriculture (GIAHS) is built on "natural ecological processes" rather than "against them; . . . endowed with nutrient-enriching plants, insect predators, pollinators, nitrogen-fixing and nitrogen-decomposing bacteria, and a variety of other organisms that perform various beneficial ecological functions;" and characterized by "small farm size" and "diversified production based on mixtures of crops, trees, and animals with high genetic variability, maximum use of local resources, and low dependence on off-farm inputs" (such as synthetic chemicals manufactured in distant locations).[14] Or, as the historian Peter Garnsey observed in 1988, the ancient Greek and Roman small farmer "traditionally practiced mixed farming, the polycropping of arable and trees on the same land with the addition of a little livestock."[15] Nice indeed, unless one remembers that subsistence farming everywhere always delivered very little return and low standards of living for all the hard labor required.

Of course, what really sets Furuno and other modern polyculture "pioneers" apart from their predecessors is that they benefit from much more advanced technologies and knowledge—agricultural machinery, electricity, carbon fuels, refrigeration, transportation, electric fences, the help of agricultural extension scientists, etc.—and much wealthier customers, thanks to the fact that they ply their trade in societies in which long-distance trade, urbanization, and commercial agriculture have long displaced subsistence agriculture. Like all subsistence farmers before them, however, practitioners of "modern" polycultures exhibit comparatively low productivity and thus entail many more man-hours per unit of output. According to one sympathetic report, Furuno's approach "requires far more intensive and continuous management than does its industrial counterpart" and he "must carefully monitor the performance of each crop and apply any new insights the following season—requirements that add considerably to a farmer's labor hours."[16] According to Matt Liebman, Iowa State University's cropping system diversification and polyculture expert, this method can require almost twice the labor hours as that of a conventional agribusiness approach. Lower productivity and longer hours are then translated into higher price tags for consumers.[17] There are good practical reasons why subsistence agriculture systems were supplanted by large-scale monocultures in all developing economies a long time ago and they are still very relevant today. The importance of differences in soil and climate, along with the overall resources (including manpower) required to produce food, cannot be overlooked.

In the end, the fact that many otherwise prosperous locations are not amenable to a locavore lifestyle is too obvious to be ignored by proponents of locavorism, although they sometimes find a simple way around it. Perhaps the most telling example in this respect is that of writer Barbara Kingsolver who left her home outside of Tucson, Arizona, and relocated full-time with her family to a farm in Washington County in rural Virginia, "a place that could feed us: where rain falls, crops grow, and drinking water bubbles right up out of the grounds."[18]

She chronicled their experiences in a book that became a bestseller, *Animal, Vegetable, Miracle: A Year of Food Life*. We have no doubt that life in Washington County is pleasant if you can make a go of it. To most people, however, a location like Tucson—despite the fact that it was in its third year of drought when the Kingsolvers left and residents wouldn't last long without massive food imports—offers more opportunities for personal development.

The Importance of Latitude

Latitude is another geographical consideration whose importance and benefits are widely misunderstood and underappreciated. The key issue here is that otherwise comparable production locations situated some distance from each other on a north-south axis will experience different ripening periods for the same commodity. Latitude was of comparatively little economic importance until the development of transportation and preservation technologies that could move perishable items quickly and cheaply over long distances, but it became crucial as soon as this was accomplished. To understand why, however, one must first understand the typical problems of "local" markets in perishable food items before these developments.

In short, neighboring farmers everywhere always grew similar things that reached maturity simultaneously. In good years, local producers would flood area markets with their produce, severely depressing prices and wasting much of their crops in the process. In bad ones, when insects, plant diseases, bad weather, or floods had taken their toll, very little if anything might be available.

In what might be termed a typical case of the "curse of good years," the historian Blake McKelvey observes that, at the beginning of the 19th century, settlers in the greater Rochester region in upstate New York knew perfectly well that "theirs was a great fruit country," but unfortunately the "slow and costly transport facilities practically prohibited the shipment of fruit." Knowing they couldn't make a living specializing in their production, they instead directed most of their efforts to less perishable items like forest products and grain—by 1838, Rochester was the largest flour-producing city in the world and consequently nick-named the "Flour City." Nonetheless, a fair number of apples and peaches were produced in the area. While apples could always be turned into cider, peaches were more problematic. In good years, the local mar-kets were "glutted . . . during the ripening season" and, often enough, "unwilling to sell at twenty cents a bushel," farmers would "dump . . . wagon loads into the Genesee [river]."[19] In following years, grains pro-duced more efficiently in the American Midwest became available at cheaper prices than could be produced in the region. On the other hand, improvements in transportation made it possible to deliver fresh pro-duce to more distant consumers and a number of farmers profitably switched from growing grain to cultivating orchards. In the meantime, other local entrepreneurs had developed a thriving nursery industry (where plants are propagated and grown to usable size), which also re-lied on a much broader geographical customer base. The *Flour City* had become the *Flower City*. Lower consumer prices, a wider range of prod-ucts, new job creation, and better overall standards of living had been made possible by improvements in transportation and the regional spe-cialization of agricultural productions.

Similar developments occurred all over North America and Western Europe. Regional specialization in perishable products mirrored what had happened earlier with grain markets. As observed in 1838 by George Richardson Porter, the head of the Statistical Department of the British Board of Trade, new forms of transportation were "stimu-lating production and equalizing prices" of perishable items:

Before the establishment of steam-vessels, the market at Cork [Ire-land] was most irregularly supplied with eggs from the surround-ing district; at certain seasons they were exceedingly abundant and cheap, but these seasons were sure to be followed by periods of scarcity and high prices, and at times it is said to have been difficult to purchase eggs at any price in the market. At the first opening of the improved channel for conveyance to England, the residents at Cork had to complain of the constant high price of this and other articles of farm produce; but as a more extensive market was now permanently open to them, the farmers gave their attention to the rearing and keeping of poultry, and, at the present time, eggs are procurable at all seasons in the market at Cork, not, it is true, at the extremely low rate at which they could formerly be sometimes bought, but still at much less than the average price of the year.[20]

The statistician then observed, "a like result has followed the introduction of this great improvement [in transportation] in regard to the supply and cost of various other articles of produce."[21] True, because of "external" demand local farmers could now extract a higher price from local customers than had previously been the case at harvest time. On the other hand, consumers whose access to fresh produce had been limited to a few weeks each year could now purchase these commodities over much longer periods of time at ever more affordable prices. Now, commodities identical to those produced locally were not only being produced on a large scale elsewhere, but they reached maturity at a different time of the year.

To give a striking illustration of these processes, in American cities at the turn of the 20th century, the earliest supplies of new potatoes to hit the market before Christmas came from both southern Florida and the islands of Bermuda, which, although at a more northerly latitude, benefited from the moderating influence of the Gulf Stream. Potatoes produced from further north in Florida all the way up to the northern potato belt that stretched from Maine to Minnesota would then reach maturity between March and early September. (See map on next page.)

Of course, what was true for American potatoes was also true for countless other crops. For instance, in 1880 in England, the city of Manchester's supply of green peas first came from Algeria, then from Spain and later on France. These were followed in time by English-grown

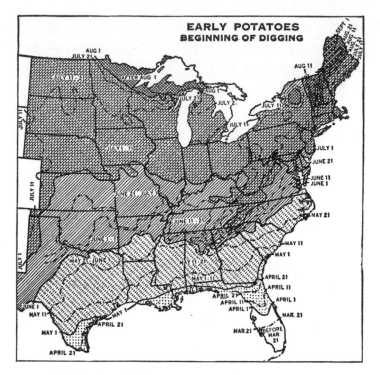

Source: V. C Finch and O. E. Baker. 1917. *Geography of the World's Agriculture.* US Government Printing Office, page 66.

green peas, first from southern regions and then all the way up to the Scottish border. The local onion market was supplied, depending on the variety, by Bedforshire in southeast England (from August to May), Holland (between July and April), Germany (September to June), Belgium (August and September), Bordeaux, France, (from October to January), and Portugal (May to July).[22] In time, seasonal products also came to be shipped in from the southern hemisphere where seasons are inverted (meaning that summer months in countries like Argentina, Australia, and New Zealand coincide with the winter months in the United States, the United Kingdom, and Germany). This pattern also historically applied to nonedible agricultural commodities such as cattle hides that were of higher quality in summer months in both the northern and southern hemispheres.[23] Shipping fresh produce grown in certain latitudes to distant consumers located in other latitudes provided not only superior alternatives to local produce when not in season, but also drastically reduced the energy costs and waste due to spoilage inherent to long-term storage.

Unfortunately, local food activists and agri-intellectuals seem to be unaware of the economic rationale underlying the export of most of a region's perishable products at harvest time and of importing similar products from growing areas located in different latitudes the rest of the year. A case in point is the food commentator Barry Estabrook, who, upon learning that 99% of produce grown in Santa Barbara County is exported while more than 95% of the produce eaten there is imported, coined the expression "Santa Barbara Syndrome" to express how "completely dysfunctional our modern food system" has become.[24] The data mentioned by Estabrook had been compiled by David Cleveland, a University of California at Santa Barbara professor of environmental studies,[25] who, during a talk in which he presented his results, reportedly stressed the absurdity of "two produce-laden tractor-trailers passing on the highway, one bringing food into the county; the other hauling it out." Two crucial facts not mentioned by Estabrook, however, are that according to Cleveland's data, Santa Barbara County produces roughly nine times the amount of produce it consumes each year and that much of its imports come from countries located in the southern hemisphere, such as Chile, Argentina, and New Zealand.

Based on historical precedents, one can logically infer a few unavoidable outcomes of an all-out adoption of locavorism in Santa Barbara County. First, faced with the loss of their export markets, local farmers would have no other choice but to sell all their production locally at harvest time. This deluge of produce would quickly bring their price below production costs. While this situation may prove a boon to customers the first time around, most producers would soon either go bankrupt, drastically decrease the acreage devoted to produce in favor of other crops less suited to the local soil and climate, or get out of the agriculture business altogether. In the process, workers with unique expertise in the growing, harvesting, preparation, marketing, and ship-ping of produce would be laid off and in most cases be unable to earn as much income as they had before (otherwise they would not have been in this line of work in the first place). Local businesses that catered to these workers would suffer as a result. Some volume of local produce would then have to be preserved in one form or another in order to be consumed out of season. Whatever the preservation option selected, out-of-season local produce would be of lesser quality and more expen-sive than formerly imported fresh produce. In bad years—after all, even Santa Barbara County is not immune to pests, floods, and earth-quakes—local residents might have to get by with very little, if any, pro-duce. Seen in this light, the "Santa Barbara syndrome" strikes us as a blessing rather than a proof of economic derangement.

Economies of Scale

So far we have discussed the advantages of long-distance trade for agricultural producers and final consumers, but its importance for food processors and manufacturers should not be overlooked. The issue here is economies of scale in production—meaning, the more units of a good that are produced, the lower the cost per unit. Economies of scale can be achieved either by increasing the size of operations in a firm or by one firm working with another, typically located nearby. Perhaps the best historical case to illustrate the economic benefits of both types of economies of scale is the Chicago meat-packing district in the second half of the 19th century, a subject to which we will now devote a few lines.[26]

Although self-styled reformers maligned the meat packers for their alleged sins of collusion and greed—long before Upton Sinclair's 1906 novel *The Jungle* indicted them for alleged unsanitary practices[27]—a case can be made that the real source of the industry's success and its true economic impact has been mischaracterized by contemporary critics who were essentially local food activists. The main argument on behalf of the packers, as stated in 1908 by the pastor George Powell Perry, was that it was a common mistake "to attribute the financial success of some of these moneyed corporations to cheat and chicanery in business methods" for "to say that all this phenomenal accumulation of wealth has resulted from shrewd trickery that enabled a few to cheat their fellows of their dues is a false representation of the true workings of a system of savings that has done as much as anything else to make possible the extraordinary prosperity of our nation during the past century." In his opinion, the fundamental truth of the matter was that "men of great business capacity and of untiring energy have been gathering up the fragments that nothing might go to waste."[28]

American meatpacking first became big business in the early decades of the 19th century with the large-scale butchering of hogs, whose meat could be packed in barrels of brine and shipped over long distances. This process, however, proved unsatisfactory in the case of beef, whose meat became hard and tasteless when prepared that way. As a result, until the second half of the 19th century, most cattle destined for meat consumption were grazed in relatively close proximity to their final destination in order to minimize loss attributable to injury and shrinkage as they were walked to their deaths.[29] Animals were then typically killed in relatively small-scale operations from which the meat was quickly sold to local consumers to avoid spoilage.

In time, the advent of a national railway network made possible the movement of cattle in railroad cars while the development of refrigeration led to the provision of "dressed meat" across the United States. At the forefront of the movement of cattle and meat on rails were the Chicago meat-packing industrialists whose strength lay not only in their ability to cut down costs by integrating forward in marketing, backward in purchasing, and by obtaining their own materials directly,[30] but also in their capacity to turn what was once the waste of their "disassembly" activities into valuable commodities. In other words, far from encouraging them to throw their polluting production residuals back into the environment (in modern economic parlance, to "externalize" their pollution costs), the packers had every incentive to create wealth out of waste. After all, they had paid for whole animals, so why would they have thrown out "free" raw materials from which they could devise some innovative ways to earn extra money?

Writing in 1889, the economist David Ames Wells attributed the success of meat-packing districts to economies of scale, "which are not possible when this industry is carried on, as usual, upon a very small scale." Crucially, the scaling up of operations had made it possible to turn animal parts such as hide, hoofs, horns, bones, blood, and hair, which in the hands of small butchers were "of little value or a dead loss," into a range of profitable products that spanned the manufacturing spectrum, from glue and bone-dust to fertilizers.[31] In the early days of the Chicago packing district, large refineries took the steam-rendered lard of packers, refined and bleached it, and sold it on the open market. Glue works made glue from bones, sinews, and various other residuals. Fertilizer plants carted off the pressed tankage and raw or pressed blood, dried and sold it as such, or manufactured mixed fertilizer. Soap factories bought various grades of tallow. Butterine manufacturers used neutral lard and oleo oil from packing plants for manufacturing oleomargarine. Other nonedible portions were turned into pharmaceutical products and lubrication oil.[32] A few decades later, many of these operations had been integrated within larger firms. While meat-packing districts were noisy, smelly, and polluted, slaughtering animals in large agglomerations of firms of all sizes resulted in much less waste material being released in the environment than would have been the case in more numerous, isolated, smaller, and less efficient operations.

Most citizens benefited from these developments. Because they were able to create more wealth out of every single animal, the Chicago packers were able to outbid their less efficient competitors and to pay a higher price for cattle, something that was obviously welcomed by producers in this industry. Higher purchase prices, however, did not ultimately mean higher selling prices to final consumer, because, through their more efficient and creative use of raw materials, Chicago packers

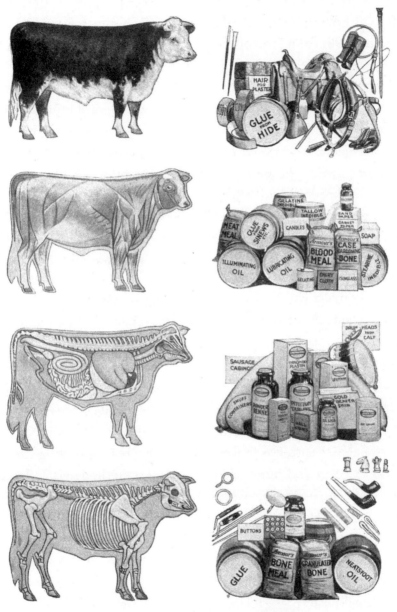

BY-PRODUCTS FROM CATTLE

Source: Rudolf A. Clemen. 1927. *By-Products in the Packing Industry.* University of Chicago Press (insert, no pagination)

were able to sell their meat cheaper and still make a profit. Not surprisingly, a growing number of American meat consumers switched their meat purchases from local offerings to those delivered by rail from the Windy City.

The main businesses hurt in this process were the traditional competitors of the large packers, small but numerous local butchers, who, unable to offer similar products at comparable prices, took to the political arena where they created a vocal and politically powerful lobby that called for a boycott of the nonlocal meat. The reasons invoked ranged from the unknown health effects of new preservation technologies to worries about the shady unsanitary practices of distant producers. Besides, the unchecked concentration of economic power in the hands of a few large corporations would surely result in "monopolistic profiteering" at the expense of the consuming public.

The public relations campaign launched by small-scale butchers was fierce and quickly relayed by journalists and politicians with a natural proclivity to go after the "big guys." The protest movement became more organized in 1886 with the formation of the Butchers' National Protective Association in Saint Louis. As the environmental historian William Cronon pointed out in 1991, however, while the stated goal of the movement was to "secure the highest sanitary condition" for consumers, public health was in fact "a convenient way of putting the best face on a deeper and more self-interested economic issue."[33] In fact, health complaints about smaller slaughterhouses and urban dairy operations long predated the rise of the Chicago packers and were common in other countries.[34] According to economists Donald Boudreaux and Thomas DiLorenzo, the most plausible explanation for the adoption of the first antitrust legislation in Missouri in 1889 is to view it as an attempt by politically powerful local producer groups, mostly independent retail butchers, to shield themselves from the lower prices and intense competitive pressures of Chicago packers.[35]

In the meantime, other small-scale attempts to circumvent the packers were set up in locations closer to production sites. One such initiative was spearheaded by a Frenchman, the Marquis de Mores, who not only built a number of slaughterhouses and cold storage houses in Montana and in what is now North Dakota, but also procured refrigerator cars. The venture, however, failed miserably. As the economic historian Fred A. Shannon observes: "Because the supply of matured beef was not year-round, slaughtering on the Plains proved impractical except for taking care of the local market . . . Furthermore, only medium-grade cattle were offered, and the small slaughterhouses were not equipped to make use of the by-products that furnished so much of the profits for the greater packers."[36] Despite small-scale butchers and some cattlemen's recriminations,[37] consumers ultimately voted with their wallets and purchased the offerings of the more efficient large-scale operations. As with many other mature urban industries, however, in time the advent of new technologies (in this case, mostly trucking) and the development of better alternatives to animal by-products (such as petroleum-derived plastics to replace animal bones in the making of countless products) led to their delocalization closer to their sources of supply.

The trend towards the increased concentration of American slaughtering operations has also been pronounced in more recent times, with their number declining from 1,211 in 1992 to 809 in 2008.[38] This development has made locavorism a difficult reality for idealistic livestock producers who find themselves forced "to make slaughter appointments before animals are born and to drive hundreds of miles to facilities, adding to their costs and causing stress to livestock." As a result, many new small-scale operators are reportedly "scaling back on plans to expand their farms because local processors cannot handle any more animals."[39] Not surprisingly, Michael Pollan and others have urged the U.S. government to step in and fill this need at taxpayers' expense,[40] but one should at least understand the economic and environmental (and, as we will argue later, food safety) benefits of large-scale operations before denouncing the regional concentration of these activities and the need to subsidize less efficient ones. Small might be beautiful, but bigger is ultimately often better for consumers who want to stretch their food budget as much as possible. Of course, if there is at some future point in time enough of a price premium associated with the locavores' approach to meat production, small and flexible processing operations might be profitable enough to be worth building.

The Debate Over Land Use

In the realm of food production, prices factor in (albeit imperfectly, mostly because of subsidies and barriers to trade) the opportunity costs associated with energy consumption, transportation costs, irrigation, growing season, fertilization, and labor costs. As such, they help agricultural producers and corporate buyers determine the most suitable crops and animals for specific locations. Prices also convey important information about alternative land uses. As the economist Steven Landsburg observes, locavores should not only care about the energy signature of a California tomato trucked to New York City, but also about the other potential products that were sacrificed in order to grow the tomatoes; the other kinds of work that the California tomato growers might have done; the longer morning commutes that would be needed if New York greenhouses were to be built in the place of a conveniently located housing development; the alternative employment that hypothetical New York greenhouse workers might find; the other applications to which the inputs required to produce additional fertilizers and farming equipment might have been used for; and so on.[41] When looking at the broader economic picture, Landsburg argues, the energy costs that so worry locavores turn out to be "quite small compared to the many other social costs involved with growing a tomato."

In the context of locavorism, the most basic land use trade-off is whether grounds within or on the margins of rapidly growing cities should be devoted to food production or to something else. Understanding the relevant trade-offs, however, requires a basic understanding of why large urban agglomerations make some individuals and activities much more productive than if they were located in rural settings. This basic fact of economic life explains why agricultural producers have long been driven out of urban land markets by other lines of work.

Unfortunately, local food activists do not see any value in converting some agricultural land to other uses and favor a number of policies to prevent the process. To quote an important player on this issue, the American Farmland Trust website states that "[s]ustaining local farms and farmland is a sound community investment, as it ensures the public will continue to receive the multiple benefits of agriculture. This involves protecting a strategic land base, providing property tax relief for farmland owners, supporting the business of farming, and investing in agricultural and community economic development."[42]

While "running out of land" to feed future generations might sound like a dire prospect and somewhat worth investing much taxpayers' money to prevent, local food activists blow the issue out of proportion. As we will now argue, far from being deplorable, land conversion around thriving urban areas is the most sensible way to use our scarce resources.

One way to better illustrate basic trade-offs in terms of urban land and agricultural production is to look at why "vertical farming" or stacked agricultural production projects—essentially, high rise buildings devoted to agricultural production, whose basic concept has existed for decades but is now mostly associated with the work of public health professor Dickson Despommier[43]—never materialized in practice. To their proponents, their most distinctive qualities are that they would allow 24 hour a day cultivation (as opposed to being dependent on natural sunlight), eliminate the use of pesticides because their production would take place indoors, and obliterate the need for long distance transportation because of their location. The first two items, however, are untenable because conventional greenhouses can already be operated around the clock if so desired while the claim that a pest-free agricultural environment can be maintained on this planet is simply implausible. After all, insects and plant diseases found their way into the Biosphere 2 project, a self-contained ecosystem built in the middle of the Arizona desert.[44] This leaves the basic economic trade-offs of such proposals, which essentially boil down to the fact that their additional costs (from building these structures to lighting, heating, and powering them) negate any economic benefits attributable to an urban location. In a critique of urban designer Gordon Graff's "SkyFarm" project, a 59-story-high and a half-dozen-story deep tower in which hydroponic plants would be grown year round,[45] agricultural economist Dennis Avery argues:

- Even if a pilot building was erected, about 500,000 such skyscrapers would be needed to make up the 400 million acres of American farmland;
- Using the average price per acre of Iowa cropland, the usable surface of this building in Iowa would cost about $5 million, a sum that would buy about an acre of land in Manhattan on top of which a very costly vertical structure would need to be built;
- Each floor of this high-rise building would have to support about 620,000 pounds of either water or water-soaked soil (by comparison, two hundred people and their office furniture weigh about 40,000 pounds);
- Replacing sunlight with "grow lights" and heating the structure in winter would require gigawatts of power;
- Sky farms would need to rely on outside suppliers to feed their chickens and pigs. Since a few pounds of grain are required to produce one pound of meat (typically a four-to-one ratio in the case of pigs), it makes more sense to transport pork chops rather than animal feed into cities;
- As in the past, slaughterhouses would need to be located much closer to downtown centers or else city-reared animals would need to be trucked elsewhere to be processed before being brought back to the city in a usable form;
- City taxes and labor costs are always much higher than in the countryside.

No wonder, Avery tells us, that such proposals will always remain "pigs in the sky."[46] Urban land can be much better used for other purposes, which is exactly what urban land prices have long indicated. Of course, additional trade-offs are also present in the case of more modest urban agriculture proposals, from rooftop gardening to the raising of backyard chickens, whose small size and consequent inability to generate economies of scale (try using a tractor on top of a high-rise building or obtaining large-scale discounts on the costs of inputs when farming small backyards) will always confine the practice to the realm of hobby gardeners, or, at best, high-margin luxury producers—either way, a result that is a far cry from the affordable and abundant food promised by locavores.

"Protecting" the farmland that surrounds large cities from "urban sprawl" (in other words, preventing residential, industrial, and commercial development on agricultural land) through strict zoning is equally problematic. While restricting development might suit the sensibilities of people who already own residential property in thriving cities, it also unavoidably drives up housing prices, thus affecting disproportionately people of more modest means and newcomers (to say nothing of farmers' children who would like to get out of this line of work and cash in on the family property). Evidence also clearly demonstrates that the creation of "green belts" around thriving metropolitan areas in which nothing can be built is also undesirable, for the economic attraction of cities is such that development will in time simply leapfrog these areas. The result will be even greater sprawl and longer commutes for residents.

If agriculture is the most desirable use of a particular piece of land, the market (meaning, ultimately, food consumers) will ensure that it remains so. If, on the other hand, residential and commercial developers are willing to put their own money into new projects, this signals that more people believe that agricultural land should be converted to other uses. (Of course, many individuals argue that markets are too short-sighted and that future agricultural land shortages are looming. Yet, because in advanced economies we now produce much more food on the same piece of land than in the not so distant past, much more agricultural land is currently reverting to a "wild" state than swallowed by "urban sprawl."[47]) Also, nothing prevents environmentalists from purchasing land they deem worth preserving rather than using political power to declare private farmland part of a "greenbelt" and prevent its owner from selling it to developers or converting it to other uses. Prohibiting the redevelopment of agricultural land might appeal to the sensibilities of well-off or already established urbanites and environmentalists, but it is a selfish policy that ignores the economic benefits of urbanization and the needs of people of lesser means. [48]

Time and Trade-offs

Finally, another point lost on many locavores is that the one thing that money cannot buy is more time, thus making it the scarcest commodity of all. Once this is factored into many proposals to increase the production of "cheap and healthy" food, the end result doesn't look affordable anymore. For instance, the National Sustainable Agriculture Information Service recommends that food miles be reduced by having people eat minimally processed, packaged, and marketed food in season; can, dry, and preserve fruits and vegetables by themselves; and plant a garden and grow as much of their own food as possible.[49] Add in the inconveniences of shopping at farmers' markets compared to conventional supermarkets and the time devoted to preparing meals increases drastically.

No doubt, people can accomplish many things cheaply—such as, say, growing organic tropical products in Maine—if their time and extra trouble are not factored in. In real life, however, most of us are happy to buy a house built by other people who specialize in various trades. The same is true where our food is concerned. Sure, many people are currently (re)discovering the joys of gardening or supporting local farmers out of a sense of duty. Michael Pollan might wax poetic over the fact that, by the end of the Second World War "more than 20 million [Victory] home gardens were supplying 40% of the produce consumed in America," but this relative success (after all, 40% was still not even a majority of the supply) owed much to a drastic reduction in the number of male farm workers and didn't last once more abundant and cheaper produce again became available through normal commercial channels.[50] As a writer in the *Ladies' Home Journal* observed in 1929, "Primitive men spent nearly all his time getting, caring for, and preparing food. In a real sense, the aim of human progress has been to make these processes ever easier and easier. The less time we are forced to spend thinking about food, the more we have for higher things, so called."[51] Many people might be yearning to connect with nature, community, and local food, but much historical evidence suggests that most won't find it as rewarding as they first believed it to be.

As a result of urbanization and long distance trade in agricultural and other products, consumers in advanced economies now enjoy a much larger, diversified, and affordable year-round food supply than would have otherwise been the case. Because of the dramatically increased productivity that resulted from geographical specialization and economics of scale, numerous remunerative jobs were created in both the agricultural and nonagricultural sectors. For instance, according to 2000–2002 numbers, the average value of agricultural production per worker was about $50,000 in the United States and $40,000 for the United Kingdom compared to the much more "local" and labor intensive agricultural sectors of Nigeria and India, where these figures are respectively about $700 and $400.[52] The United States and the United Kingdom could easily create the kind of jobs that Nigeria and India have in abundance, but much wealth would be destroyed in the process and a lower standard of living ensured for all. Besides, as the celebrity chef Anthony Bourdain observes, the "labor-intensive pastoral vision" of local food activists implies that "either lots of the citizens of wealthy countries like America and Italy are going to have to take up farming again," something which he rightly thinks unlikely, or else, "importing huge numbers of poor brown people from elsewhere—to grow those tasty, crunchy vegetables for more comfortable white masters. So, while animals of the future might be cruelty-free . . . what about life for those who have to shovel the shit from their stalls?"[53]

Why is it that American and British agricultural workers are so much more productive than their Nigerian and Indian counterparts and, as a result, enjoy a much higher standard of living? Hard work is not the issue, for if anything Indian and Nigerian subsistence farmers work even harder than food producers in the U.S. and U.K. Rather, the difference between the two groups is that those in more advanced economies—where people specialize in what they do best in the most favorable locations and trade extensively with each other—belong to a much more sophisticated and geographically extended division of labor than subsistence farmers enjoy. Greater self-sufficiency has always been a one-way road to poverty, even at the national level. As was obvious to the geographer Jacques Redway more than a century ago:

> If a country or an inhabited area produces all the foodstuffs and commodities required by its people, the conditions are very fortunate. A very few nations, notably China and the United States, have such diverse conditions of climate, topography, and mineral resources, that they can, if necessary, produce within their national borders everything needed by their peoples. The prosecution of such a policy, however, is rarely economical; in the history of the past it has always resulted in weakness and disintegration. China is to-day helpless because of a policy of self-seclusion; and the marvelous growth of Japan began when her trade was thrown open to the world.[54]

Of course, China's economic growth in the last few decades was entirely contingent on its becoming part of the international division of labor and on relying ever more on foreign goods and markets. Suffice it to say here that it is now the world's largest importer of soybeans (over 50 million tons a year as of this writing) to feed its hogs and chickens, even though soybeans are native to China and the country is the world's fourth largest producer of this commodity (although it lags significantly behind the top three, the U.S., Brazil, and Argentina).[55]

True, increasing agricultural productivity and letting in cheaper imports will always hurt inefficient agricultural producers and their workers. On the other hand, cheaper prices mean that consumers have more income available to spend on other things—and all of us are consumers. In the end, if the economic case made by locavores was sensible, it would not stop at the "foodshed next door" but would revert all the way back to subsistence agriculture. And why stop there? Why not adopt a stance similar to that of the Horse Association of America a century ago? When faced with the advent of gasoline and diesel-powered engines, it "emphasized that reliance on horses kept money within the community whereas the use of tractors required an outflow of the cash required to purchase and operate the equipment."[56]

The real key to economic development and improved standards of living, as Adam Smith identified so long ago, is to make "a smaller quantity of labour produce a greater quantity of work."[57] Creating miserable "local" jobs is easy, but creating prosperity and a higher standard of living requires long distance trade.

4

Myth #3:
Locavorism Heals the Earth

Fire, the ax, the plow, and firearm have been the four fundamental tools of our modern culture, and in some of the
most fertile and productive regions of the earth they have
raised the environmental resistance to such a height that
the carrying capacity has been brought nearly as low as that
of the Gobi or the tundras of Siberia. Hundreds of millions
of acres of once rich land are now as poor as—or worse
than—the city gardener's sterile plot. Despoiled forests,
erosion, wildlife extermination, overgrazing, and the drop-
ping of water tables are unforeseen and unwanted by-blows
of a vigorous and adolescent culture on the loose.

—WILLIAM VOGT. 1948. *Road to Survival.*
William Sloane Associates, Inc., p. 33

Local food activists who are willing to concede some usefulness to
market prices nonetheless strongly believe that their prescription
will deliver environmental benefits to which prices are oblivious. Once
again, however, they fail to take a broad enough look at the relevant

issues to understand some inherent shortcomings of their prescription. Before we address these problems, though, we must first paint a more accurate portrait of natural evolution and of the true environmental impact of primitive agricultural production technologies.

On the Unbalance of Nature

Perhaps the most deeply-felt conviction of environmental and food activists is that "Nature" is a fragile and finely balanced web of interrelationships among living things upon which the first modern humans had little impact because of their small numbers and primitive technologies. By embracing industrialized civilization, however, we became nothing short of a deadly cancer to our planet. Although widespread, these beliefs are now known to be mistaken. Far from being "balanced," landscapes and ecosystems are to the contrary dynamic environments where living and nonliving components constantly interact with each other. Because of factors such as keener predators, invasive species, animal diseases, tectonic processes, frost, lightning strikes, hurricanes, and ice ages, nature has always been in flux.[1]

Our ancestors have also long had a profound influence on all regions of the globe from the moment they developed technologies (such as seafaring vessels, warmer clothing and shelter, and better hunting tools and strategies) that made it possible for them to colonize habitats that had previously been too harsh or whose potential offerings (from large land, freshwater and seawater animals to small prey and grasses) had been too dangerous or too difficult to tap into profitably. In the process, not only did they become the ultimate "invasive species," but also they profoundly reshaped their surroundings. For example, many large mammal and bird species disappeared soon after humans reached the shores of the Americas, Australia, New Zealand, Madagascar, and countless small islands.[2] Perhaps their most profound impact over time, however, was that they profoundly altered the natural fire regime of countless ecosystems through deliberate and regular burning of the landscape, a practice which both opened and reduced forested landscape and created or "refreshed" prairies and meadows, the process resulting in a significant increase of large herbivores and better hunting conditions.[3]

With the invention of agriculture came the creation of cropland and pastureland out of forests and wetlands; the opening up of forest canopies through the cutting of tree sprouts and limbs for fodder and the grazing of animals; the removal of predators and competing wild herbivorous mammals; and the worldwide transfer and adaptation of domesticated plants and animals.[4] In the words of Norwegian botanist Knut Faegri, apart from "some small and doubtful exceptions, all vegetation types were created or modified by man. . . . The 'natural' landscapes of preceding generations," Faegri tells us, "are now understood for what they really are: relics of earlier types of land-use, which were maintained by extensive methods demanding little machinery and much manpower and which therefore became uneconomical... By abandoning these methods and discontinuing traditional land-use, the landscape was left to regenerate in response to other uses or non-use."[5] Even much of the Amazon basin is now widely believed to be the recent evolution of massive orchards made up of hundreds of different crops of fruit, palm and nut trees that were created long ago by significant populations who were later decimated by European diseases and conquest. "Native" Amazonian agriculturalists, it turns out, not only profoundly altered local tree compositions and densities, but also their genetic makeup, just as wheat farmers had transformed wild wheat varieties into domesticated ones.[6]

Another widespread misconception is that human activities can only reduce species' richness; actually, landscapes created or impacted by human actions often display greater levels of biodiversity than natural ones. This is not controversial on a small scale, such as when inhabitants open a road in the middle of a forest and create a niche habitat for specific plants that would not otherwise be present in this location. The same effect can also be observed on a much larger scale, especially in environments where humans initially had little impact. For example, non-native settlers introduced more than 4,000 plant species in North America in the last 400 years and were directly responsible for what is now nearly 20% of the continent's vascular plant biodiversity.[7] Some, like kudzu, purple loosestrife, and water hyacinths, are problematic, but most are not. The state flowers of Vermont and New Hampshire, red clover and purple lilac, are of European origins. In New Zealand, Europeans added approximately 2,000 plant species to a roughly equal number of native species, with only three native plant species believed to have disappeared in the process. Even in the case of small island habitats, the later introduction of foreign species often brought back local bird biodiversity to levels comparable to those that preceded human arrival.[8] According to biologist Mark Davis and his collaborators, the "introduction of non-native species has almost always increased the number of species in a region" and the only invasive species that might prove significant threats are pathogens and predators in lakes and on islands.[9] (A related yet different complaint is that the last century has been a disaster in terms of commercial crop diversity losses, yet a case has been made that overall commercial crop diversity has been sustained by the creation and addition of thousands of new varieties.[10])

True, much like critics of globalization who disdain the increased homogenization of urban areas—which are becoming more similar by having each become more diverse in the same way, say by harboring the same or similar food and retail outlets, sushi joints, Irish bars, etc.—many landscape ecologists are not fond of what they refer to as the "homogecene" (i.e., humanity's homogenization of the world's flora and fauna through transport of species across once insurmountable barriers), arguing that richness is only one component of biodiversity and that invasive exotics can relegate existing populations of native species to marginal habitats, leading to genetic bottlenecks and eventual decline, extirpation, and/or extinction over time. Yet, no specialist denies that much human-caused biodiversity losses long predate the advent of modern agri-business and that only very wealthy societies can afford to care about the fate of native species with no direct economic value. As we see things, plants, insects, and other animals that have a major negative impact on human health and economically valuable resources should obviously be kept under control, but whether they are "native" or "invasive" should be irrelevant, for, in the words of Davis and his collaborators, the fight against invasive species ultimately amounts to "an impossible quest to restore the world to some imaginary, pristine state."[11]

If one is willing to consider that something along the lines of doubling the world's food output by 2050 is required, and that, as the molecular biologist Nina Fedoroff observes, agriculture is always "ecologically destructive, whether it is performed at the subsistence level for a single family or on an industrial scale,"[12] then the most environmentally sensible course to pursue is to minimize the amount of land devoted to food production by increasing agricultural yields. In other words, the smaller the total area in active human use, the more environmentally friendly is the landscape. [13] If past achievements and trends provide any indication, this is a realistic goal[14]—as long as one embraces long-distance trade and rejects locavorism, as we will now argue.

Locavorism and the (Mis)management of Natural Resources

An article of faith among locavores is that because their impacts are so concentrated in a few locations, modern industrial agriculture does more damage to the environment than smaller-scale and less technology-intensive operations. Ironically, the low productivity practices now advocated by locavores are the ones that previous generations of environmental activists believed were the cause of problems such as deforestation, massive soil erosion, depletion and compaction, and outright ecological collapse.

In an often quoted passage, Plato complained more than 2000 years ago that if Athens' hinterland hills had once been "covered with soil," the plains "full of rich earth," and the mountains displaying an "abundance of wood," by his time many mountains could "only afford sustenance to bees" while, as in small islands, all the "richer and softer parts of the soil [had] fallen away, and the mere skeleton of the land [was] being left."[15] Even though some scholars now suggest that the Greek philosopher was exaggerating to make a point,[16] fears of widespread land mismanagement and irremediable top soil losses recurred from then on. To give but one more recent illustration, in their 1939 classic *The Rape of the Earth: A World Survey of Soil Erosion*[17] (a book which reviewed the vast literature of the time on the topic), British writers Graham Vernon Jacks and Robert Orr Whyte argued that "as the result solely of human mismanagement, the soils upon which men have attempted to found new civilizations are disappearing, washed away by water and blown away by wind;" that the "destruction of the earth's thin living cover is proceeding at a rate and on a scale unparalleled in history, and when that thin cover—the soil—is gone, the fertile regions where it formerly lay will be uninhabitable deserts," just as had happened to "former civilizations and empires whose ruined cities now lie amid barren wastes that once were the world's most fertile lands." [18] Erosion, they proclaimed, was the "modern symptom of maladjustment between human society and its environment. It is a warning that nature is in full revolt against the sudden incursion of an exotic civilization into her ordered domains."[19]

As is now obvious, although much damage was done in some areas, the global catastrophe predicted by past activists never materialized because of the adoption of a number of tools and strategies, from contour plowing, windbreaks, legume fallow crops, mulching and alley cropping to deferred and rotational grazing, drip irrigation, re-vegetation and no-till agriculture. Unfortunately, one of the greatest advances in combating erosion in the last decades—"no-till" agriculture, which leaves the root systems of previous crops undisturbed, thereby retaining organic matter and greatly discouraging erosion—is decried by many activists because of its reliance on rDNA-modified plants and synthetic herbicides.

Be that as it may, the key point is that by concentrating the growing of crops in ever more suitable locations, long distance trade not only maximized output and drastically lowered prices, but also significantly reduced the environmental impact of agriculture. For instance, the agricultural economist Dennis Avery observes that with the rise of the American corn and wheat belts in the 19th century, grain growers in Virginia's Shenandoah Valley could no longer compete with producers whose yields were three times higher than theirs and whose farm machinery didn't get damaged by buried rocks. In short order they had no choice but to switch to cattle grazing and wood production for which their land was better suited. As a result, in today's Shenandoah Valley wildlife is more common than in colonial and pre-colonial times, the area has gained beauty and the "huge soil erosion losses that cropping inflicted on its steep, rocky slopes" has long ended. True, the ecosystems of grain producing states from Indiana to Montana have been profoundly altered, but because their land is more productive and less prone to erosion, more grain is now being produced on fewer acres and, overall, more habitat is available for wildlife. Avery further argues that, because of similar land use changes in many other locations, severe erosion problems are now largely confined "to poor countries extending low-yield farming onto fragile soils."[20]

Of course, Avery was far from being the first agricultural analyst to observe this phenomenon.[21] To quote but one other writer, the Marxist theorist Karl Kautsky observed in 1899 that "as long as any rural economy is self-sufficient it has to produce everything which it needs, irrespective of whether the soil is suitable or not. Grain has to be cultivated on infertile, stony and steeply sloping ground as well as on rich soils." In time, however, the emergence of commodity production and overseas competition meant that "it was no longer necessary to carry on producing grain on unsuitable soils, and where circumstances were favorable it was taken off the land and replaced by other types of agricultural production," such as orchards, cattle, and dairy farming.[22]

International trade is also beneficial in terms of overall water usage, as exporting food from locations where it is abundant to regions where it isn't reduces the need to drain surface waters and aquifers in these less-productive areas. For instance, a country that imports one ton of wheat instead of producing it domestically is said to save about 1,300 cubic meters of local (or "indigenous") water. As food production represents approximately 70% of human water use, the issue is not insignificant. Trading agricultural products grown in water-rich regions to drier ones is now often subsumed under the labels of "virtual," "embedded," "embodied," or "hidden" water[23] to describe the environmental benefits of the practice, but it has long been a reality because of simple economic incentives.

Perhaps the least heralded triumph of high-yield agriculture and international trade is that, along with urbanization, they have played a crucial role in the expansion of forested areas in significant parts of the Earth in the last two centuries. Contrary to the common belief that massive deforestation is a recent occurrence (with the bulk of it taking place in the tropical regions of the world during the last five decades), it is now acknowledged by specialists that perhaps as much as nine-tenths of all deforestation caused by human beings since the emergence of civilization occurred before 1950 as people needed to clear vast tracts of forested land in order to provide themselves with shelter, food, warmth, and a multitude of implements.[24] A reversal of these trends (not attributable to wars, epidemics, or collapse of civilizations) began in the early decades of the 19th century in certain European countries through a process since labeled "forest transitions." In France, the forest area expanded by one-third between 1830 and 1960, and by a further quarter since 1960. Similar processes, although of varying intensity and scope, have been occurring in all major temperate and boreal forests and in every country with a per capita Gross Domestic Product (GDP) now exceeding U.S. $4,600 (roughly equal to the GDP of Chile) and in some developing economies, most notably China and India.[25]

While in some cases this outcome can be traced back to aggressive governmental policies,[26] these efforts would have been unthinkable without drastically improved agricultural and forestry productivity (including the development of tree or "fiber farms") that reduced harvesting pressures in other locations. Of course, this transition also owed much to the more efficient transformation of wood into various products and to carbon-fuels that were the basis of substitutes for organic fibers, dyes, and animal feed (when automobiles, tractors, and trucks became substitutes for horses).[27]

Turning our back on the global food supply chain, and, in the process, reducing the quantity of food produced in the most suitable locations will inevitably result in larger amounts of inferior land being put under cultivation, the outcome of which can only be less output and greater environmental damage. Such problems would obviously be made worse by the locavores' rejection of technology-based approaches such as no-till farming. Unfortunately, these considerations are never addressed by locavores, whose primary focus is on reducing the distance that foodstuff travels between producers and final consumers.

The Basic Problems with Food Miles

The locavores' only original addition to the rhetoric of past generations of food and environmental activists is the concept of "food miles"—the distance food items travel from farms to consumers—which they use as a proxy for greenhouse gas emissions. In short, the more distance traveled, the more greenhouse gases emitted and the more overall environmental damage. Despite its popularity, the concept and its underlying rationale have been convincingly debunked in numerous Life Cycle Assessment (LCA) studies, a methodology that examines the environmental impact associated with all the stages of a product's life cycle, from raw material extraction to disposal of the finished product. Not surprisingly, it turns out that food miles can only be taken at face value in the case of identical items produced simultaneously in the exact same physical conditions but in different locations—in other words, if everything else is equal, which is obviously never the case in the real world.[28] What follows is a brief summary of the most relevant findings of LCA researchers.

Production vs. Transportation

The fact that retailers are able to sell profitably food items that have traveled long distances clearly indicates that they can be produced more economically elsewhere for reasons that range from better growing conditions to cheaper labor costs. If this were not the case, transportation costs would act as an insurmountable trade barrier.

In the most comprehensive literature review to date, in 2007 New Zealand researchers Caroline Saunders and Peter Hayes[29] surveyed 27 studies (17 of which were funded by U.K. sponsors) that all unambiguously demonstrated the relatively insignificant carbon dioxide emission impact of transporting food. For instance, in 2005, researchers associated with the U.K. Department of Environment, Food and Rural Affairs (DEFRA) published[30] a comparison of U.K. and Spanish tomatoes sold in the U.K. that factored in both the production and delivery by land transportation of Spanish tomatoes to British consumers. According to their estimates, U.K. tomato producers emitted 2,394 kilograms of carbon dioxide per ton compared to 630 kilograms per ton for their Spanish competitors. This huge gap could be traced back to differences in the climate between the two locations. Because they live in a much cooler and overcast part of Europe, producers in the United Kingdom had no choice but to use heated greenhouses. Their Spanish competitors, by contrast, are located along the much warmer Mediterranean coast and can obtain much higher yields in non-heated greenhouses, which emitted much less carbon dioxide, thanks to nature providing the heat free of charge.

Tomato production is but one instance of a much larger phenomenon. As American researchers have documented, in their country the "food miles" segment (from producer to retailer) contributes only about 4% of total emissions related to what Americans take home in their grocery bags, while 83% of households' carbon dioxide footprint for food consumption can be traced back to the production stages.[31] Again, these credible LCA studies document the commonsensical notion that producing food requires a lot more energy than moving it around. This is especially the case for food that requires significant heating and/or cold protection technologies when the same items can be produced elsewhere in much more favorable climates. A schematic overview of the globalized food supply chain can also help put the relative (un)importance of transportation in broader perspective:

LCA SCOPE AND INPUT IN FOOD MILE ANALYSIS

SCOPE	PLAYER	INPUT
1. Raw material for production	Farm	Seed, land, fertilizer, water herbicide, pesticide, etc.
2. Production		Capital (machinery, facility buildings, etc.)
3. Packaging		Energy (fuel, electricity, oil) Labor
4. Distribution	Supply chain	Storage Waste Transportation Labor
5. Consumption	Consumer	Transportation Preparation Waste
6. Disposal		Recycle Waste Transportation

Transportation Mode/Load

Another general conclusion of the LCA studies is that the distance traveled matters less than the mode of transportation employed, whether boat, railroad car, truck, or individual car. Using 2002 data, the authors of the aforementioned 2005 DEFRA study developed two different types of measurements for food transport. The first was vehicle kilometers—the distance traveled by vehicles carrying food and drink regardless of the amount being transported. The second was ton kilometers—the distance multiplied by load, which gives a better sense of the amount of energy required for each item transported.[32] The researchers observed that 82% of the estimated 30 billion food miles associated with U.K.-consumed food are generated within the country, with car transport from shop to home accounting for 48% and tractor-trailers (what they call HGVs—heavy goods vehicles) representing 31% of food miles. Remarkably, air transport amounted to less than 1% of total food miles. The large share accounted for by cars was the result of individual families making numerous trips to the supermarket. By contrast, delivering these goods to stores using much more efficient means required much less energy per item. In other words, transporting a large volume of broccoli in a refrigerated container that had been moved around on a boat, a railroad car, and a truck to a distribution point required a lot less energy than a few thousand consumers bringing the same volume of broccoli back to their homes.

Significant differences also exist between transportation modes. By far the most efficient is maritime transportation, as modern container ships float on water and are powered by highly efficient diesel engines that can cover huge distances using very little fuel. According to the authors of the DEFRA study, in the U.K. sea transport accounted for 65% of food miles—the actual distance traveled by numerous food items that were imported from distant locations—but overall *maritime* food miles accounted for less than 1% of the total vehicle kilometers of the country. So moving New Zealand apples to the U.K. using highly efficient container ships consumed very little energy per apple, when compared to moving the fruit by car and in very small volumes from a supermarket to relatively close residences. Distance may be important, but in truth the transportation mode is typically a much more significant issue.

Seasonality and Storage

Advances in transportation have historically been associated with the increased outsourcing of perishable food items at the expense of local production and storage. Not only were imported items fresher than stored local produce, but they also reduced the costs associated with storage, especially in terms of energy (refrigeration) and spoilage. As we have already discussed, the timing of local harvests has long influenced the geographical distribution of food production. This consideration is lost on food activists, but was tackled head-on in a study published in 2006 by New Zealand researchers Caroline Saunders, Andrew Barber and Greg Taylor. Their work took into account the energy required for out-of-season cold storage as well as the related carbon dioxide emissions equivalent for U.K. apples and assumed that they would be kept in this state for an average of 6 months.[33] According to their scenario, the amount of energy needed to store these apples was 2,069 megajoule per ton (MJ/ton), and emissions for production was 85.5 kilograms of carbon dioxide per ton (CO_2/ton). These amounts are comparable to the energy consumption required to ship New Zealand apples to the U.K. (2,030 MJ/ton), but far exceed those required to produce New Zealand apples (60.1 kg of CO_2/ton). In other words, because New Zealand is located in the Southern Hemisphere where the growing season coincides with the Northern Hemisphere's winter, shipping freshly picked New Zealand apples and quickly selling them to U.K. consumers during their late winter season results in less greenhouse gas emissions than the purchase by U.K. consumers of U.K. apples that have been in storage for several months. Another study published by Llorenc Milà i Canals et al. in 2007 factored in seasonal storage and storage losses and reached a similar con-clusion.[34] In this scenario, local apples stored between 5 and 9 months with normal storage loss rates increased the energy used by 8–16%. What these studies show is that the smart thing to do is also the most eco-nomical: avoid cold storage as much as possible and purchase produce grown in different latitudes instead.

Consumer Behavior

The LCA and other studies have also highlighted additional consid-erations that, while less crucial to our argument, help put the food miles rhetoric in broader perspective. For one thing, consumers' trans-portation choices, such as walking, biking, or taking a crowded bus (as opposed to driving) can obviously reduce the total carbon dioxide emissions associated with food purchases. The authors of the DEFRA study showed that, in the worst-case scenario, a U.K. consumer driv-ing 6 miles to buy Kenyan green beans emits more carbon dioxide per bean than does flying the vegetables from Kenya to the U.K. There are, however, good reasons why most of us use a car to shop. Among other things, when we drive to the store we are able to buy more gro-ceries and thus reduce the number of shopping trips and amount of time devoted to this activity.

Another largely overlooked issue is the amount of food that is wasted. According to some estimates, between 30 to 40% of raw food materials and ingredients are lost between the points of production and consumption.[35] In less advanced economies, food losses in the produc-tion, harvesting, and on-farm storage stages are primarily attributable to the lack of infrastructure, knowledge, or investment in the means to protect agricultural products from damage and spoilage due to rodents, insects, molds, and other microorganisms. (Postharvest losses as a result of these factors are believed to account for at least 30% of the harvested crop in some parts of the world, a dramatic waste of seeds, water, fertil-izer, and labor.) By contrast, in industrialized countries, food losses are more significant in retail and food service establishments and in homes.[36] For instance, a 2008 British study conducted by the Waste & Resources Action Programme analyzed the trash of 2,138 households and estimated that more than 6.7 million tons of food—roughly a third of the food bought by consumers—was thrown out every year. According to its authors, 61% of this food waste (consisting mostly of fresh fruits, vegetables, and salads, and amounting to approximately 70 kilograms per person annually) could have been avoided with more care and planning. The costs involved were estimated to be about £10.2 billion (about $19.5 billion USD) and the cause of 18 million tons of carbon dioxide emissions per year in the U.K.—an amount equivalent to the emissions of one fifth of the British car fleet during this time period.[37]

We have already documented in chapter 2 how locavore initiatives such as Community Supported Agriculture result in more waste of fresh produce than is the case when people shop at supermarkets. Another misconception promoted by activists is that the absence (or much smaller volume) of packaging material at farmers' markets has significant environmental benefits, a notion that conveniently ignores the fact that food packaging has the dual advantage of protecting food from microbes and greatly prolonging shelf life. These advantages, in turn, significantly increase the probability of the food being consumed instead of ending in a landfill or incinerator.[38]

Clearly, if we are serious about decreasing the overall environmental impact of food production, food miles are nothing but a misleading distraction. To quote one of the world's leading authorities on the LCA analysis of agricultural productions, Dr. Adrian Williams of the National Resources Management Centre at Cranfield University (U.K.), the "concept of food miles is unhelpful and stupid. It doesn't inform about anything except the distance travelled."[39] A much more constructive approach to further minimize the environmental impact of agriculture would instead focus on further reducing production and postharvest losses as well as educating consumers on their food handling behaviors.

Blame It on the Poor People[40]

In recent years, about 40% of the U.K.'s air-freighted fresh fruit and vegetable imports have originated in sub-Saharan countries such as South Africa, Ghana, Tanzania, Uganda, Zambia, and Kenya. These goods drew the ire of uncompetitive European producers and activists who claimed that they were the epitome of unsustainable consumption and therefore deserving of retaliatory measures. In the words of Patrick Holden, Director of the U.K. Soil Association (the main U.K. organic certification organization and lobbyist), Britain should aim "to produce most of its organic food domestically and import as little as possible" because there "is a strong demand" for this "from the public and many of our licensees."[41] Yet, as the basic facts surrounding Kenyan products convincingly illustrate, in order to truly do what is best for the environment, one should avoid decisions based on emotional reactions and poorly disguised protectionist rhetoric and embrace instead price signals.

In 2004, Kenya's export of vegetables, roots, tubers, and other edible plants totaled $161 million, making it the 27th largest exporting country in this category.[42] Kenyan producers also exported $470 million worth of live trees, plants, bulbs, and cut flowers, making the country the 7th largest such exporter in the world at the time. Indeed, Kenyan cut flower exports amounted to $250 million, accounted for about 10% of the agricultural sector's contribution to the country's gross domestic product that year, and had a 25% market share in the European Union.[43] Not surprisingly, the livelihood of millions of Kenyans has come to depend on those export-based industries.

Because of their light weight, high value, and perishable nature, 91% of the fresh fruits and vegetables exported from Kenya to the U.K. were air freighted,[44] adding, for example, an additional 2–18 pence to the cost of each pack of organic Kenyan green beans.[45] Intercontinental air freight adds to the atmosphere 8 kilograms of carbon dioxide per kilogram transported—about 200 times more emissions and 12 times more energy than sea transport.[46] However, a much larger volume of carbon dioxide emissions is released by U.K. passenger flights each year. In fact, passenger flights amount to 90% of all emissions from airlines, with cargo amounting to about 5%. Furthermore, air freighted imports of fresh fruits and vegetables account for less than 0.1% of the total U.K. emissions of carbon dioxide. Interestingly, 60 to 80% of Kenyan fresh agricultural products are transported in the cargo hold of passenger flights.[47] When the passenger-related emissions are factored in, carbon dioxide emission levels for air freighted exports are actually much lower.

A study from 2007 provided another striking illustration of the impact of environmental differences between production locations. Here the authors considered the contrast between cut flowers grown in Kenya and the Netherlands and destined for the U.K. market.[48] For each 12,000 cut roses produced, Kenyan producers released 6,000 kilograms of carbon dioxide as opposed to 35,000 kilograms of carbon dioxide for their Dutch competitors. Overall, Kenyan rose production is said to be much more efficient and environmentally friendly compared to Dutch production, reflecting, among other things, the fact that 99% of Dutch emissions were caused by heating and lighting intensive production systems, whereas Kenyan flower production relies mostly on sunshine. In contrast, 91% of Kenyan emissions were attributed to the 4,000-mile air-freight transport from Kenya to the U.K.

When the food miles controversy over African perishable products reached its peak in early 2007, supporters of Kenyan exporters were quick to point out that greenhouse gas emissions associated with air-freighted produce were miniscule in comparison with the impact of tourist air travel by citizens of importing nations. They further argued that Kenyan agriculture typically relied on manual labor and organic fertilizers because they couldn't afford sophisticated farm machines and chemical pesticides and fertilizers. As such, the carbon dioxide emissions attributable to the production phase are rather negligible. Another relevant fact is that while carbon dioxide emissions per capita vary widely from country to country, the global average is currently estimated to be about 3.6 tons per person per year, with the U.K. average being approximately 9.2 tons, the African average 1.04 tons and the Kenyan average 0.2 ton.[49]

Green Cities and Trade

Another environmental consideration that is directly relevant to any discussion of locavorism is urbanization. As we argued in chapter 1, there can be no sustained economic development without cities, and, for at least a few millennia, urbanization has been impossible without significant long distance trade in food. Locavorism, though, is inherently anti-urban as it effectively mandates low density settlements distributed over the arable landscape (in our experience, though, a number of locavores do not grasp this implication). This vision of small and self-sufficient communities obviously holds much appeal for people who are not fond of the greater densities and sprawling suburbs of metropolitan areas, to say nothing of the associated higher air pollution and noise levels, crime, and failing public schools.

While most people, including those who are not willing to live there, will acknowledge the unique economic and cultural opportunities offered by thriving metropolitan areas, their environmental benefits are less readily understood, especially if one pictures congested, unpleasant, and unhealthy third world shantytowns. And yet, as observed by commentators whose basic argument parallels that of defenders of high-yield farming, thriving cities are not an environmental problem, but rather the best means to lighten up humanity's impact on nature. To quote the applied scientists and policy analysts Peter W. Huber and Mark P. Mills, the skyscraper is "America's great green gift to the planet" for it "packs more people onto less land, which leaves more wilderness undisturbed in other places, where the people aren't. . . . The less real estate we occupy for economic gain," they add, "the more we leave undisturbed as wilderness. And the city, though profligate in its consumption of most everything else, is very frugal with land. The one thing your average New Yorker does *not* occupy is 40 acres and a mule."[50]

In the words of economist Edward L. Glaeser, "residing in a forest might seem to be a good way of showing one's love of nature, but living in a concrete jungle is actually far more ecologically friendly . . . If you love nature, stay away from it."[51] The journalist David Owen further observed that because spreading people thinly across the landscape would increase environmental damage, "even part-time agricultural self-sufficiency . . . would be an environmental and economic disaster."[52] The basic point made by the likes of Huber, Mills, Glaeser, and Owen is thus that, by virtually any measure, residents of high-density urban areas drive, pollute, consume, and throw away much less than people living in greener surroundings.[53] Apart perhaps from self-selected migrants to environmentalist meccas such as Portland, Oregon, or Missoula, Montana, urbanites are not intrinsically greener than rural inhabitants, but when space is at a premium, wastefulness turns out to be prohibitively expensive.

True, growing cities have always been surrounded by lower density suburbs (*suburbium* originally referred to the area beyond the walls of Ancient Rome), but these always become denser in good economic times.[54] This phenomenon has arguably accelerated in the last few decades with the development of "edge cities" (or suburban downtowns) and row housing and garden apartments in new residential developments located far from older urban centers. Actually, for quite a few years the densest metropolitan area in the United States (including both downtown and suburban areas) has been Los Angeles—and by a fair margin—a result that can be traced back to its numerous high-rise buildings spread out over its territory, high population numbers per individual housing unit, and costly water supply infrastructure. Overall, though, cities, suburbs, roads, and highways cover perhaps less than 5% of the land area of the lower 48 American states, and for several decades, because of high yield technologies, far more American agricultural land has been reverting to wilderness than has been converted to suburbia. Worldwide, cities occupy approximately 2% of the earth's surface, an area that should double to 4% in the next half century.[55] If the world's

7 billion individuals were living at a density comparable to New York City, all of them could be housed in Texas.[56] Provided that economic growth is strong and local governance reasonably effective, large metropolitan areas will prove to be significant environmental assets rather than liabilities.

Although agriculture will continue to have a major impact on the landscape, what is clear from the available evidence is that the world envisioned by locavores would have a significantly larger surface area devoted to growing food (and therefore a much more severe impact on the landscape) than a world where farming is practiced in the most suitable production zones. Moving ever closer to a world dominated by modern agriculture technologies and international trade will not eliminate our impact on the environment, but will nonetheless drastically curtail it. Because of increased competitive pressures, food producers will have no other choice but to constantly find new and better ways of doing things, including generating economies of scale and relocating their operations or increasing their purchases from businesses located in more suitable areas, in the process sparing nature and increasing output. Because it would be inherently wasteful in its use of resources, the world of locavores can only, by contrast, deliver greater environmental damage.

5

Myth #4: Locavorism
Increases Food Security

We have had unmistakable warnings, too, in the last few
years, that we cannot afford to be dependent for the staples
of our food and industry on any single place or production.
The potato disease was one of those warnings.

—THOMAS EDWARD CLIFFE LESLIE. 1862.
"The Reclamation of Waste." *The Saturday Review of Politics,*
Literature, Science and Art 356 (14) (AUGUST 23): 225

One of the greatest benefits to be expected from the improvements of civilization is that increased facilities of communication will render it possible to transport to places of consumption
much valuable material that is now wasted because the price at
the nearest market will not pay freight. The cattle slaughtered
in South America for their hides would feed millions of the
starving population of the Old World, if their flesh could be economically preserved and transported across the ocean.

—GEORGE PERKINS MARSH. 1864.
Man and Nature; or Physical Geography as Modified by Human Action.
Charles Scribner, p. 37

"Food security" has traditionally been defined as providing access at all times to enough sufficient, safe, and nutritious food to allow people to maintain healthy and active lives.[1] This goal long remained elusive as historically most people were malnourished most of the time and frequently struggled with food shortages and famines.[2] These perennial worries have disappeared from the collective memory of the citizens of advanced economies and are now confined to the least developed and more conflict-prone parts of our planet.[3] Even wartime tragedies such as the *hongerwinter* (hunger winter) of 1944–1945, in which at least 20,000 Dutch citizens and one in six babies starved to death, and the roughly 100,000 individuals who suffered the same fate in Tokyo in the three months that followed the Japanese surrender in 1945, are now almost completely forgotten.

True, important food challenges have yet to be met. For instance, even if in the aggregate enough food is produced to feed each human being substantially more than the minimum caloric intake required for survival, close to a billion people remain malnourished and approximately nine million reportedly die every year of hunger, malnutrition, and related diseases.[4] Significant food price spikes have also made a noticeable comeback in recent years.[5] Not surprisingly, locavores blame these problems on unfair international trade and the greed of large multinational corporations. Along with so-called "food sovereignists," their preferred solution is that "people and community" should be given the "ability to sustain themselves" and the right "to define their own agricultural, labor, fishing, food and land policies" without outside interference.[6] What these activists envision, however, is not increased individual freedom to patronize either domestic or foreign suppliers, but mandatory government policies to subsidize and protect local producers (with the proviso that their policies do not hurt other countries) despite the wishes of individual consumers or taxpayers.[7] Moving in this direction, they claim, will not only make the provisioning of vulnerable communities more secure, but also more "culturally appropriate," "dignified," respectful of the environment, and "socially just."[8]

The case for increased food sovereignty now essentially revolves around three basic "security" claims. First, because local food systems must not only be smaller in scale but also more diversified (after all, you cannot feed a community a healthy diet by producing only a few commodities), they are inherently more resilient to pests of all kinds than large monocultures. Second, the sudden decline in the demand for or collapse in the production of an agricultural commodity in which a community has overspecialized means that it will be left unable to import the nonlocal food on which it has come to depend. Finally, in times of rapidly rising commodity prices, political turmoil, or all-out war, no community will be better served than by itself. In addition to these claims, many locavores further promote their prescription by invoking an impending oil shortage and drastic climate change. Better anticipate and prepare for the unavoidable, they argue, by accelerating the inexorable transition towards local food systems. We will examine each argument in turn, but before we do so a brief overview of the history of famines in mostly "self-sufficient" local economies is warranted.

The Third Horseman

The third horseman of the *Apocalypse of John* (otherwise known as the *Book of Revelation*) famously carried a pair of weighing scales, which would have been used to weigh bread during hungry times. Like his fellow riders (conquest, war, and death from pestilence), he was until recently a familiar presence in most human societies. As the geographer Brian Murton observes, famines have plagued humankind for at least 6,000 years and have long been used by scholars and chroniclers to "slice up history into manageable portions."[9] While researchers still disagree on the widespread, recurring, and severe character of prehistorical hunger, there is a general consensus that, with the invention of agriculture, famines typically resulted from a succession of mediocre harvests rather than from an isolated crop failure. Some could be traced back to human factors such as wars, ethnic and religious persecution, price controls, protectionism, excessive taxation, and lack of respect for private property rights. Others were due to natural origins, such as unseasonable temperatures, excessive or insufficient rainfall, floods, insect pests, rodents, pathogens, soil degradation, and epidemics that made farmers or their beasts of burden unfit for work.[10] In many cases, a number of these factors were involved.

To give a glimpse of past horrors and calamities, suffice it to say that during the Hundred Years War in Medieval Western Europe (1337–1453), a combination of crop failures, epidemics and warfare is thought to have reduced the population by two-thirds. Chinese inhabitants suffered an average of perhaps 90 famines per century in the last two thousand years. Between 1333 and 1337, approximately six million Chinese died of starvation whereas perhaps as many as forty-five million perished in the first half of the 19th century. In the 1920s, Chinese peasants "recalled an average of three crop failures during their lifetimes that were serious enough to cause famines. These famines lasted on average about ten months, and they led up to a quarter of the affected population to eat grasses and strip bark from trees" while forcing "one in every seven people to leave their hungry villages in search of food."[11] In the recent past, at least forty-three million people are now thought to have died during the famine of 1959–1962 as a direct result of the "Great Leap Forward" policies of Mao Zedong, making it the single largest famine of all time.[12]

Political and individual strategies for coping with famines have always been similar the world over. In the absence of charitable giving and emigration opportunities, authorities could call upon heavenly assistance, impose price controls and seize private reserves, lower import tariffs, expel strangers, identify and make an example out of scapegoats and "profiteers," and dispatch envoys to find additional supplies. Among private citizens, wealthier individuals could reduce discretionary spending and tap into or stop accumulating savings in order to purchase increasingly scarce and expensive food while poorer people were more likely to stretch available resources by temporarily lowering their food intake. Whenever possible, too, individuals would borrow money to purchase food. Much harder times would command the consumption of seed grains, farm animals, and famine foods, including grass, leaves, bark, clay, and dirt; the selling or mortgaging of familial assets, from clothes and furniture to animals, land, and children (once a famine had receded, children were sometimes sold into slavery so that parents could buy back their land[13]); reducing the number of mouths to feed through infanticide or senilicide; and cannibalism. In most places the burden of food shortages historically fell disproportionately on the shoulders of the elderly, pregnant and lactating women, and poor and landless people. In many cultures, too, the survival of boys was given priority over that of girls.

The Slaying of the Third Horseman (with Long Distance Trade)

In advanced economies, what ultimately limited famines to wartime periods is long distance trade and economic development. Writing in 1856, George Dodd observed that in the "days of limited intercourse, scarcity of crops was terrible in its results; the people had nothing to fall back upon; they were dependent upon growers living within a short distance; and if those growers had little to sell, the alternative of starvation became painfully vivid."[14] In the classic *Annals of Rural Bengal,* published in 1871, William Wilson Hunter, the Scottish historian and member of the Indian Civil Service, noted that an important set of preventative steps against famines included "[e]very measure that helps towards the extension of commerce and the growth of capital, every measure that increases the facilities of transport and distribution... [and whatever tends] to render each part [of a country] less dependent on itself."[15] More recently, the economic historian Cormac Ó Gráda similarly observed that "the historical record suggests that the integration of markets and the gradual eradication of famine are linked." By the late 19th century, he adds, even "disaster relief was truly globalized."[16] As a group of British food policy experts stated in 2010, "international trade is a key underpinning of food security at all levels" and in the relatively recent past "food crises have occurred, not simply because domestic production fails, but when financial resources are lacking, trade is blocked, distribution channels are inefficient or crippled, and governance is poor."[17]

In times of political stability and open trade, the provisioning of urban populations has always been more abundant and stable overall than that of subsistence farmers, a fact that can be inferred from the typical migration of rural peasants to cities in times of famine.[18] (This is not to say that poor urban dwellers were necessarily well fed, but they were certainly better off than their rural counterparts.) In a 1768 essay promoting the liberalization of grain markets, the French economist and ecclesiast Nicolas Baudeau observed that even though no grain production took place in the heavily urbanized Netherlands, freedom to trade had long eradicated famine in the region. Inspired by the Dutch success, in 1689 English rulers adopted a similar policy and achieved beneficial results. Another success story at the time was the Republic of Genoa whereas, by contrast, government restrictions on commerce in the nearby Papal States and Sicily had resulted in the inhabitants of once exporting regions struggling to feed themselves.[19]

The basic fact about food security, Baudeau argued, was that when freedom to trade was secure and goods could be moved between political borders, differences in physical geography and seasonal weather ensured that the surplus of regions that had enjoyed good harvests could be channeled to those that experienced below average ones. The Mediterranean basin has always been striking in this respect as, according to some classifications, it possesses no fewer than 64 climatic subtypes and experiences significant weather variability from one growing season to the next. As Aristotle observed more than two millennia ago: "Sometimes there is much drought or rain, and it prevails over a great and continuous stretch of country. At other times it is local; the surrounding country often getting seasonable or even excessive rains while there is drought in a certain part; or, contrariwise, all the surrounding country gets little or even no rain while a certain part gets rain in abundance."[20] This is even more so on a planetary scale.

Of course, the state of transportation and information technologies at any given point in time was also crucial in moving goods around in the right amounts and at the right time. Historically, regions that could rely on maritime transportation always had a clear advantage over land-locked ones. To give but one illustration, a 4th century AD observer noted that in the town of Edessa (modern Turkish Sanliurfa) located more than 350 kilometers away from the nearest seaport:

[t]here was a famine, the most severe within the memory of man. The city was in distress, but there was no help forthcoming from any quarter, nor any remedy for the calamity. The maritime cities support without difficulty occasions of want like these, since they can dispose of their own product and receive in exchange those which come to them by the sea. But we in the inland can make no profit on our superfluous products, nor procure what we need, having no means of disposing of what we have and importing what we lack.[21]

In 1774, Benjamin Franklin observed that in "inland high countries, remote from the sea, and whose rivers are small, running from the country, not to it, as is the case of Switzerland, great distress may arise from a course of bad harvests, if public granaries are not provided and kept well stored." It might also have been the case in ancient times, Franklin observed, that "before navigation was so general, ships so plenty, and commercial connections so well established," that "even maritime countries might be occasionally distressed by bad crops." In the second half of the 18th century, however, he commented that "an unrestrained commerce can scarce ever fail of procuring a sufficiency for any of them."[22]

This is the context one needs in order to appreciate the importance of the railroad in drastically improving food security in the last two centuries. As the historian Christian Wolmar observes: "France… had periodically suffered famines as a result of adverse weather conditions right up to the 1840s, but once the railways began reaching the most rural parts of the country, food could easily be sent to district[s] suffering shortages. Moreover, it was at a price people could afford." Wolmar further quotes the journalist Nicholas Faith to the effect that "'only' half a million Chinese died in a famine in 1920/21 whereas 25 times as many had perished in a similar disaster fifty years earlier, before the railways had reached the regions involved."[23]

Agricultural Resilience: Diversification vs. Monocultures[24]

Agricultural producers have long had to strike a balance between the greater resiliency and lower productivity of growing different types of food simultaneously and the greater productivity, but increased vulnerability, of focusing all of one's efforts on a single lucrative commodity. Subsistence farmers the world over have understandably always elected to spread risks through crop and animal diversification. When you cannot easily tap other food sources, you better make sure that you have something to fall back on if a crop fails. In the words of agricultural economists George Norton, Jeffrey Alwang, and William Masters, in subsistence agriculture livestock acts as "a savings bank and an insurance plan."[25] In topographically diverse environments, farmers often deliberately used contrasts between various microclimates by, for example, working more than one parcel of land on different sides of a mountain. These strategies helped mitigate the impact of unpredictable weather, such as a late frost or an isolated hailstorm. Diversification was also eminently sensible in the presence of insect pests and diseases that targeted one or a few related plants and animals.

Building on the incontrovertible fact that unbroken fields of a single crop increase predation, disease, and risk of crop failure, critics of modern farming have argued for decades that monocultures are by their very nature unsustainable. For example, in 1962 Rachel Carson wrote in *Silent Spring* that under "primitive agricultural conditions the farmer had few insect problems. These arose with the intensification of agriculture—the devotion of immense acreage to a single crop. Such a system set the stage for explosive increases in specific insect populations. Single-crop farming does not take advantage of the principle by which nature works; it is agriculture as an engineer might conceive it to be. Nature has introduced great variety into the landscape, but man has displayed a passion for simplifying it. Thus he undoes the built-in checks and balances by which nature holds the species within bounds."[26] A few critics even take this argument to its logical conclusion, noting that, no matter how diversified, local agriculture can in theory never be as resilient as hunting and gathering, a point that is also often raised in controversies surrounding the development of agriculture some 10,000 years ago.[27]

Despite its intuitive appeal, the notion that local polycultures are an inherently better way to improve the security of a community's food supply ignores the fact that large-scale monocultures have always been part of a much broader geographical division of labor. In other words, despite their fondness for diversity in all its forms, locavores are oblivious to the fact that their prescription mandates that a community puts all of its agricultural eggs into *one geographical basket* while monoculture regions can rely on a broad range of distant suppliers in troubled times. As the historical record clearly shows, local polycultures have always been perilously unstable because they remained vulnerable to natural events that destroyed much in their path (from tornadoes and floods to hailstorms and earthquakes), highly contagious diseases that could affect a broad range of animals, and omnivorous insect pests. To give but one example, during the mid-1870s, Rocky Mountain locusts are said to have "launched attacks of such fury" that the governor of Missouri proclaimed a day of public prayer and fasting "for the interposition of Divine Providence to relieve the calamities cause[d] by [their] devastation." Fortunately for the local inhabitants, the federal government was able to send emergency shipments of food, clothing, and seeds to hundreds of Mississippi Valley farmers.[28]

And let's not forget that not all monocultures are the same. Some, like the corn and soybean rotation in the American Corn Belt, involve deliberate efforts to reduce pest buildups. Others, like vineyards, will include different types of vines that will react differently to weather conditions. It is also worth remembering that the now-dominant varieties of most crops—which are not only higher yielding, but also much more resistant to disease and stress than most landraces (local varieties of *domesticated* animal or plant species that have developed largely by natural selection processes in response to their surrounding environments)—were bred from multiple types that originated from different locations.

Most important, though, is the fact that, because of their lower productivity, local food systems can only support a much smaller fraction of the human intellect, capital, and sophisticated division of labor made possible by large monocultures and international trade. When things go wrong in the local polycultures of less advanced economies, only a few individuals with limited means can be called upon to perform such measures as crushing bugs by hands or diverting flood waters with picks and shovels. Large-scale monocultures, on the other hand, have long been able to rely on the work of numerous plant and animal breeders, researchers combating disease, and countless other experts whose very existence has always depended on the wealth generated by specialization and exchange. Despite low crop and animal diversity in commercial agriculture, highly skilled specialists continue to improve resistance to parasites, insect pests, diseases, and environmental stresses in monocultures over time. Unlike subsistence farmers who only ever had access to a limited number of local varieties of seeds, plant researchers can tap into large seed banks (which include hundreds of thousands of varieties for major crops like rice) and ever more sophisticated breeding technologies. As the economist Thomas R. DeGregori observes: "Monoculture today is in fact not only consistent with an incredible diversity of means for crop protection, it is the *sine qua non* for them, because it is not possible to have such resources for all the less widely planted crops."[29]

This basic fact of modern agricultural life should help put in perspective the claim that lethal "monoculture" disease outbreaks will inevitably force us down the locavores' road. A case in point are Gros Michel bananas, the variety among a thousand that made a tropical fruit the most affordable fruit option in temperate advanced economies over the last century. At the beginning of the 20th century, they were exported in large quantities from tropical locations to North America and Europe because of their thick skin, year-round availability because of their nonseasonal character, ease of long-term storage without much packaging, and simultaneous ripening in ethylene-filled rooms. The variety was essentially wiped out of commercial production by fungus problems decades ago. Yet, our supermarket shelves are still stocked with bananas because Gros Michel were replaced by the more resistant Cavendish variety (which, despite its name, is of southern Chinese origins) while resistance to the diseases that had plagued banana production was finally found in New Guinea.[30]

Of course, bananas were neither the first nor the last monoculture to suffer significant setbacks and recover in one form or another thanks to scientific research. To give a few additional illustrations, in the West Indies and Java in the late 19th century, the main variety of cane used on sugar plantations suffered dramatic disease outbreaks (especially from the sugarcane mosaic virus) and consequent yield reductions. In time, though, new varieties were bred that introduced genes from a wild relative, *Saccharum spontaneum* L., that were not only more resistant, but also richer in sucrose.[31] In the United States, a rust epidemic destroyed most of the wheat crop in the northern plains in 1878 and struck again periodically afterwards, but the problem was brought under control at the time through better breeding and the eradication of wild barberry bushes that hosted spores capable of creating new strains of the disease. The grape phylloxera, a small North American insect pest of commercial grapevines, destroyed between two-thirds and nine-tenths of European vineyards in the late 19th century. At first, chemicals such as carbon bisulfide were used to curb its impact, but in time the pest was dealt with more successfully through the grafting of cuttings onto resistant rootstocks of North American origins and through hybridization efforts.[32] More recently, the Southern corn-leaf blight of the early 1970s destroyed 15% of the American corn harvest, but the problem was quickly resolved through scientific research.[33] In 1970 coffee rust made its first appearance in Latin America and in 1994 damaged a significant portion of the Brazilian crop. Coffee breeders then turned to wild-growing coffee plants found in Uganda and Mauritius for resistance genes and were able to address the problem.[34] In the early 1970s, leafspot disease inflicted huge losses on California alfalfa producers, but a genetic solution was eventually found in 1974 in a single wild alfalfa plant (*Medicago hemicycla* Grossheim), and was soon transferred to a cultivated type of alfalfa by a team of scientists at the University of California-Davis.[35]

Large "monocultural" herds and flocks of farm animals have similarly suffered from various epidemic diseases long before the advent of modern agribusiness.[36] For instance, in the 19th century the railroad and steamships not only facilitated the movement of livestock, but also of diseases which rapidly spread among animals in different locations that until then had been relatively isolated from each other. Rinderpest (or cattle plague, an infectious disease of cattle, buffalo, yaks and numerous wild species) in particular became more endemic than it had ever been. Between 1857 and 1866, "Europe was almost denuded of cattle" while in later decades Indonesia, the Philippines and much of East Africa would experience cattle losses ranging between 90 and 95% that caused widespread famine and deaths, especially among pastoralist groups such as the Maasai. In time, though, medical advances in combination with older procedures, such as quarantine and culling, made eradication of this plague a reality.[37] In 1914, a foot and mouth disease outbreak in the United States became rampant after it turned up in the Chicago stockyards, affecting over 170,000 cattle, sheep and swine. It was nonetheless swiftly controlled at a cost of U.S. $4.5 million (approximately $100 million in today's dollars). (Interestingly, some contemporaries first suspected terrorists "equipped with hypothermic syringes" whose objective would have been to prevent U.S. meat shipments to "warring countries in Europe."[38])

While it is true that monocultures, like any other commercial line of work, have always been subjected to financial risks, suffered major setbacks, and will remain plagued by various problems in the future, their alleged shortcomings in terms of crop failure and food security should be contrasted to those of traditional "localized" polycultures. The basic facts here are unambiguous. Subsistence farmers periodically starve while commercial agricultural producers who rely on monocultures for their livelihood don't—and these days, when subsistence farmers in poor economies escape famine, it is typically because relief efforts were able to deliver the products of large-scale monocultures grown in distant locations. The best way to improve the security of humanity's food supply is therefore not to revert to inherently unstable systems, but to press forward with constant research, development, adaptation, and reliance on the broad range of genetic material conserved in the cold storage vaults of the world's approximately 1,400 gene banks. Nature is a powerful and extremely creative foe against which many more generations of agricultural scientists and commercial producers will struggle. Despite this, however, past successes—ranging from ever more sophisticated pest control technologies to more resistant crop and animal varieties—have clearly demonstrated that, paradoxically, large-scale monocultures backed up by scientific research and international trade are significantly more resilient than more diversified but less technologically sophisticated local food systems.

Overspecialization and Food Security

In the first edition of Thomas Robert Malthus's *Essay on the Principles of Population as it Affects the Future Improvement of Society* (1798),[39] the English clergyman and economist sought to debunk the view that standards of living could be constantly improved through scientific and technological advances. Although he later adopted a more nuanced stance, his general argument is now widely understood to be that human populations have a tendency to grow more rapidly (geometrically or exponentially) than their means of subsistence (arithmetically or linearly). Population growth will therefore inexorably outstrip food and other supplies, resulting in ever increasing misery, famine, disease, war, environmental destruction, and population crashes.[40]

Commenting on Malthus's dire predictions, the British economist Kenneth Smith observed in 1952 that the clergyman's previsions on the fate of the English and Welsh populations (he considered both regions full and on the verge of collapse with a population of approximately 10 million individuals—there are now approximately six times more people living in Wales and England today) had failed to materialize "because the development of overseas territories opened up an enormous source of additional food." He added that individuals "are not compelled to subsist on the supplies grown in the area where they live; in a trading community it is only the total which must suffice" and that just as "townspeople live on the products of the countryside, so do industrialized nations draw their supplies from more primitive countries which specialize in the production of raw materials and foodstuff." Englishmen and Welshmen were thus "able to draw on the whole of the world."[41]

Although Smith's core economic insight was eminently sensible, his insistence that "primitive" regions should specialize in the production of a particular foodstuff has long been challenged on the grounds that a sudden drop in demand for a local specialty item—whether because of new competitors, changing consumer tastes, or the development of better substitutes—or an epidemic disease of massive proportion will rapidly make it impossible for laid off workers to purchase the food imports on which they have come to rely. The concern is valid, but the problem is not unique to agriculture. In a time of rapid technological change, all of us invest in personal skills that are likely to become obsolete during our lifetimes. Similarly, as the economist Alfred Marshall observed more than a century ago, "a[n industrial] district which is dependent chiefly on one industry is liable to extreme depression, in case of a falling-off in the demand for its produce, or of a failure in the supply of the raw material which it uses."[42] Fisheries can collapse. The remains of once prosperous mining communities litter the American landscape. The real issue is therefore not whether a poorly diversified economic base is undesirable, but rather whether specialized agricultural regions should revert back to greater self-sufficiency and subsistence economies to prevent economic downturns. The answer is an unequivocal no, but again, one needs to look at the bigger picture to appreciate why.

First, while virtually all commercial products and economic skills will eventually sink into obsolescence, they are still worth producing as long as there is a market for them. Phonographs, vinyl disks, and tape cassettes are now at best collectors' items, but they created ample employment in earlier times by providing consumers a greater range of musical experiences than would have been the case in their absence. Should investors have refrained from putting their capital into this line of work? Should employees have refrained from acquiring once valuable skills? Obviously not. Similarly, profitable monocultures should be pursued as long as they remain viable in a particular location. If they are suddenly no longer worth pursuing, other alternative crops can often be grown in their place. In the 19th century, coffee production in what is now Sri Lanka was wiped out by a fungus infection, yet the local economy nonetheless forged ahead as tea, rubber (through rubber tree plantations), and coconut production proved profitable.[43] At the turn of the 20th century, Pierce's disease was a significant factor in dooming the wine-making industry of Southern California (the other was the poor quality of the product), but citrus fruits better suited to the local climate more than made up for it.

But, critics readily object, what about *people* being thrown out of work *now* when no viable substitutes have been found? The short answer is that agricultural workers are ultimately no different than the former employees of horse-drawn carriage manufacturers. Old jobs need to be terminated so that resources can be redeployed to better uses, which will in turn create more and better jobs. Besides, skills developed in one context can often be used in another. Well then, activists typically add, what about the fate of local communities? Shouldn't people have a right to live where they want and where they belong? As we see things, humans gave up that "right" the moment they left Africa a very long time ago. True, having to leave one's rural community in search of better opportunities elsewhere might not be everybody's wish, but it sure beats the traditional "starving in fresh air" fate of subsistence farmers. Besides, the fact that humans are not plants and can escape from droughts, floods, and other natural and economic calamities should be viewed as a blessing, not a curse. It could also be pointed out that the food price spike of 2008 was somewhat softened by record remittances dispatched by migrants to their countries of origin that totaled close to $340 billion, a 40% increase from the $240 billion sent in 2007.[44] In the end, too, abandoned agricultural lands quickly revert to a more "natural" state, a fact that should please environmental activists.

Like financial investors, producers in a monoculture region can reduce the risk of economic collapse through the diversification of their "economic portfolio." More than a century ago Alfred Marshall observed that the economic meltdown of mono-industrial districts could "in a great measure [be] avoided by those large towns or large industrial districts in which several distinct industries are strongly developed." Regional diversification, however, doesn't imply giving up on specialization, but rather developing multiple profitable specializations. Unfortunately, mainstream economists have long been in the habit of discussing the benefits of the geographical division of labor using the simple model of two countries, each only able to manufacture two different commodities. Basic economic reasoning then leads to the conclusion that each region or nation should specialize in the production of only one good, but this result is for all intents and purposes built into their unrealistic assumptions. Why they persist in using this example is something we never quite understood given the realities of vast geographical entities made up of diverse landscapes and millions of people with different abilities. What ultimately matters is the fact that individuals with different aptitudes and interests living in specific places specialize and trade with other individuals, in the process profitably concentrating on all kinds of endeavors and making abstract "entities" such as cities, regions, and nations more rather than less diverse over time.[45]

Many diverse cities are found throughout the American cornbelt, yet corn producers in this area remain highly specialized. Should things go wrong with corn farming, local producers could find other lines of employment in their region, although this might entail a long commute or relocation to another city or town. The key point to improve food security in the long run is to ensure that as many resources as possible are invested in the development of the profitable activities of tomorrow rather than squandered in a vain attempt to cling to the industries of yesterday. As long as new lines of work are developed and people are free to move, the fate of agricultural workers in declining monoculture regions and towns will be positive by any historical standard and certainly better than in a world shaped by locavore ideals.

One more way to convey this point is to look at the circumstances of the inhabitants of regions that were once agriculturally diversified and regularly subjected to hunger and famines, but which later became large-scale monocultures and practically famine-proof. Because almost all monoculture regions in advanced economies would qualify, we will limit ourselves to the case of a few square miles in the so-called "American bottom," the approximately 175-square-mile Mississippi flood plain east of Saint Louis in southern Illinois. This area—once the home of the largest Native American settlement north of what is now Mexico—includes a six-square-mile complex of man-made earthen mounds, the Cahokia Mounds, the largest earthwork built during pre-Columbian times.

At its peak in the 13th century, Cahokia might have had a population of as many as 40,000 people (a high-end estimate that would have made it larger than London at the time), a figure that would only be exceeded in the United States by Philadelphia at the turn of the 19th century. As with all sizeable urban settlements in history, evidence has been found of goods that were brought in from long distances, in this case from as far away as the Gulf Coast (shells), Lake Superior (copper), Oklahoma (chert, a flintlike rock), and the Carolinas (mica). The local inhabitants grew corn, squash, goosefoot, amaranth, canary grass, and other starchy seeds, beans, gourds, pumpkins, and sunflowers which they supplemented by wild fruits and nuts, fish, waterfowl, and a few game animals. Despite corn storage in granaries, though, the Cahokians were subjected to recurring hunger and famine.[46] By contrast, today, the main mounds are part of the city of Collinsville, Illinois, which is not only the home of the largest ketchup bottle in the world, but is also the self-described "world's horseradish capital." Even if America's (and the world's) fondness for horseradish were somehow to fade away, the area's agricultural labor force could find work elsewhere or help local horseradish producers switch to other crops. As such, they are much more food secure than the ancient inhabitants of the site.

As the above cases illustrate, monocultures can only be a serious threat to food security *in the absence of broader economic development, scientific and technological advances, trade, and labor mobility.* The Irish potato famine, the standard case used by opponents of monocultures, is also a more telling illustration in this respect than most imagine. Without getting into too many details of a complex and still controversial story,[47] a key feature of the Irish famine of the 1840s is that it was not the result of a uniquely "Irish" disease, but rather of a problem that was then rampant in North America and Continental Europe. A little appreciated feature of the Irish economy at the time is that it was the home of a thriving export-oriented food sector that had long shipped out goods such as dairy products, grains, livestock, fish, and potatoes to the rest of Europe and various American colonies.[48] Not surprisingly, the best lands were devoted to the most lucrative products while a rudimentary form of potato cultivation was concentrated on less fertile soils and had displaced oats as the main staple of poor people because it delivered much higher yields. Potatoes, rich in vitamin C, also proved to be a fitting complement to then-abundant dairy products rich in vitamins A and D. As a result, despite many local and partial potato harvest failures and significant famines in 1799 and 1816, the Irish population grew faster in the 18th century than in any other European country, from around 2 million people in 1750 to about 8.2 million people in 1845.

The downside of this demographic boom, however, was that on the eve of the great famine, about a third of the population depended on potatoes for most of their food intake and that relatively few potato varieties had been introduced from the Americas. As serious disease problems began to emerge in Western Europe and North America in the late 18th century, new South American varieties were introduced in an attempt to increase resistance. Unfortunately, they probably brought in or heightened vulnerability to the so-called late blight of potato caused by the oomycete (a fungus-like microorganism) *Phytophthora infestans* that attacked both tubers and foliage.

The disease that would forever be associated with Ireland actually first showed up in central Mexico and then reached Pennsylvania in 1843, from which it swept across an area stretching from Illinois and Virginia to Nova Scotia and Ontario over the next three years. It probably entered Belgium in 1845 through a shipment of American seed potatoes and soon ravaged potato fields all the way to Russia. As if things were not dire enough, below average wheat and rye crops also plagued Europe at the time, giving rise to the moniker "the Hungry Forties." In Ireland, the disease destroyed a third of the potato crop in 1845 and most of the harvest in 1846 and 1848. The resulting loss of foodstuff was of such magnitude (approximately 20 million tons for human consumption alone) that the banning of ongoing Irish grain and livestock exports at the time, a measure requested by many, would have covered at most one-seventh of it. Nearly a million people died in total, the majority from hunger-related diseases such as typhus, dysentery, and typhoid rather than outright starvation. Another notable fact is that the areas that specialized in livestock and cereal production were largely unaffected by the famine.

In Continental Europe, the potato blight resulted in perhaps 100,000 deaths while, to our knowledge, no specific death toll was recorded in North America. While the European number was large, it was literally and proportionately only a small fraction of Ireland's despite the fact that many poor Western Europeans were also heavily dependent on potatoes for their sustenance. Much evidence suggests that the key difference between Ireland and Western Europe at the time was that the latter was by then offering more employment and food options to its inhabitants, such as artisanal or cottage production, as salesmen working for local markets, or as part-time workers in various industries. Many of the relatively poor Europeans were thus able to purchase other food commodities that were then no longer available to the most impoverished segments of the Irish population. Many individuals whose nutritional intake was also heavily dependent on potatoes moved permanently to industrializing areas, for example from the Scottish highlands to the Scottish lowlands. By and large, however, the potato blight did not result in massive emigration from Western Europe. In New England, farmers gave up on potatoes (often the only crop that grew in their poor soil), culled their cattle and swine for want of feed, and moved away to rich grain (wheat and corn) lands further west or else found manufacturing or other employment in the then-rapidly developing American industrial belt.

Apart from massive death and emigration, the Irish famine had at least two significant consequences. One was that it put an end to quasi-subsistence domestic food provisioning among the poorer classes of Irish people, a welcome development inasmuch as it ensured that serious failures of the potato harvests in the early 1860s and late 1870s did not increase mortality even though they did cause local hardship. The other was that it accelerated efforts to develop more productive and disease-resistant varieties that, together with the development of fungicides, laid the foundation for massive potato production in both Europe and North America in subsequent decades. Potato monocultures are found in many regions of the world today (being essentially water and extremely cheap, potatoes are not traded in large volumes between continents) and their producers are still struggling with a number of diseases and pests, but a repeat of the Irish tragedy is unthinkable in our globalized world.

Locavorism and Military Security

Writing in the year following the end of the First World War, the American geographer Joseph Russell Smith observed that two generations of Americans and Europeans had become so used to an abundant food supply that they no longer considered the possibilities of famine nor understood "the troubles of the past, nor as yet the vital problems of the present." Dependence on world trade, he argued, had in the end given modern man "the independence of a bird in a cage, no more." "The world market is excellent," Russell Smith added, "when it is well supplied." In wartime, however, the places where food is produced "determined the lives of nations."[49]

This experience drastically shaped European food politics in later years. In Italy, the fascist dictator Benito Mussolini launched a "Battle for Grain" in 1925 that, through high tariffs, farm subsidies of various kinds, "local content" milling requirements, newer seeds, and technical education, was supposed to free Italy from the "slavery" of food imports. In practice, however, his policy came at the cost of converting a lot of the Italian landscape from profitable export crops such as fresh produce, citrus fruits, and olives to grain production, resulting in a more monotonous and costlier diet for Italian consumers. In the words of the historian Denis Mack Smith, the battle for grain was ultimately won "at the expense of the Italian economy in general and consumers in particular."[50] Meanwhile, in Germany, national socialist ideology promoted both agricultural autarky, or self-sufficiency, and *Lebensraum*—the required vital space of Eastern Europe from which inferior races were to be cleared and food produced to supply the German Fatherland.[51] We all know how this one ended. The leaders of the Soviet Union also pursued agricultural autarky until 1973 when confronted with a severe domestic grain shortfall that forced them to open up to food imports from their main competitor for world influence and domination.

The appeal of autarky for imperial and totalitarian regimes is easily understood. As the Austrian economist Ludwig von Mises observed several decades ago: "A warlike nation must aim at autarky in order to be independent of foreign trade. It must foster the production of substitutes irrespective of [economic] considerations. It cannot do without full government control of production because the selfishness of the individual citizens would thwart the plans of the leader. Even in peacetime the commander-in-chief must be entrusted with economic dictatorship."[52] Many economists otherwise supportive of trade liberalization have also been willing to make an exception to their stance when national security was thought to be at stake. Perhaps the most famous was Adam Smith, who observed, "defence... is of much more importance than opulence."[53] In short, Smith implied, autarkic policies come at a significant price, but it pales in comparison to starvation in time of conflicts. We will now argue, contra Adam Smith himself, that the "autarky for food security" rationale doesn't stand up to scrutiny.

First, we currently live in what is undoubtedly the most peaceful time in human history.[54] Reverting to autarky and, in the process, making life more difficult in countries not well endowed with agricultural resources is therefore more likely to promote military problems than prevent them. As the old saying goes, if goods don't cross borders, armies eventually will. Second, while geopolitics can always take a turn for the worse, nothing prevents a country from stockpiling large quantities of food and agricultural inputs purchased on the international market while ramping up local production if the threat of prolonged conflict becomes real. Third, putting all of one's food security eggs in a single geographically limited agricultural basket rather than purchasing food from multiple foreign suppliers is antithetical to any notion of spreading risks. Food policy observers are periodically reminded of this reality when protectionist countries experience domestic production problems. For example, Finland, a country with a grain self-sufficiency policy, suffered its wettest crop year in recorded history in 1987. Not only were yields low, but the wet grain that was somehow harvested in muddy fields soon sprouted in storage. The Finnish government then had no choice but to quietly purchase two-thirds of the country's yearly wheat supply on world markets (and for only half the price they would have had to pay their own farmers).[55]

Another problem is that reliance on long distance trade only proved a less desirable alternative than autarky in the context of prolonged blockades and stationary fronts. In the context of aerial bombing, however, the destruction of critical local infrastructure would soon cripple locavore communities with no capacity to tap into the agricultural surplus of more distant regions. Autarkic policies also always mandate the use of more marginal agricultural lands whose long-term productivity is more likely to be affected by erosion and other problems. Finally, postwar reconstruction is much easier when distant resources can be accessed. While future world conflicts are always possible, distant and hopefully remote possibilities should not be invoked to maintain hundreds of millions of people in a state of hunger and malnutrition in the present time. In our opinion, it would be better to work towards world peace and greater global economic integration. Countless city walls were torn down in the last two centuries. Agricultural tariffs, quotas, and subsidies should meet the same fate.

This being said, the study of past military blockades and agricultural countermeasures is helpful in terms of getting a more concrete appreciation of the real world consequences of locavorism. True, in wartime many valuable resources are diverted towards destructive goals that would be put to good agricultural use in the locavores' utopia. Nonetheless, the basic trade-offs for increasing local food production would remain the same. For instance, in Europe over the last two centuries, the following substitutions in terms of both food production and consumption were widespread among warring countries that had been cut off to a large degree from international trade:[56]

- a switch from livestock and fruit production to high yielding crops (the conversion of grassland and orchards to cropland devoted to grain and potato production);
- a switch from beef to dairy cattle (the replacement of meat by dairy production);
- the culling of chicken and hogs whose feed could be consumed by humans;
- the elimination of a large number of "luxury animals" such as horses and dogs;

- a significant reduction in the volume of grain used for brewing, distilling, and luxury products, such as pastries;
- the replacement of white bread by bread made with whole wheat flour and further diluted with potato and barley flour.

A brief discussion of specific cases can also provide further insights. We begin with the Allied Blockade against Germany during the First World War,[57] an Empire whose technical and scientific capabilities were comparable to any other country at the time; whose landscape was reasonably large and varied; and whose territory remained virtually untouched by opposing forces during the First World War. Most notable, though, is that while German political authorities had built up some food stocks before the beginning of the hostilities, they had not launched large-scale autarkic agricultural efforts.

In spite of some protectionist policies, before the beginning of the hostilities, the Reich's agricultural sector was, in the words of agricultural economist Karl Brandt, very much integrated in the "international co-operation and division of labor,"[58] and, as a result, in 1913, German agriculture was more productive than ever before, some commentators even suggesting that the subjects of the Kaiser were perhaps even "better or more richly fed than the inhabitants of France or England."[59] To give a sense of progress in previous decades, between 1878 and 1912, Germany's total rye production rose from 6.9 million metric tons (MMT) to 11.6 MMT; wheat from 2.6 to 4.4 MMT; oats from 5 to 8.5MMT; barley from 2.3 to 3.5 MMT; and potatoes from 23.6 to 50.2 MMT. While some of this progress could be attributed to increased acreage, most of it could be traced back to greater yields. Because the German population grew from 41 million people in 1871 to 68 million in 1913, the Reich's inhabitants relied on foreign imports for approximately a third of their direct food supplies, and, through the importation of large quantities of fertilizers and high-protein animal feed, for much of their "local" crop and livestock production. Like many of their Northern European counterparts, many German producers had reoriented their activities towards livestock and, when possible, fruits and vegetables.

Although they had made preparations for blockades and counter blockades, German military leaders never envisaged a prolonged conflict and were soon unable to find substitutes for imported phosphates (a critical fertilizer) while the absence of imported concentrated feeding stuff for livestock not only drastically reduced milk and meat production, but also the volume and quality of animal manure. Many animals eventually died from inanition despite attempts to develop substitutes for forage that included "drying lees, grinding straw, weeds, carcasses, fish [and] working up food refuse."[60]

Making matters even worse were weather conditions so bad they "would have caused a large diminution in the agricultural yield of the country even if all other conditions had been normal."[61] Largely because of this, in 1916 the potato crop failed at a time when it occupied about a fifth of German arable land. From a prewar figure of 52 million tons, only 21 million tons were harvested which, due to bad handling and inadequate storage by government authorities, translated into only 17 million usable tons of potatoes. By 1917 they had been replaced by turnips and cabbage. Despite the introduction of meat ration cards and meatless days, valuable breeding stock that had been developed over decades was gradually gobbled up by starving individuals, often in a deliberate attempt to preserve for human consumption what had previously been considered substandard fare. All sorts of leaves, berries, roasted acorns, and beans were also at the time being steeped in hot water as tea and coffee substitutes.

By late 1917, a two-pound can of preserved marmalade made of apples, carrots, and pumpkins was sold to each German household during the Christmas season and was expected to serve the family for the following year. By the end of the war, malnutrition might have killed as many as 700,000 civilians on top of the Empire's 1,800,000 battlefield casualties. As one contemporary observer commented, in "the condition of dull apathy and mental prostration resulting from the deprivation of food the course of the War no longer seemed of importance. Food filled [Germans'] thoughts by day and their dreams by night, and the only desire was to end the War by any possible means that might lead to a slackening of the blockade and the free entry of food into the country."[62] Things got even worse for the German population after the armistice as Allied occupying forces presented numerous obstacles to the re-opening of trading activities. While the partition of Germany that came out of the Treaty of Versailles is often blamed for later German belligerent attitudes and the rise of Nazism, the Allied food blockade both during and after the war played a crucial part in fueling future German aggressions.

Lest one thinks that the previous example was deliberately chosen because of its dire outcome, we will now turn to a brief discussion of what is generally acknowledged to have been the most successful case of local agricultural production under wartime conditions: Denmark during World War II. [63]

In their massive study on the *Management of Agriculture and Food in the German-Occupied and Other Areas of Fortress Europe*, Karl Brandt and his collaborators, Otto Schiller and Franz Ahlgrimm, observed that Denmark "received by far the most gentle treatment of all the German-occupied countries;" that there was no German military government; that "the Danish contributions to the German war-food economy were among the most important;" that the "production record of Danish agriculture in World War II is one of the most remarkable in the annals of world agriculture," comparable to and probably even superior to "the achievements of American farmers;" and that the war actually "became a period of extraordinary prosperity for [Danish] agriculture."[64] This outcome can undoubtedly be traced back to the German "quasi-benevolent" attitude towards the country because of its racial profile (Danes were said to be Aryans), the country's military insignificance, and the fact that, proportionally speaking at least, the Danes did not need to devote many resources to the direct war efforts. Yet, this case is hardly a vindication of locavorism.

Like their counterparts in Great Britain, the Netherlands, and Belgium, 19th century Danish political authorities did not react to the "invasion" of cheap North American and Eastern European grains by imposing higher tariffs to protect their domestic producers. On the contrary, a majority of Danish farmers were opposed to the idea as they realized that cheap foreign animal feed would give them the opportunity to specialize in more lucrative livestock and dairy farming, making it possible to expand dairy production from summer to year-round. Although mostly comprised of small- and medium-sized independent operations, the creation of large agricultural cooperatives gave Danish farmers the capacity to develop significant economies of scale and a reputation for excellence that made their products highly sought after in lucrative foreign markets such as Great Britain. The result was that, from the mid-1870s to the mid-1920s, the Danish cattle herd doubled, the pig herd multiplied by more than six, and the chicken flock by four. Even more remarkable, Danish crop growers expanded their production by a factor of almost three as the five-year average of all crops expressed in a measurement known as barley equivalent (i.e., as if they had been converted to barley) went from around 27 million tons to no less than 74 million tons during this period.[65] By 1938, the British and German markets absorbed more than 76% of Danish exports, which were mostly made up of livestock products such as butter, eggs, lard, and bacon.

As Karl Brandt argued in 1945, far from proving the assertions of agricultural protectionists that all trade liberalization "would financially ruin millions of European family farms and reduce the farmers to abject misery and poverty... [or a] general depression of their living standards," Danish agriculture from the middle of the 19th century to the eve of World War II illustrated that, by embracing free trade, Danish farmers had not only learned to "discover the fields of production in which they had the best opportunity to compete successfully with the farmers of the world, but they also were able to develop their own abilities, their agricultural production and marketing plants to almost functional perfection," the result being "a most remarkable degree of culture and the art of decent living."[66]

The Nazi invasion of Denmark in April 1940, however, quickly cut off the importation of foreign oilseeds and grains along with access to the British market. Based on their past experience, German administrators devised plans for the massive slaughter of dairy cows, hogs, and chickens in order to save as much grain as possible for human consumption. Danish farmers overwhelmingly opposed these measures and threatened to engage in general passive resistance if they were enforced. Meanwhile, Danish authorities let it be known to their occupiers that they weren't concerned with where food surpluses would end up (i.e., feeding members of the Third Reich) as long as the local population did not go hungry. Because of this and the difficulty of effectively rationing a large agricultural sector made up of numerous small production units, German administrators settled instead upon economic incentives such as export quotas, boosting the prices of farm products, and keeping the price of farm inputs such as nitrogen and potash fertilizers artificially low, thus ensuring that "farming was made exceptionally profitable."[67]

As could be expected, Danish farmers responded by maintaining the land area devoted to grain to prewar average; increasing slightly the area devoted to root crops; converting perhaps as much as 16% of their pastureland to flax, vegetable seed, and vegetable production; reducing fallow land by about two-thirds; and hiring individuals previously unemployed or active in other lines of work. The end result was that, in terms of barley equivalent, the harvests during the last three years of the war were actually higher than the prewar average.

Reminiscent of the situation of the Second Reich during the previous conflict, however, phosphate fertilizer use fell to around one-tenth of the prewar level while the quality of animal manure declined because of poorer nutrition. German authorities also enforced a number of restrictions to ensure greater volumes of export surpluses, such as prohibiting the manufacture of margarine, full-fat cheese, fluid cream, and beer with a high alcohol content; increased rates of extraction in flour mills; and a reduction in the fat content of fluid milk. The reduced availability of animal feed also meant that by 1942 the culling of two thirds of the hog and chicken population had become unavoidable, although by 1945 production levels eventually came back to above half of prewar levels.

At the end of the war, the per capita food consumption in Denmark was about 20% less than at its beginning and the country had experienced a decrease of 5% of its overall national wealth. True, these results were not bad considering the context, but still the Danish case does not support the notion that increased self-sufficiency delivers economic and security benefits. As one University of Copenhagen economist observed at the time, the Danish agricultural performance was only as good as it turned out to be because the "Germans paid for the war effort," and, overall, the Danish economy consumed some of its accumulated capital and suffered "heavy financial loss[es]."[68] In Denmark, as elsewhere, increased national self-sufficiency would have been unsustainable in the long run and the adoption of this policy on an ever smaller geographical scale (i.e., locavorism), even less so.

Peak Oil and Locavorism[69]

Another common belief among locavores in terms of food security is that their prescription prepares us for the unavoidable re-localization of our food system that will follow the imminent peak and later depletion of our supply of "cheap petroleum" in the next century. This argument, however, is fallacious, whether or not one believes in the peak oil rhetoric. For starters, even assuming a world in which hostile aliens have emptied all of our best oil fields, all credible analysts (there are always a few pessimistic outliers) tell us that, with minimal efforts to look beyond the ample economically recoverable reserves available at the moment, we could easily have enough coal to last us several centuries.[70] It is true that rebuilding our global food supply chain around (mostly liquefied) coal would be more

expensive, inconvenien,t and environmentally damaging than around petroleum-derived liquid fuels (which is why they displaced coal in the first
place), but it does not present any insurmountable problem—indeed,
South Africa's Sasol, the world's largest producer of coal-based liquids, already manufactures a completely synthetic jet fuel. Locavores should remember that relatively inefficient and expensive coal-powered railroads
and steamships laid the foundations of our global food supply chain. The
world didn't simply go from a hearty diet of local organic deliciousness to
eating globalized petroleum in one fell swoop—there was a substantial
course of coal in-between.

Reverting to coal in the 21st century would also not mean reverting
to 19th century engine technologies, but simply to a more expensive
and inconvenient fuel that would compete with other unconventional
sources (from shale oil to Canadian oil sands). Furthermore, because
the liquid fraction of petroleum used to power container ships is for the
most part the dirtiest and cheapest (so-called "bunker fuel") for which
there is at present little other demand,[71] higher crude prices would have
a much more pronounced effect on other segments of the food supply
chain than on long distance maritime transportation.

At any rate, the Peak Oil rhetoric should not be taken seriously. Pessimistic energy forecasts have a long history—predictions of imminent
petroleum shortages were even made before the first oil well was drilled
in Western Pennsylvania in the middle of the 19th century—and a
truly awful track record.[72] The main problem historically is that energy
doomsayers never quite understood that humans are not only mouths
to feed, but also brains to think and arms to work, along with the fact
that resources are not fixed and permanent things that exist in and of
themselves, but instead are created by always renewable human intellect
and labor.

Despite the obvious finiteness of their surroundings, humans have
long been able to develop profitable new technologies to achieve the
same or better results while using less resources; to extract valuable materials from more remote locations (for example, offshore drilling) or

from less interesting materials (such as less concentrated ores); and to create substitutes out of previously worthless raw materials and industrial residuals that proved their advantage over previous alternatives, such as being more powerful and/or abundant; stronger and/or lighter; and/or easier to produce, handle, transport, and/or store. For instance, because they did not burn cleanly without modern technologies, coal and petroleum were not very valuable for most of human history. In recent years, in North America alone, the advent of shale gas, increased onshore oil production from shale rock, new recovery techniques that make it economical to extract oil left in old wells, new oil field discoveries in the Gulf of Mexico, and advances that have drastically reduced production costs in the Canadian oil sands, have all ensured an abundant supply of affordable transportation fuels for at least several decades, if not for a few centuries.[73]

Sure, one day humanity will move beyond fossil fuels, but it will not be because we have run out of them, but rather because better alternatives have come along. Justifying a preemptive move towards locavorism because of irrational fears of an imminent energy shortage is an untenable proposition. At any rate, if one truly believes that economic resources are finite, then sustainable development becomes a theoretical impossibility, for humanity will unavoidably run out of everything and collapse at some future date. Saving for the future in this context is therefore nonsensical, for it at best delays the unavoidable. Better then to save farmers from labor-intensive toil now while also sparing future generations a horrible fate by making sure that we consume as much energy as we can in the present and collapse in style as soon as possible!

In the end, while the specific details of our energy future are unknowable, provided that current anti-technology sentiments and public finance insanity can be kept under control, past experience warrants an optimistic outlook. After all, if this hadn't been the case, how could a human population of a few million individuals at the dawn of agriculture now count nearly six *billion* well-fed individuals?

Climate Change, Locavorism, and Food Security[74]

The fate of agricultural productions has always been dependent on and shaped by singular weather events (from droughts to torrential rainfalls) and more long-term climatic trends (from warmer to cooler and back). Not surprisingly, unfavorable events and trends were often attributed to human actions, be they insufficient offerings to climate deities, sinful behavior, swamp drainage, agriculture, and massive deforestation to the invention of lighting conductors, extensive gunfire during the First World War, the development of short-wave radio communication, nuclear explosions, supersonic transport, space traffic, and air pollution. Carbon dioxide produced through human activities—primarily the burning of carbon fuels—is now the focus of much policy attention, but it is just the latest suspect in a long line of potential large-scale "climate criminals."[75] (Of course, carbon dioxide is also plant food, and, as such, higher concentrations of this gas should ultimately prove beneficial for agricultural production, but we will not address this issue here.)

While we claim no expertise in climate science, we cannot imagine how locavorism can ever be considered more desirable in the context of a warming or cooling climate than the global food supply chain. First, as we illustrated in chapter 4, the fact that the international division of agricultural labor produces less greenhouse gas emissions per unit of food than less efficient "local" growers is pretty much "settled science." Second, singular weather events and climate change will not stop even if humans drastically reduce their carbon dioxide emissions. As in the past, crop failures caused by hailstorms, floods, droughts, and other weather-related events will cause much harm to communities that cannot tap into the agricultural surplus of more distant regions that have enjoyed better growing conditions.

Last but not least, as the agricultural economist Dennis Avery observes, wheat, rice, and corn are all originally warm weather plants that, through thousands of years of modifications, are now able to withstand a wide range of conditions. Corn most likely originated in the hot and wet lowlands of Mexico and required 4,000 years of careful seed selection to become acclimatized to the conditions of the U.S. "Corn Belt." Wheat is native to the hot and dry Fertile Crescent, and, in locations like the Punjab, can now tolerate summer temperatures as high as 100 degrees F. Domesticated rice was developed in Chinese regions with summer heat comparable to those of the Punjab, but now also thrives in locations like Manchuria with summer temperatures of only 80 degrees F. (The real enemy of crops, Avery notes, is not heat but droughts, which have historically been more often associated with cooler than warmer periods.)[76] Given enough freedom and adequate incentives, agricultural producers have long demonstrated that they can adapt to warming and cooling trends and provide consumers the basic necessities of life. For instance, in England during the Roman Warming period (250 BC to 450 AD), grapes were produced where none are to be found today. In colder times, though, farmers reverted to grain production (thus ensuring that alcohol remained available in the form of beer and whiskey). Another fact worth pondering is that Canada is now largely recognized as a net marijuana exporter. Clearly, humans can achieve much when they put their minds to it…

Call us old-fashioned (or even Canadians!) if you will, but a warmer world doesn't worry us all that much in terms of food production. As long as economies develop, scientific and technical knowledge expands, people are free to adapt, and international trade allows the movement of foodstuffs between regions, humanity will thrive as it did in the last century and a half, a period of warming. Whatever the climate change problem may be, locavorism is not the answer.

Until very recently, hunger and famines loomed large in the human experience. In relatively recent times, though, modern agricultural technologies and long-distance trade played a crucial role in turning the "third horsemen" into a distant memory for most people on our planet. The globalized food supply chain did come with some problems of its own, but it should be kept in mind that the vast majority of today's malnourished people are African and South Asian subsistence farmers and rural landless laborers who cannot readily access international food markets.[77] Lifting them out of poverty and malnutrition will require more innovation, trade, and, until something better comes along, greenhouse gas emissions. This prospect might worry some, but the evidence is pretty clear: wealthy people can adapt and live well from Singapore to Edmonton while poor people are miserable everywhere.

As estimated by the authors of a recent report from the Food and Agriculture Organization of the United Nations (FAO) on humanity's capacity to feed itself in 2050, even if most of today's less advanced economies are expected to provide for most of their future needs by expanding their own production, they would still need to double their net imports of cereals, from 135 million metric tons in 2008–09 to 300 million by mid-century, and therefore require not only infrastructure improvements, but also a "global trading system that is fair and competitive."[78]

Paradoxically, a world where in a few decades 9 billion people could afford to purchase their food from 90 million highly efficient farmers using the planet's most productive locations would be incredibly more food secure than one in which a few billion farmers feed their neighbors but lack the infrastructure to ship their products over long distances. Food insecurity is mainly due to a lack of income opportunities rather than geography, as poor and hungry people cannot afford to purchase food from the international market. Economic development through trade liberalization is what food security should really be about.[79]

6

Myth #5:
Locavorism Offers Tastier,
More Nutritious, and Safer Food

Of all the frauds practiced by mercenary dealers, there is none more reprehensible, and at the same time more prevalent, than the sophistication[1] of the various articles of food. This unprincipled and nefarious practice, increasing in degree as it has been found difficult of detection, is now applied to almost every commodity which can be classed among either the necessaries or the luxuries of life, and is carried on to a most alarming extent in every part of the United Kingdom.

FRIEDRICH CHRISTIAN A. ACCUM. 1820.
A Treatise on Adulterations of Foods, and Culinary Poisons.
Longman, Hurst, Rees, Orme, and Brown, pp. 1–2

Michael Pollan's influential "Farmer in Chief" essay, published in the October 2008 issue of the *New York Times Magazine*, is a useful summary of the widespread claims that locavorism delivers tastier, more nutritious, and safer food than the offerings of agribusiness. First, the journalism professor observes, "food eaten closer to where it is grown will be fresher and require less processing, making it more nutritious." We're not quite sure about the "less processing" part (for example, whether local or imported, potatoes must be cooked, but there is obviously no such need for salads), but what we infer from Pollan's remarks is that food sold at farmers' markets will have been picked in a more ripened state, ensuring superior taste and nutritional value.

Farmers' markets also offer fewer options in terms of "oversalted, oversweetened, transfat rich, and highly preserved" foods designed primarily for microwave ovens. So far, so good. (Well, sort of, as the farmers' markets we visited over the last few years had no shortages of sausages, pates, and sugar-laden homemade pies. One could also remind Pollan of Benjamin Franklin's observation two centuries ago that "[i]n general, mankind, since the improvement in cookery, eats twice as much as nature requires."[2])

Pollan then points out that a lone factory "grinding 20 million hamburger patties in a week or washing 25 million servings of salad" is not only highly vulnerable to "a single terrorist armed with a canister of toxins," but "equally susceptible to accidental contamination" because "the bigger and more global the trade in food, the more vulnerable the system is to catastrophe." The obvious way to avoid such threats, he asserts, is decentralization. Unfortunately, this strategy is now hampered by "a tangle of regulations originally designed to check abuses by the very largest food producers" that now mandate "a huge investment in federally approved facilities" for such innocuous things as farmers smoking a ham and selling it to their neighbors. Food-safety regulations, Pollan argues, should "be made sensitive to scale and marketplace, so that a small producer selling direct off the farm or at a farmers' market is not regulated as onerously as a multinational food manufacturer." This is not, he adds, "because local food won't ever have food-safety problems—it will—only that its problems will be less catastrophic and easier to manage because local food is inherently more traceable and accountable."

Although we agree with the basic proposition that government inspection and regulation should be much less intrusive in the realm of personal transactions between consenting adults than they currently are (who needs SWAT teams to take down a raw milk retail operation?), Pollan's view on food safety is too careless not to be dissected. Before we do so, however, we need to illustrate how, over the last few centuries, the globalized food supply chain and agri-business have delivered historically unparalleled nutritional and health benefits.

The Changing Human Body[3]

Local diets have always been more monotonous and less nutritious than our present day food cornucopia. True, some past locavores used available resources rather creatively. For instance, some Native Americans seasoned wild rice with the excrements of rabbits, roasted entrails with their original content, and used Caribou droppings to thicken blood soup.[4] The fact remains, though, that throughout history most people were not only always on the verge of hunger and starvation, but also that whenever the food supply was sufficient it was typically problematic on some level. For instance, the historians Frances and Joseph Gies tell us that the diet of Western Medieval European peasants was not only low in calories and proteins, but also often lacking in lipids, calcium, and vitamins A, C, and D.[5] Until the mid-1800s, most Europeans remained "in a chronic state of undernourishment" while only the upper class could expect a daily intake of white bread and meat.[6] The standard fare of an 18th century German rural laborer was "gruel and mush," a soupy combination of grains and lentils.[7] Despite improvements over past circumstances, the diet of a typical English farm worker at the turn of the 19th century still consisted of "bread, a little cheese, bacon fat, and weak tea, supplemented for adult males by beer," its monotony only "relieved to some degree by the harvest period" and, on good days, modest amounts of beef and mutton. Hot meals were also few, since cooking fuel was expensive. For this pittance, the laborer spent nearly three-quarters of his income, with starches such as bread accounting for the bulk of that expenditure.[8] And in the United States, vitamin deficiency diseases such as anemia, beriberi, and pellagra were common before 1940.[9]

As a result of nutritional inequalities, members from the richer groups in Western Europe and the United States were historically "taller and heavier than those from poorer backgrounds," suffered less from chronic and debilitating diseases, lived longer, and were capable of harder and more sustained work.[10] For instance, British aristocrats were about 6 inches (15 centimeters) taller than average in 1800.[11] The same trend could also be observed in other locations, such as in pre-Columbian times in the Mayan city of Tikal, where well-fed nobles were on average 4 inches (10 centimeters) taller than commoners.[12] (Of course, taller does not necessarily mean healthier in the context of a group, but height is considered a good indicator of the quality and quantity of nutrition over a lifetime and is especially relevant when used as a measure of the change in the average of a group over time.) Gaps of this kind have now largely been closed in advanced economies thanks to improved overall nutrition made possible by the development of the globalized food supply chain. British aristocrats are now only only 2 inches taller than average and, as the Marxist historian Jeffrey M. Pilcher observes, while there is much debate as to the actual timing, there is no controversy over the fact that "when nutrition did improve for common [British] people, it came at the price of a growing distance between producer and consumer."[13]

Probably the most underappreciated benefit of the global food supply chain is the role it played in transforming human bodies. In the words of Nobel laureate economist Robert W. Fogel and his collaborators, "in most if not quite all parts of the world, the size, shape, and longevity of the human body have changed more substantially, and much more rapidly, during the past three centuries than over many previous millennia."[14] For instance, the average adult man in 1850 America was about 5 feet 7 inches tall, weighed about 146 pounds, and could expect to live until about 45 years of age. His countrymen of the time expected to develop chronic diseases in their forties and fifties and, since they were the lucky ones who had survived childbirth, to die in their fifties and sixties. In the 1980s, a typical American man in his early thirties was about 5 feet 10 inches tall, weighed about 174 pounds, was likely to pass his 75th birthday and then die of a stroke, cancer, or heart or respiratory disease since he was no longer dying of other things, such as diphtheria, smallpox, polio, cholera, and malaria. In the last few decades, the onset of these ailments, along with nonlethal ones like arthritis, has since been delayed on average between ten and twenty-five years. In 1900, 13% of people who were 65 could expect to live until 85, whereas the proportion is now closer to 50%.[15]

Other American data suggest that the average consumption of proteins, vitamins, and minerals is now virtually identical among poor and upper middle-class children, in both cases being comparably excessive and well above recommended norms for most children (in other words, too many kids eat too much). Poor American boys today at ages 18 and 19 are taller and heavier than middle-class boys of similar age in the late 1950s. They are also a full inch taller and 10 pounds heavier than American soldiers who fought in World War II. The major dietary problem facing poor Americans is now, like most Americans, eating too much and being overweight.[16]

Similar positive and sometimes problematic trends can be observed in all developed and rapidly developing economies. For instance, gains in height between the preindustrial world and today were about 12 centimeters (about 5 inches) in Japan and 7 centimeters (about 3 inches) in England. The height of Chinese students increased rapidly following the introduction of economic and agricultural reforms in 1979.[17] In what is perhaps history's most dramatic case of anthropometric divergence in a genetically homogenous population, preschool children raised in (autarkic) North Korea are up to 13 cm (about 5 inches) shorter and up to 7 kg (slightly more than 15 pounds) lighter than children who were brought up in (globalized) South Korea; North Korean women weighed up to 9 kg (almost 20 pounds) less on average than their southern counterparts; and North Korean refugees between 20 and 39 years of age (admittedly, not the most representative sample) were on average 7 centimeters (almost 3 inches) smaller than their southern counterparts. Interestingly, before its partition, the north was the most prosperous portion of the Korean peninsula and its inhabitants were on average between 1.1 and 1.4 centimeters (about half an inch) taller than their southern counterparts.[18] In better but still problematic news, according to the World Health Organization, more than half of the population in 18 countries today is either overweight or obese while in 7 countries—including Egypt, Mexico and South Africa—more than two-thirds of all adults are overweight or obese.[19] Overall, there are now at least one and a half overfed individuals for every malnourished one. While the problem is not insignificant, as the journalist Greg Easterbrook observes, "four generations ago, the poor were lean as fence posts, their arms bony and faces gaunt. To our recent ancestors, the idea that even the poor eat too much might be harder to fathom than a jetliner rising from the runway."[20]

Of course, nutrition alone does not explain all positive trends; advances in sanitation (from improved water supplies to sewage systems), medicine (from antibiotics and disinfectants to hand washing and sterilization in hospitals), and food preservation technologies (especially refrigeration, but also packaging) obviously played their part. Yet, many infectious diseases that plagued previous generations, especially those afflicting children, were made worse by calorie, protein, minerals, and vitamin deficiencies. And again, none of the technological advances that made current living standards possible would have taken place in the absence of long-distance trade and urbanization. With these facts in mind, let us turn to the locavores' case on behalf of taste, nutrition and food safety.

Taste

Freshly picked ripened local produce is tastier than identical items shipped over long distances. No one—not even us!—will argue over

that. The important issue here, though, is freshness, not "local" character. After all, leave the local item on a shelf for as long as it takes to
bring in the nonlocal alternative and then good luck telling them apart.
Or what about two identical varieties of strawberries grown in different
locations that have both been flash frozen as soon as they were harvested? In season, tasty local produce does not need a locavore movement to find its way to nearby supermarkets and restaurants. As John
Page observed in 1880: "Home-grown fruit has, and must always have,
a great advantage over the imported by being delivered in our markets
fresher and in a generally better condition."[21]

The issue though is not as straightforward when dealing with "similar" (as distinguished from "identical") products. In our corner of
Canada, we seem to be involved in an ongoing argument regarding local
versus California strawberries. The imported berries, our debating opponents tell us (tongue-in-cheek) only succeed because they apparently
never decay, no matter how long they remain on supermarket shelves,
and because their cheap price can help consumers forget about their
bland taste. We disagree. For one thing, California strawberry producers (whose output now accounts for about 80% of the U.S. supply)
gained significant market share a few decades ago not only because of
the suitable climate in the west, but also because of considerable research that resulted in the development of new varieties and ever more
efficient production, storage, and transportation technologies. It was
only by offering both lower prices and higher quality (including taste)
that they were able to displace most producers in other states (the re-
maining market share is now mostly represented by producers in Oregon and Florida). The circumstances are no different in Ontario today
than they were in Delaware and other places not too long ago. Like it or
not, California strawberries might travel some distance, but they do it in
a matter of days and in impeccable storage conditions. Not only are they
cheaper and better looking, but also typically tastier—at least according
to our unscientific assessment in purchasing both kinds over the last
several years. Competitive local products will always find a market, both

locally and in more remote locations. Uncompetitive offerings will not. Tastes are subjective, but it is up to the producers to cater to them. Food production is not a local charity.

Notwithstanding this personal perspective, let us for a moment grant our opponents' point and assume that all local produce is inherently superior when in season. What about the rest of the year then? Should Ontarians limit themselves to frozen berries and jam? How is shutting the door to imported fresh products improving the sensory experiences of food consumers? If the spectacular growth of fresh produce sections in the last few decades is any indication, the verdict is already in: transporting fresh fruits and vegetables over long distances resoundingly beats canning and freezing the local varieties.

Nutrition

The capacity of the modern food supply chain to deliver ever more abundant calories at ever more affordable prices is so overwhelming that it is not debated by agri-intellectuals and food activists. Rather, their ire is directed at two alleged nutritional deficiencies, namely that the most significant advances in terms of availability and affordability have been achieved in the realm of "junk food" and that today's fresh produce grown with "synthetic" methods are less nutritious than those grown with traditional inputs. Regarding the former claim, the food policy analyst Robert Paarlberg states in no uncertain terms that "the charge that junk-food prices have fallen while fruit and vegetable prices have not is… bogus," for both the price of traditional in-season fruit and vegetable products has fallen while the variety and year-round availability of fresh products have dramatically increased. American supermarkets now carry as many as 400 different produce items, up from an average of just 150 four decades ago.[22]

While it is obviously impossible to compare the nutritional value of perishable food items from the past to similar ones produced today, a reasonable case can be made for using present-day organic foods as

proxies, at least inasmuch as the whole rationale of the organic movement is to avoid the use of synthetic chemicals (fertilizers, pesticides,
herbicides, fungicides, etc.), antibiotics, growth hormones, rDNA technologies (or what locavores prefer to call genetically modified organisms), and concentrated animal feeding operations (CAFOs). This is
not to say, of course, that organic growers do not use pesticides of all
kinds (pests apparently feel no urge to spare organic crops because their
producers are nicer to them), but rather that they make abundant use of
"botanical extracts" and "rockdusts" which are nothing but old-fashioned
pesticides like pyrethrum and copper sulfate[23] that were around at the
time of the Model T and are much less effective than pesticides created
later on through scientific research. (Rigorous tests have shown that
many pesticides used by organic producers display higher toxicity for
mammals, persist longer in the environment, and do more collateral
damage to non-pests.[24])

What makes these older technologies acceptable to organic growers
is the fact that they were created through geological and biological,
rather than through industrial, processes. In other words, two identical
molecules can be deemed different if one was created in a manufacturing plant and another in a (real) plant or in a bird's digestive system. As
the agricultural policy analyst Gary Blumenthal observes, "the marketing of organic foods is not on the basis of what they are, but rather what
they are not."[25]

Be that as it may, on the issue of what they are nutritionally, the evidence gathered from decades of scientific research is clear: organic
foods are not better than conventional ones and have at best tiny, in-
termittent and overall insignificant differences in nutrient levels from
one study and research sample to the next. In the most comprehensive
review ever published, researchers affiliated with the London School
of Hygiene and Tropical Medicine and commissioned by the U.K.
Food Standards Agency looked at all the scientifically sound studies
published on the topic in the last five decades. Their conclusion was
that there was "little, if any, nutritional difference between organic and

conventionally produced food and that there is no evidence of additional health benefits from eating organic food." As the lead author declared: "A small number of differences in nutrient content were found to exist between organically and conventionally produced crops and livestock, but these are unlikely to be of any public health relevance. Our review indicates that there is currently no evidence to support the selection of organically over conventionally produced foods on the basis of nutritional superiority."[26] These findings made major news headlines when they were published in 2009, but they were hardly surprising in specialist circles. Indeed, because of the incontrovertible evidence on the topic, organic spokespersons had long before begun to claim environmental benefits for their products rather than nonexistent nutritional advantages.[27]

True, overnutrition (in essence, eating too much) and unhealthy diets are problematic, especially among the poorest segments of the population of advanced economies. Still, compared to the previous realities of malnutrition and famine, these are lesser concerns. Besides, overnutrition can't be blamed entirely on poverty nor food systems. According to a 2010 Organization for Economic Cooperation and Development (OECD) report, one in 2 people are overweight and obese in almost half of the 34 OECD countries and this problem can mostly be traced back to unhealthy diet choices and sedentary lifestyles.[28] As with everything, cheap calories can be a mixed blessing. They can make a hungry person more productive, but they may also make him (or her) fatter and less productive. There is no point in blaming the cupcake, though, as it doesn't spontaneously jump into someone's mouth. Besides, substituting organically produced sugar (or "evaporated cane juice," as listed on some "health food" packages) for conventional sweetener would not affect this situation, nor would it encourage people to eat better and to exercise more. For all its imperfections, today's food supply is more diversified, abundant, and cheaper than ever, while comparable items, say an apple produced today and another grown a century ago, are at a minimum just as nutritious as they have ever been.

Better education in terms of eating and cooking habits seems a more sensible way to address the problem than locavorism.

Nonetheless, for the sake of argument, let's pursue this topic a little further. The locavores' claims regarding the inherently more nutritious character of local fare boils down to two main points: 1) fresher products have lost less of their nutritional value than products that travel long distances and spend time in storage; and 2) local products are typically riper when they are picked and therefore inherently more nutritious. Granting these assumptions, what are the implications when local produce is no longer in season? As with taste, locavores can't have it both ways. If local is more nutritious because it is fresher, then it is less nutritious most of the year when it is only available in preserved form. This argument alone is sufficient to put the locavores' stance on nutrition to rest, for eating better food a few weeks during the year and lesser quality food during the remainder cannot deliver a more nutritious diet overall. Other considerations must be brought in, too. For instance, the fortification of food items ranging from milk and butter to salt, flour, and pasta, can be accomplished much more effectively and cheaply (especially if vitamins and minerals are produced in large volumes) through large-scale facilities that serve a significant customer base. Food imports can also be crucial for people who suffer from food allergies ranging from celiac disease to lactose intolerance if adequate substitutes are not available locally.

Most damaging to the locavores' stance on nutrition, though, is the undeniable fact that while human consciousness might care about the geographical origins of food items, human bodies don't. From a physiological perspective, what matters is that they provide sufficient energy and nutrients and are not poisonous. Furthermore, from a nutritional point of view, the composition of individual items counts less than the nutrient content and overall balance of the diet as a whole. In other words, even if imported items were slightly less nutritious than local ones, what is important is the overall intake, especially in terms of eating a variety of different foods, not the specific characteristics of each item. Eating insufficient amounts of monotonous but high quality food is less desirable than eating slightly lesser quality food but in sufficient quantity and variety. Because locavorism can only result in decreased variety and increased prices, it is more likely to have a negative impact on the quality of human diets. As in the past, these conditions will set the stage for greater nutritional inequalities than is presently the case. True, average waistlines will undoubtedly be reduced if this ever happens, but such an approach is not the most effective way to address current dietary challenges.

Food Safety[29]

Food safety issues have been a perennial problem ever since our remote hunter-gatherer ancestors displayed symptoms like nausea, fever, vomiting, abdominal cramps, or diarrhea, or even died after consuming contaminated prey and water. Without providing a comprehensive list of all the bad "natural" things they were subjected to long before "synthetic" chemicals came along, suffice it to say that various diseases and infections transmitted by wild animals and their parasites included rabies, tuberculosis, brucellosis, the plague, leprosy, tularaemia, leptospirosis, Chagas disease, yellow fever, encephalitis, anthrax, salmonellosis, rickettsiosis, herpes, staphylococcal and streptococcal infections, treponematosis, haemorrhagic fever, gangrene, botulism, tetanus, encephalitis, and trypanosomiasis (sleeping sickness). True, some traditional herbal, fungal, and mineral remedies displayed some analgesic, antiseptic, and antibiotic properties, but they typically brought little meaningful relief even if accompanied by shamanic incantations.[30]

Other evidence of the type of "natural" ailments that plagued our distant ancestors can be found in the mummies of the Chinchorro, a Native American fishing culture that lived several thousand years ago on what is now the north Chilean coast. Despite the absence of modern pollutants and a fully local and natural diet that consisted of up to 90% of fish, shellfish, marine mammals, and seaweed, a quarter of the local children perished before reaching the age of one, a third of the population suffered from infections that eroded their leg bones, and the vertebrae of one fifth of their female population was so porous that they splintered from the weight of their own flesh. Not surprisingly, their average life expectancy was around 25 years of age. Other mummified remains and coprolites (i.e., fossilized excrements) from past Native American populations document, among other things, heart failures resulting from nematodes having invaded muscles along with intestinal walls pierced by thorny-headed worms. As the archeoparasitologist Karl J. Reinhard put it: "The hard data of paleopathology show that many [early Native Americans] were as sick as dogs."[31] To quote a public health researcher of our acquaintance, "Nature is filthy!"[32]

Fortunately, comparatively recent advances—such as proper canning, pasteurization, refrigeration, water chlorination and sanitary packaging, and food irradiation, along with greater scientific understanding of problematic agents and the development of ever more efficient countermeasures—have helped eradicate once widespread foodborne illnesses and have made our modern food system by far the safest in human history. Because many different agents can contaminate food and because different diseases have various symptoms, however, food safety at both production and processing sites is a complex issue that easily lends itself to much mythmaking. Unfortunately, the broader beliefs of most locavores on the issue are at odds with the established science and must therefore be addressed, if only superficially, before the food contamination problems inherent to locavorism are discussed in somewhat more detail.

The public debate on food safety has long been skewed by activists, who, in economist Thomas DeGregori's apt characterization, equate "preservatives with contamination and microbes with health," and are obsessed with the pesticide-residue molehill while ignoring the germ mountain.[33] In short, for a long time agriculturalists have relied on pesticides which are, technically speaking, any substance or mixture of substances that kill, repel, control, or mitigate the actions of any pest likely to damage humans and crops. Unlike animals that could always potentially escape predators, plants have always had a strong evolutionary incentive to develop toxic chemicals and digestive inhibitors as a primary defense mechanism. All plants produce on average a few dozen toxins to protect themselves against fungi, insects, and animal predators. Tens of thousands of these natural pesticides have been discovered. When plants are stressed or damaged by pests (as sometimes happens when synthetic pesticides—meaning pesticides produced by humans in factories—are not applied), they greatly increase their output of natural pesticides, sometimes to levels that are acutely toxic to humans. While both synthetic and natural chemicals can cause cancer in animals at high doses, we typically ingest through our regular diet at least 10,000 more (by weight) of natural than synthetic pesticides. In other words, about 99.99% of all pesticides in our diet are entirely "natural;" a single cup of coffee contains natural carcinogens roughly equal to at least a year's worth of carcinogenic synthetic residues in our diet.[34] As Paracelsus (1493–1541), the founder of toxicology, observed a few centuries ago, it is the dose that makes the poison. Any substance, even water, can be hazardous at high enough concentrations. Needless to say, though, public opinion was long ago tainted by beliefs that "natural" substances are not only inherently more benign than synthetic ones, but also that human intervention to control "natural" organisms through "artificial" means will ineluctably prove lethal to *genus homo*.

In terms of food safety, pesticides are a very minor—and in most cases insignificant—issue. While the media is keen to generate public panic over the feeding of unrealistically high doses of a synthetic chemical to experimental animals, it is almost completely silent on the fact that old-fashioned food production and "modern" organic agriculture are much more greatly endowed in harmful microorganisms than the offerings of agri-business. Over 250 different foodborne diseases are caused by consuming beverages and foods that have been contaminated by a wide range of viruses, bacteria, parasites, toxins, metals, and prions, and through nonfood mechanisms, such as the consumption of contaminated water or contact with animals. According to the latest research from the U.S. Centers for Disease Control and Prevention (CDC), each year approximately 1 in 6 Americans—48 million people—gets sick, 128,000 are hospitalized, and 3,000 die of foodborne diseases. Of these, by far the most significant are bacteria, viruses, and microbes[35] and, significantly, the vast majority of all U.S. food-related hospitalizations and fatalities nowadays *do not* originate from contaminated batches of agri-business products produced in large facilities, but rather are the result of careless handling and improper preparation inside the home, such as poorly refrigerated foods, unwashed hands and produce, cross-contamination of food through unwashed cutting boards, and insufficiently cooked meat.

To repeat and clarify, the foodborne illness cases in American emergency wards are *not* attributable to the synthetic pesticide and herbicide residues that worry the public so much, but rather can be traced back to "natural" pathogens such as *Campylobacter jejuni, Salmonella,* and *E. coli* O157: H7 that often find their way into our food supply through the use of animal manure in agricultural production.[36] Another very good source of illness is raw milk, a prime vector for tuberculosis, diphtheria, severe streptococcal infections, and typhoid fever, among other things.[37]

Humanity's food supply has never been inherently "pure, natural, and safe" and only recently corrupted by man-made chemicals and careless industrial practices. On the contrary, it was always afflicted by a large number of "natural" pathogens that are all around us and have been significantly, but not completely, brought under control in the recent past, in large part because of the development of industrial-scale food safety technologies.[38] In other words, there are such things as economies of scale in food safety, both in terms of producing and processing food. To give but one illustration, the science writer Steve Ettlinger describes two of many surprises he encountered while visiting a Wisconsin whey plant a few years ago:

The first is the sticky doormat just inside the door. Thinking I have stepped in some spoiled spilled milk, I stare dumbly at my gooey feet. My guides, two athletic-looking women, get a good laugh: the mat I've stepped on is designed to remove dirt from shoes. Inside another door, I gingerly step into an unavoidable mound of white foam, thinking once again that I did something bad. The women laugh once more: the foam is disinfectant, sprayed continually on the floor. Cleanliness is clearly paramount here.[39]

Among other striking features, Ettlinger noticed a network of steel pipes that brought sanitizing products in and out of the operation to keep things clean, that the floors were spotless, and that there was no smell in the plant. Of course, what the science writer observed is typical of all large-scale and state-of-the-art food manufacturing operations, which have extremely detailed and complex food safety management systems that analyze and control biological, chemical, and physical hazards from raw material production, procurement and handling, to manufacturing, distribution, and consumption of the finished product.[40] Large-scale operations obviously have much self-interest in preventing foodborne illness outbreaks, if only because of the attendant litigation and decline in sales.

One must keep these basic facts in mind when assessing the locavores' claim on behalf of a highly decentralized system made up of innumerable small farms and processing operations, for, as the agricultural economist Dennis Avery observes, "[s]almonella bacteria are pretty much everywhere, and always have been," from lettuce, spinach, peanut butter, and unpasteurized juices to ground beef, live chicken, and eggs. The USDA has never tested a cattle herd for *E. coli* O157:H7 without finding it, while the spinach *E. coli* outbreak of the same type of a few years ago that killed three people was traced back to nearby cattle and the wild pigs running around both the cattle and the spinach field. Interestingly, the spinach field was in transition towards organic production, meaning that chemical fertilizers could not be used. In addition, the manure on the field might not have been composted at a high enough temperature to kill the dangerous type of *E. coli* that has also been found in wild pigs, mice, coyotes, cowbirds, and crows.[41]

The main problem with the locavore's prescription for food safety is that the threat of food contamination by natural pathogens is much more serious in small than massive food production and processing operations because smaller operations can never possibly assemble the same quality of equipment and food safety know-how as much larger firms. True, large operations are not perfect and from time to time the media has a field day reporting on large food recalls and problematic processing plants. In truth, however, the perception that food is becoming less safe is probably driven by increased reporting of smaller outbreaks that were detected through recent technological advances. In other words, the greater media coverage is not driven by more significant problems, but because they can now be more easily detected and acted upon.[42] Although a locavore's system would ultimately make more people sick and kill more of them, the symptoms they would exhibit, such as nausea, vomiting, diarrhea, and fever, would often be difficult to trace to a specific food item as people eat many different things and, additionally, just as many problems can be traced back to the way food is handled at home. In a locavore's world, only the very worst outbreaks would be publicized.

Sadly, this chapter was being completed as the culprit of the deadliest outbreak of foodborne illness (25 deaths and counting) in a quarter of a century in the United States had just been identified. Not surprisingly, the guilty party in a multi-state outbreak of listeriosis turned out to be not a large agri-business plant with top-of-the-line food safety technologies, but a "pesticide free" and "four generation strong," family-operated cantaloupe farm located in Southeast Colorado, Jensen Farms, that not only marketed some of its output at local farmers' markets, but also had benefited from the "buy local" campaigns of large retailers in its area, such as King Soopers, Safeway, Wal-Mart, and Sam's Club.[43] According to FDA inspectors,[44] a number of factors had most likely contributed to the introduction, spread, and growth of *Listeria monocytogenes* in the cantaloupes, namely:

Introduction:
- There could have been low-level sporadic *Listeria monocytogenes* in the field where the cantaloupe were grown, which could have been introduced into the packing facility.
- A truck used to haul culled cantaloupe to a cattle operation was parked adjacent to the packing facility and could have introduced contamination into the facility.

Spread:
- The packing facility's design allowed water to pool on the floor near equipment and employee walkways.
- The packing facility floor was constructed in a manner that made it difficult to clean.
- The packing equipment was not easily cleaned and sanitized; washing and drying equipment used for cantaloupe packing was previously used for postharvest handling of another raw agricultural commodity.

Growth:
- There was no pre-cooling step to remove field heat from the cantaloupes before cold storage. As the cantaloupes cooled there may have been condensation that promoted the growth of *Listeria monocytogenes*.

Interestingly, according to food industry blogger Jim Prevor (otherwise known as the "Perishable Pundit"), Colorado is an especially unsafe location to grow cantaloupes because their rough skin makes them particularly susceptible to contamination as bacteria can hide out in their crevices. Because rains splatter mud on them, Colorado melons have to be washed post-harvest, a process that can result in cross-contamination among melons and create ideal conditions for bacteria to thrive. By contrast, the dry summers of Arizona and California are much safer for this fruit because they are watered by drip irrigation and much less likely to get dirty. Cantaloupes produced in those state can thus bypass the rinsing phase and are packaged dry, sometimes right in the field. What to outsiders might look like corporate attempts to cut corners was to the contrary the result of much research sponsored by the California cantaloupe industry.

Prevor adds that the food safety science in cantaloupes was pretty clear before the listeriosis outbreak: "The safest cantaloupes are what are called high desert cantaloupes. Jensen Farms washed all its cantaloupes. Since the science says don't get them wet, this washing is not a food safety matter. It is a marketing matter." He then goes one step further and observes, "whatever the specific cause of this outbreak, the more general cause is the local food movement. More specifically, the willingness of large buyers [such as Wal-Mart] to waive food safety standards so they can buy regionally." "The priority," he says, "can be safe or the priority can be local, but it cannot be both."[45] Words to ponder...

Of course, what is true for produce is also valid for livestock. Another late 2011 news item was an egg recall from a relatively small Minnesota organic producer.[46] While no system is perfect and some operations can be badly managed, large confined egg-producing operations have a number of inherent food safety advantages over such small cage-free farms, such as protecting laying hens from predators, soil-borne diseases, and extreme temperatures. The health of confined animals can also be monitored closely at low unit costs and various systems, such as screens through which feces fall so that they are not walked on or eaten and conveyor belts that move feed and eggs without being touched by human hands, can benefit from significant economies of scale. Salmonella can contaminate any animal-based food from any kind of farm operation whatever its size, but bigger is typically better in terms of food safety.[47]

In the retail sector, there can be no doubt that large supermarkets are inherently safer than farmers' markets which are, in most cases, temporary outdoor events with few facilities and whose vendors have, in general, received only the most basic training in food hygiene. While customers typically raise no concerns over these issues, during our trips to such markets we couldn't help but notice practices that seemed problematic, including freezer doors left open for significant periods of time and different kinds of raw meat being handled on the same cutting board. Perhaps we would all be better served by heeding the warning of Welsh health experts that "given the restricted facilities at farmers' markets and the early phase of implementation of hygiene management systems by market traders, it may be precautionary to restrict the sale of farm products at farmers markets to those that are regarded as low-risk."[48]

Finally, let us address the claim that local food is inherently safer than similar items purchased in countries with less stringent health and environmental regulations. Again, what matters is how the food is produced, processed, shipped, and conserved, not where it is grown. While there are no ultimate guarantees anywhere, large-scale producers in foreign countries are visited by various purchasers and inspectors while food shipped to a country like the United States is regularly inspected at large transit points. Exporters also have greater economic incentives for shipping good products because having these items rejected would cost them more than if they sold them in their home market due to the additional shipping costs. Export operations established by producers from advanced economies in poorer parts of the world typically implement state-of-the-art technologies which are then implemented in the domestic market. Paradoxically, food produced by small operators and sold at local farmers' markets in advanced economies rarely if ever undergoes the same level of scrutiny.

Of course, distrust of foreigners is something local producers have long tapped into by invoking—often dubiously—that their production methods are inherently safer. For instance, between 1880 and 1891, Germany declared a "Pork War" on the United States. The implicit message was that America should "reform its slaughterhouses and packaging methods and, most important, that it introduce a reliable system of microscopic examination for exported pork" in order to prevent the spread of trichinae—parasitic nematodes or roundworms, the reason for the widespread advice to cook pork thoroughly. (Again, this trade conflict began nearly three decades before Upton Sinclair published *The Jungle*.) As was widely known at the time, though, trichinosis was also a significant problem in Germany, as it had claimed at least 513 lives before 1880. [49] Slightly more than four decades later, American exports of apples to the United Kingdom were blocked after arsenic-based pesticides had been discovered on some fruit. This ban on imports—pursued, of course, with only the best interest of consumers in mind—was fortuitous as the local apple industry was then struggling. As one commentator had observed in 1925:

> It is unfortunate that, just when the majority of growers are ready to sell their bulkiest crops and best varieties the market should be filled with imported fruit. [Non-British] Imports begin earlier every year; and the period during which we have our own markets more or less to ourselves becomes correspondingly shorter... Very large quantities of apples are now coming from the United States, Ontario, British Columbia and Nova Scotia, and low prices are the general rule... The very large supplies of imported apples have naturally affected the value of home-grown, and further have made sales very difficult to effect. This state of affairs is very discouraging to home-growers in a season when apples are, in most cases, the only satisfactory crop. [50]

With the development of the global food supply chain, consumers were given access to a more diverse and affordable diet that contained more fresh produce and animal products than was the case before. In localities where fresh produce was competitive, consumers benefited from excellent products (because of their freshness) for a few weeks each year and from very good ones (because they were shipped some distance) for the remainder of the 52 weeks. The safety of the food they consumed also drastically improved over time, as the wealth creation that resulted from long-distance trade and urbanization paved the way for scientific advances that drastically curtailed the incidence of pathogens that had long plagued humanity.

Were we to turn our back on these advances, we would not progress towards a new system built around heirloom produce varieties and increased freshness, but rather regress towards the grain and potato-based diet that our ancestors eventually escaped from, for the priority of local food eaters, as it was back then, would have to be caloric intake over quality, diversity, and taste. As if this is not bad enough, the locavore's world food supply would not only be more monotonous and less nutritious, it would be inherently less safe as small producers would never be able to devise food safety protocols that require significant economies of scale to be cost- and capital-effective.

Many consumers might believe that agri-businesses only care about their profits and ignore consumers' nutrition and health, but the facts tell another story. Humans who benefit from the global food supply chain are now taller, healthier, and live longer than ever before. In the United States, deaths from foodborne illness have proportionally dropped by perhaps as much as 100-fold since 1900.[51] Besides, as the food policy analyst Robert Paarlberg observes, approximately 700,000 people die every year from food- and water-borne diseases in Africa where "many foods are still purchased in open-air markets (often uninspected, unpackaged, unlabeled, unrefrigerated, unpasteurized, and unwashed)," versus only a few thousand in the United States.[52] Our modern food system is not perfect, but it is a significant improvement over the past practices that locavorism would bring back with a vengeance.

7

Well-Meaning Coercion, Unintended Consequences, and Bad Outcomes

Of all things, an indiscreet tampering with the trade of provisions is the most dangerous, and it is always worst in the time when men are most disposed to it: that is, in the time of scarcity. Because there is nothing on which the passions of men are so violent, and their judgment so weak, and on which there exists such a multitude of ill-founded popular prejudices.

—EDMUND BURKE. 1795. *Thoughts and Details on Scarcity*
In Edmund Burke. 1800. *The Works of the Right Honorable Edmund Burke*,
vol. 4, John West and O.C. Greenleaf, p. 235,
http://books.google.ca/ebooks?id=TaNCAAAAYAAJ

In the name of greater food security and economic benefits, countless political rulers have historically sought to increase local food production while keeping foreign imports at bay. Because people only bothered to import foodstuffs from great distances if they provided cheaper and better alternatives, however, protectionist policies have always and everywhere resulted in a higher price tag. Not surprisingly, the available evidence strongly suggests that in most places and most of the time, "food patriotism" needed to be forced down consumers' throat with coercive measures. Although they might have said something different in public, given a choice, most people apparently always found the notion of paying more for lesser quality food rather unpalatable.[1]

Things have not changed all that much today. Sure, many consumers will interrupt their dinner to sing the praise of local food to pollsters. When a (typically much) higher price tag stares them in the face though, they sing a different tune.[2] Like previous food protectionists, today's locavores and food sovereignists have therefore increasingly come to embrace old-fashioned coercive policies which they have similarly sugar-coated in alleged broader benefits. Sure, they tell us, forcing schools, prisons, university and military bases to spend more on local food might seem costly to taxpayers, but think of all the jobs created! Yes, preventing farmers from selling their land to build subdivisions might make housing a tiny bit more expensive, but isn't that a small price to pay for increased food security? As we have already argued, these claims can't withstand scrutiny. In the remainder of this section, we will briefly explain why other long-standing coercive policies that have been co-opted by an increasingly large numbers of food activists are similarly misguided.[3] Trade barriers, production subsidies, supply-restriction schemes, government-run food reserves, prohibitions on food exports and price controls on agricultural products, we will argue, not only make everybody poorer and more food insecure, but also entail a significant environmental cost. First though, let us begin with a brief discussion of how ancient and pervasive such measures really are.

A Brief Historical Overview of Government Intervention in Food Markets

Political rulers have long intervened in food production and markets. Among the oldest measures are the building of infrastructure for transportation (such as ports, roads, and canals) and agricultural production (such as water reservoirs and dikes), as well as the creation of government-run grain reserves, which have been in existence at least since Pharaonic Egypt and Han China (around 200 BC). In Babylon about 4000 years ago, the Code of Hammurabi specified the exact annual wage for a field laborer, a herdsman, and a shepherd, along with the annual rental fee for a draught ox and the price of a milk-cow. In ancient China, the *Official System of Chou* prevented food merchants from raising their prices above government-decreed levels during calamities and famines, while a whole class of bureaucrats surveyed fields and determined the amount of grain to be collected or issued in accordance with the condition of the crop. Several restrictions on the trade and profits in grain are found in the *Arthashastra*, an Indian treatise on statecraft published perhaps as early as the 4th century B.C. In ancient Athens, inspectors set the price of grain at a level the government determined to be just; the exportation of local grain was prohibited at any time and punishable by death; officially sanctioned grain buyers were authorized to raise public subscriptions and use private money to secure foreign supplies; and commanders of Athenian ships leaving a foreign port were compelled to carry grain as ballast and to leave two-thirds of their grain cargo in Athens (the rest could be sold or re-exported at their discretion). [4]

Punctual or stopgap food policy measures are still very much with us today. For instance, in the aftermath of the price spikes of 2008, the governments of 35 countries released grains from public stocks and subsidized sales of food. The government of Malawi announced that all maize sales would be conducted through its Agricultural Development and Marketing Corporation (ADMARC) that would fix the price at which maize was bought from farmers and sold to consumers. The governments of Thailand, Pakistan, and India enacted measures against speculation and harsh penalties against grain hoarders while the Filipino government went as far as enacting life sentences for "plunder" and "economic sabotage." The Indonesian government implemented trade restrictions and regulations, such as "export bans, use of public stocks, price control, and anti-speculation measures" on rice and palm oil. China imposed export taxes on grains and grain products. Russia raised export taxes on wheat and Argentina on wheat, corn, and soybeans. India banned exports of rice other than basmati.[5]

Of course, such measures were on top of numerous preexisting regulations and programs. According to the Organization for Economic Co-operation and Development (OECD), in 2009 government policies in advanced economies transferred more than $253 billion worth of income to farmers and approximately 22% of all farm earnings in these countries could be directly traced back to these programs.[6] Policies take various forms and are often at odds with each other. For instance, the agricultural economists E. C. Pasour and Randal R. Rucker observed that in 2002 spending by the U.S. Department of Agriculture on initiatives designed to increase the prices received by farmers amounted to $37.8 billion, while initiatives to reduce producer prices cost taxpayers $11.4 billion.[7] To give but one illustration, the price of corn was artificially lowered by some policies (primarily income supports to corn farmers) and artificially raised by a set of import taxes, tax credits, fuel mandates, and import restrictions on cane sugar that creates an artificially high demand for corn-based sweeteners. (Because these measures largely counteract each other, the evidence on behalf of the argument that heavily subsidized and therefore artificially low corn prices are the prime reason for the American "obesity epidemic" is actually rather weak.[8])

Needless to say, the "creativity" of U.S. politicians and bureaucrats is more than matched by their "(Agricultural) Fortress Europe" counterparts whose Common Agricultural Policy (CAP) has long combined a maze of direct subsidy payments, guaranteed prices, and import quotas and tariffs. Among other wonders, the CAP has resulted in minimum prices for sugar beets which are processed into sugar costing twice that available from sugar cane. Surplus beet sugar is then dumped in foreign markets at only about a quarter of the real cost. Perhaps because defending the indefensible became increasingly challenging over time, the

CAP is now justified in the name of "guarantee[ing] the survival of the countryside as a place to live, work, and visit."[9]

It is not only advanced economies that are knee-deep in counter-productive agricultural policies; many governments in less advanced economies are even worse in this respect, although unlike rich countries they tend to use trade barriers more than other means such as produc-tion subsidies and government-led supply management schemes and mandates. As the trade policy analyst Caroline Boin observes, barriers to trade in developing countries are on average four times higher than in richer countries while African farmers pay roughly 60% more in export taxes than other African businesses. While most activists rightly de-nounce the subsidies paid to large agribusinesses and the damage they inflict on poor countries, about 70% of the world trade barriers are ac-tually between poor countries. Boin quotes a Nigerian presidential ad-viser as saying: "I can assure you that my pen is always ready to ban [importing] more items as long as they are available in Nigeria." When in doubt, he "impose[s] high tariffs." Not surprisingly, Nigeria's import bans have drastically increased the prices of such staples as maize, rice, and vegetable oil.[10]

The official rationale for government interventions has always been that international trade and market prices cannot be relied upon to pro-vide enough food at reasonable costs, especially in times of need—a view widely shared by agri-intellectuals and local food activists. Because of this, and the fact that there would be even more pressure to implement similar measures to combat the inevitable shortages and higher prices that would result from a locavore-driven economy, we will now briefly outline the consequences of some popular government interventions.

Public Food Reserves

In his influential "Farmer in Chief" essay, Michael Pollan argues that a way of improving "the food security of billions of people around the world" would be through a government-run strategic grain reserve which would "prevent huge swings in commodity prices" and "provide some cushion for world food stocks." By buying and storing grain "when it is cheap and sell[ing] it when it is dear," he argues, public-minded bureaucrats would be "moderating price swings in both directions and discouraging speculation."[11] This is the same rationale that has motivated the building and maintaining of public granaries for thousands of years and, more recently, of a wide range of public interventions ranging from the large-scale national food reserves of India and China[12] to NGO-, UN-, and World Bank–sponsored community cereal banks in sub-Saharan Africa.[13]

Unfortunately, the historical and contemporary records are pretty clear on the pitfalls of these policies. A recent case in point is Sahelian community-managed cereal banks—essentially small subsidized warehouses located in subsistence farming communities whose managers are expected to buy grain when it is inexpensive and to sell it later at a discounted (but nonetheless profitable) price when it is more costly. In practice, however, as noted by the author of a news report published by the Integrated Regional Information Networks—a respected humanitarian news and analysis service—these operations often ran out of money, borrowers defaulted, managers price-gouged or simply stole money, and villagers were in the end left as hungry as before. As one former NGO employee quoted in the news report observed, people "stole, managers disappeared, or the bank was located too far for some villagers to get their food." Not surprisingly, while supporters of such schemes acknowledge these challenges, they nonetheless justified these programs on the grounds that "even a flawed solution to fight hunger is better than no solution," while an international bureaucrat opined that such cereal banks "are a microcosm of Africa [and of] Africa's problems. There are management problems, transparency and corruption issues no matter who funds the start-up."[14]

Similar problems have also been observed in the strategic grain reserves set up throughout Africa under the aegis of the Food and Agricultural Organization of the United Nations (FAO) after the first oil shock of the 1970s.[15] As the geographer Evan Fraser and the journalist Andrew Rimas—two analysts not exactly friendly to market solutions—observed, the "seemingly limitless hoard" in silos proved "too tempting for local officials to ignore, and the program was plagued by politicking, mismanagement, and corruption. By the end of the 1980s, all that was left was the ink on a ledger sheet." During the crop failure of 2001 in Malawi, local officials were "shocked, shocked, shocked" (our words, not theirs) to discover that when the silo doors were opened, the "strategic grain reserves held no grain."[16]

Yet, blaming African political culture for these failures is misguided, for major problems in similar schemes have been uncovered elsewhere. For instance, according to a 2010 internal note of the Food Corporation of India (FCI),[17] about a third of the vast grain stock under its supervision was rotting in the open because of a lack of adequate storage space. Indeed, despite "full knowledge of the precarious condition of food grains, governments, both at the centre and in states, were unable to protect the country's precious food reserves." The FCI was also accused of being unable to move stocks after acquiring them and of having problems carrying out fumigation, "thus making preservation difficult." According to a news report on the issue, the "apathy of the people and officials responsible for feeding millions may result in more losses in years to come. The big question which needs to be answered is whether anyone would be held responsible for this seemingly criminal negligence."[18]

Far from being aberrations, such recent reports are but the latest in a long line that might go back all the way to the first government-run food reserves. Recurring complaints throughout the ages were that public officials could rarely resist the temptation to dip into them for their personal gain; that these reserves crowded out or at the very least often resulted in a decline in private inventories; and that their costs were way out of line with their alleged benefits as the long-term storage of large quantities of grain has always been expensive and technically challenging (among other problems, their operator had to aerate and turn the grain; control moisture levels; sell and replace the grain frequently if it was to be used as seeds; and repair and maintain large structures).[19] Other perennial issues raised by the Belgian historian Louis Torfs in 1839 were that public granary managers who could rely on the public purse were never as careful in their purchases as private individuals who spent their own money; that massive state-sponsored purchases drove up prices for everyone; and that safeguarding large warehouses during turbulent times always proved nearly impossible. Besides, while the building and maintenance of massive structures entailed enormous sums of money, it paled in comparison to the amounts required to provision a decent sized city for even a short period of time. As such, Torfs stated, the very notion of effective public granaries had always been impractical. Efficient provisioning, he concluded, should be left in the hands of farmers and merchants, with government intervention limited to guaranteeing freedom to trade and private property rights, a prescription that has been validated by recent scholarship.[20] Writing six decades before Torfs, the British agricultural writer William Harte had similarly concluded that the best public granaries were "vast tracts of country covered with corn," wherever they may be.[21]

Despite the sad historical record, numerous individuals working for organizations such as the prestigious *International Food Policy Research Institute* (IFPRI),[22] NGOs such as the *Institute for Agriculture and Trade Policy*[23] and *Share the World's Resources*,[24] several American consumer, environmental, religious and development groups,[25] and producers' cartels are still making the case for government-managed food reserves in the name of increased food security and reduced price volatility. Although recent proposals often take the form of special emergency reserves, international reserves, and "virtual reserves" controlled via commodity futures and options trading, their basic rationale and inherent shortcomings remain unchanged. It is beyond the scope of our book to discuss these new variants in any detail, but like more seasoned analysts, our intuition is that because they do not fundamentally differ from long-standing failed approaches, they will turn out to be ineffective and expensive while unable to outperform futures markets, which, through the buying and selling of commodities and their future delivery contracts, already smooth out long-term price volatility.[26]

Food Export Restrictions and Bans

In recent years, more than 20 countries including Russia, India, Tanzania, Ukraine, Macedonia, Moldova, Brazil, Argentina, and the Kyrgyz Republic have imposed complete or partial restrictions on the exportation of certain food commodities, such as wheat and rice.[27] In doing so, they were following another practice that is thousands of years old.

The main argument of critics of export restrictions has always been that the actual results of such measures are the exact opposite of their stated purpose. French economists such as Claude-Jacques Herbert and Anne-Robert-Jacques Turgot wrote in the mid-18th century that "a prohibition on exports made French grain prices too low and variable" and undermined the performance of the kingdom's agricultural sector. By preventing food exports, political rulers ensured that farmers earned less on their investments than would have otherwise been the case and thus removed much incentive to improve production volume and productivity. On the charges of profiteering during hard times, the French economists replied, "free entry into a liberalized grain trade would arbitrage away any resultant excess profits," competition would "eliminate excessive price differentials between different markets" and "minimize seasonal fluctuations," as differences in climate and geography between regions were the best insurance against risk.[28] In short, even though trade liberalization would shift the focus of public policy from consumer protection to greater incentives to increase production, consumers would nevertheless be made better off in the process.

At about the same time in England, William Harte reached similar conclusions, fortified by his studies of the ancient world. The leaders of Rome never understood that "by prohibiting the exportation of grain on the one hand, and giving no encouragement to trade and commerce on the other," they could only "procur[e] food for [their] subjects in a forced precarious manner." Yet, other cities such as Carthage and Tyre, although located in much less fertile surroundings, had "enjoyed food of all useful kinds in great abundance" because of their free-trade policies. Much of the explanation, Harte argued, lay in the fact that the "liberty of exportation" had sharpened human industry "to such a degree" as "to render half-barren countries fertile" and able to feed cities in both Antiquity and in his time.[29] (As the British agricultural writer Arthur Young famously observed in 1792: "Give a man the secure possession of a bleak rock, and he will turn it into a garden; give him a nine years' lease of a garden, and he will convert it into a desert."[30])

Benjamin Franklin observed that it was "common to raise a clamor" when higher prices in distant locations encouraged increased export of local grain on the "supposition that we shall thereby produce a domestic famine." Typically what followed was a "prohibition, founded on the imaginary distress of the poor." While Franklin was in favor of helping poor people in such circumstances, what was the justice, he asked, of compelling the farmer to accept a lower price for his wheat, "not of the poor only, but of everyone that eats bread, even the richest? The duty of relieving the poor is incumbent on the rich; but, by this operation, the whole burden of it is laid on the farmer, who is to relieve the rich at the same time." In his opinion, most people could afford to pay more for bread by either working longer hours or reducing their consumption of other items until wheat prices came down to previous levels. As such, there would "remain comparatively only a few families in every district, who, from sickness or a great number of children, will be so distressed by a high price of corn as to need relief; and these should be taken care of, by particular benefactions, without restraining the farmer's profit." Those who further feared that food exports would result in local shortages, Franklin added, were concerned about something that had never and could never happen. "They may as well," he wrote, "when they view the tide ebbing towards the sea, fear that all the water will leave the river." His key point was that "the price of corn, like water, will find its own level."[31]

These basic arguments are still put forward by critics of recent food export restrictions.[32] For instance, in 2010 Dr. Vicent Levalo, an economic lecturer at the University of Dar es Salaam, Tanzania, claimed that to lock farmers out of the international market would discourage the growth of the sector. He argued that this policy was "improper because exportation guaranteed farmers with a market for their produce," which in turn "will entice many people to participate in the sector as they find it profitable, hence developing the sector. You lock farmers from the market yet you expect them to get a better life from farming, how will it be achieved?"[33] The authors of a recent DEFRA report on the agricultural price spike of 2007–08 also highlighted that, to the extent that export bans are successful in curbing domestic food price inflation, "the necessary adjustment in global demand is concentrated amongst fewer countries and consumers. The more 'residual' the world market becomes as a result of such policies, the higher the degree of price volatility…" Furthermore, export restrictions also have the effect of undermining "confidence in the reliability of international markets" and will therefore encourage governments in some countries "to pursue policies that promote self-sufficiency and domestic production in ways that further fragment the international market."[34] As of this writing, Japan was leading the effort to secure a World Trade Organization (WTO) prohibition against export restrictions. Of course, Japan will be more likely to ease its import barriers and self-sufficiency goals if it has confidence it can always import the food it needs.[35]

Another type of food export control that has discouraged local production is commodity boards, through which government bureaucrats attempt to stabilize agricultural income and prevent price fluctuations. Introduced in Africa in the 1930s by British colonial administrators (but soon emulated by French and Belgian officials in their colonies),[36] their rationale was that while agricultural producers would be compelled to sell their crops for a fixed price to the bureaucrats who managed these institutions, these bureaucrats would in turn have more leverage to command higher and more stable prices in light of their size and ability to reduce interseasonal variations in terms of quantities offered.[37] As critics of these institutions observed, though, in practice the people who ran these boards typically gave producers a price that was below what could be obtained on world markets and then pocketed the differences for themselves. According to some analysts, these price control mechanisms destroyed flourishing export industries that had in most cases been created by and benefited primarily African producers who were then increasingly forced back into subsistence farming.[38]

Price Floors

The complaint that agricultural prices are too low to allow producers to earn an honest living is probably as old as commercial agriculture. Of course, while low prices are never good news to inefficient producers, to the extent that they are "market" prices means that they are still sufficiently high to allow the best farmers to earn enough profit to maintain and develop their businesses. This being said, no producer has ever complained about higher sale prices and reduced competition. Historically this has meant that wherever they carried enough political clout, inefficient domestic producers were able to keep cheaper nonlocal products at bay through import tariffs, outright bans, and government schemes which artificially restricted supplies (sometimes by killing millions of farm animals, which is what occurred in the USA during the 1930s) or created an artificial demand for some commodities (such as the ethanol program today).

Artificially high prices, however, have always hurt consumers (especially the poorest ones) and resulted in much waste of valuable resources. Policies that artificially inflate prices without reducing production also ensure increased environmental damage by rewarding the planting of crops in less suitable land that might require additional inputs (such as irrigation water and fertilizers) and be more prone to erosion.

Price Ceilings

In the last few decades, many governments in less advanced economies have been able to provide a reasonable amount of food at very cheap prices through government-purchased grain imports and their sale as subsidized bread or flour in urban markets. (The suspension or termination of these policies, often brought about by the threat of being denied stabilization loans by the International Monetary Fund, often resulted in so-called "IMF riots.") More recently, as mentioned earlier in this chapter, numerous governments addressed rapidly rising international food prices by fixing domestic prices on a wide range of foods at below-market levels.

What thousands of years of price control experiments have convincingly shown, however, is that they never achieve their stated goals of stopping inflation and remedying shortages. Far from delivering tangible benefits, they always provoked greater scarcity as local producers were no longer able to cover their production costs and had the assurance of losing more money the harder they worked. Because artificially lower prices quickly increased consumption, reduced stocks, and encouraged hoarding, essential goods rapidly became scarcer. Not surprisingly, producers and industrial purchasers always tried to find ways around these restrictions in order to cover their costs. In Europe, a classic reaction to the freezing of the price of a loaf of bread was for bakers to reduce their size in accordance with the rising price of breadstuffs. In many other cases, a price-controlled product would simply disappear from store shelves. Black markets would then inevitably emerge to satisfy consumer demands, but at a higher price than would have been the case in the absence of price controls, if only to compensate black marketers for the additional risks they took. The main victims of such developments were consistently people with lesser means.

Apart from discouraging production and distribution, in the long run price controls also killed innovation and adaptive behavior by preventing fluctuating prices from transmitting useful information and by stifling entrepreneurship. Ironically, by impeding people from buying when prices were cheap and selling later when there was greater scarcity and therefore higher prices (which is essentially what "hoarding" amounts to), political authorities have also long amplified price fluctuations.

As far as famine and price controls are concerned, the main lesson learned is that the political rulers from regions suffering a food shortage should refrain from imposing price controls. This approach was occasionally tried and proved successful (which is not to say that all hardship vanished, but rather that the final outcomes were much better than they would have been under price controls).

A case in point is Bengal, India, which in 1770 experienced one of the most infamous famines in history with a death toll ranging between 6 and 10 million people. Some researchers now attribute it to severe droughts in the previous decade,[39] but a more traditional interpretation puts the blame on price controls and the lack of tax relief by the British authorities.[40] Evidence for the latter claim is that crop failures on the same scale in 1865–66 did not result in a similar outcome in the absence of price control policies.

According to William Wilson Hunter, the Scottish historian stationed in Bengal in the mid-1860s, in 1770 "the Government, by interdicting what it was pleased to term the monopoly of grain, prevented prices from rising at once to their natural rates." In doing so, it made it impossible to send the right signals to spread out consumption of whatever was then available over the next 9 months in order to last until the next harvest. "Private enterprise if left to itself," Hunter wrote, "would have stored up the general supply at the harvest, with a view to realizing a larger profit at a later period in the scarcity. Prices would in consequence have immediately risen, compelling the population to reduce their consumption from the very beginning of the dearth." Unfortunately, this was not the case in 1770. In 1866, however, the British authorities realized that they had to stimulate private trade and prices were allowed to rise. As a direct consequence, "respectable men in vast numbers went into the trade; for Government, by publishing weekly returns of the rates in every district, rendered the traffic both easy and safe. Everyone knew where to buy grain cheapest, and where to sell it dearest, and food was accordingly brought from the districts that could best spare it, and carried to those which most urgently needed it." The result in Hunter's assessment was the equalization of prices "so far as possible throughout the stricken parts" and the pouring of rice "into the affected districts from all parts."

This outcome was also greatly facilitated by two technological advances that did not exist a century before: the telegraph, which allowed the instantaneous and accurate diffusion of regional prices, and the railroad, which could move much larger volumes at much more affordable prices. Hunter further observed that Orissa, the only region that suffered significant harm at the time, "possessed no English mercantile public, and had never expressed any desire for the means of intercommunication which is the first demand that such a public makes." Because its commerce had always been oriented towards the ocean rather than inland, it did not possess a railroad to connect it to other nearby regions. When supplies ran low the southwest monsoon had set in and, as it did every year, made local harbors impractical to use while the "only landward route was wholly unfit for the transport of sufficient food for the country, and the doomed population found themselves utterly isolated, 'in the condition of passengers in a ship without provisions.'"[41] Had the region been connected to the rest of India by the railroad and the telegraph, much suffering would have been alleviated.

On Appointing "Good" Czars

If a growing number of food activists have come to understand the absurdity of much agricultural policy, most still cling to the notion that markets cannot be trusted and that what is really needed is to appoint the right person at the helm of government. A case in point is the *New York Times*' food writer Mark Bittman. In a column titled

"Don't End Agricultural Subsidies, Fix Them!," he lamented the fact that well-meaning agricultural support policies created during the Great Depression now mostly benefit "wealthy growers [who] are paid even in good years, and may receive drought aid when there's no drought . . . homeowners lucky enough to have bought land that once grew rice now have subsidized lawns," and "Fortune 500 companies and even gentlemen farmers like David Rockefeller" who receive cash payments for no valid reason. As if this was not bad enough, agricultural subsidies also delivered "high-fructose corn syrup, factory farming, fast food, a two-soda-a-day habit and its accompanying obesity, the near-demise of family farms, monoculture, and a host of other ills." Yet, he adds, what these subsidies need "is not the ax, but reform that moves them forward" towards a "resurgence of small- and medium-size farms producing not corn syrup and animal-feed but food we can touch, see, buy, and eat."[42]

Even though he typed these words in 2011, Mr. Bittman was somehow oblivious to the fact that since "Hope and Change" had swept through the White House a few years earlier, President Obama's main achievements in terms of the writer's agenda had been a small garden at 1600 Pennsylvania Avenue and a few hundred million dollars promised to local food activists. Without being too cynical, it would seem that shoveling (or redirecting) all the corporate welfare manure out of the policy barnyard is somewhat more challenging than a food columnist imagines. Perhaps this is because, as Adam Smith observed more than two centuries ago, it is typically "the industry which is carried on for the benefit of the rich and powerful that is principally encouraged" by the political system "while that which is carried on for the benefit of the poor and the indigent is too often either neglected or oppressed."[43] In other words, the poor and middle-class can't afford top lobbyists while the path of least resistance for politicians has always been the creation of new programs rather than the phasing out or redirecting of existing ones. If history is again any guide, however, beneficial change can sometimes happen in the wake of a crisis (although plenty of bad things can happen, too . . .), as we will now discuss.

Unleashing the Invisible Hand

For nearly a century and a half, food activists and small producers of all kinds have argued that unbridled competition will destroy family farms and empower "monopolistic" corporations. True, in a free market inefficient firms are continuously being driven out of business while the most efficient ones are rewarded by consumers and growth as long as there are economies of scale to be realized—but only until the day they stop providing the best alternative available and are themselves driven out of business or absorbed by more efficient competitors. As we parse the available evidence, the fear of monopolies is misplaced, at least inasmuch as real food prices have been going down for decades, something which wouldn't happen in the presence of true monopolies. Besides, business history bears ample testimony to the fact that once-dominant firms will in time be eclipsed by creative upstarts. For instance, in the meatpacking industry, the original Chicago "Big 3" of Armour, Swift, and Morris have long been outgrown, divided, and absorbed by other firms while new upstarts, such as Tyson Foods, and older companies previously involved in other lines of work, such as Cargill, are now dominant players in this line of work. Opening up markets to competition of all sorts is the best way to reign in monopolies while government-enforced restrictions and bailouts are the best way to create and preserve them.

This being said, there is a time-tested way to help small agricultural producers reap economies of scale and remain competitive. Although rarely if ever discussed in any meaningful way by agri-intellectuals, for over a century and a half agricultural service cooperatives have helped smaller producers access cheaper supplies (from seeds and fertilizers to fuel and machinery), marketing services (including processing, packaging, storage, sales and distribution) and credit (from working capital to investment). No doubt these institutions would help small producers thrive once counterproductive policies had been eliminated, as was demonstrated most convincingly after the liberalization of the New Zealand agricultural sector. In 1984, following the near bankruptcy of the country and the election of a government with little support among agricultural producers, virtually all subsidies to agricultural production, export incentives and funding for natural disaster relief were eliminated while farm advisory services were privatized. Perhaps the best indicator of the scale of these reforms is that two decades later the portion of farm income represented by subsidies fell from 33% to less than 2%, with most of the latter figure being spent on agricultural research. True, many small independent operations and cooperatives merged to become more efficient and competitive, but a business model like the dairy co-operative giant Fonterra, which is owned by more than 11,000 dairy farmers and represents nearly 30% of the world's dairy exports, is something that should be considered by activists who truly care about thriving small operations, increased efficiency, lower prices and reduced environmental impact.[44]

Food activists are fond of saying that prices do not adequately reflect the true environmental costs of production. Fair enough, but typically the most meaningful problem in such cases is government failure. Maintaining agricultural prices artificially high usually brings more fragile and less productive land under the plough or hooves, which then requires sucking more water out of the ground, rivers, and streams along with the greater use of synthetic chemical inputs. The results are greater deforestation, soil erosion, and water scarcity for wildlife than a free market would have delivered.

By contrast, maintaining food prices artificially low discourages production and encourages waste, as when subsidized bread was used to feed cows and pigs in the former Soviet Union. Subsidizing inputs such as nitrogen fertilizer also ensures that more will end up in waterways, in the process increasing the nitrate concentrations in drinking water and causing eutrophication[45] of streams, ponds, and lakes. Subsidizing pesticide prices will encourage their abuse and typically result in the greater destruction of beneficial insects. Subsidizing the cost of irrigation water will result in more environmental damage through greater and more wasteful use of surface and underground water than would occur without these subsidies. When something is made artificially cheap, people have little incentive to use it as carefully as they would when it is not.

In countries where massive domestic food surpluses were generated as a result of government programs, further subsidies were needed to dump them on world markets and less developed economies. Governmental inability to recognize traditional community practices for the management of common resources such as fisheries, grazing lands, and irrigation systems or to clearly define and enforce private property rights also promotes short-term abuse.[46] Overall, it has been estimated that perhaps up to two thirds of the 1,000 billion dollars spent on subsidies related to agriculture, water, fisheries, energy production, forestry and transport are counterproductive as they damage both the economy (through increased budget deficits, unemployment, and trade distortions) and the environment (through increased pollution and mismanagement of natural resources).[47]

Once adopted, counterproductive agricultural policies are rarely rolled back as most politicians would rather avoid confronting powerful constituencies. Instead, when enough pressure has built up to compel them to do something, they usually adopt additional measures and subsidies, which will create new problems. For instance, policies that maintain prices artificially low are often dealt with through new production subsidies rather than by simply removing price restrictions and letting prices adjust upwards. The end result of an ever more politicized agricultural sector can only be an ever growing burden of taxes, debts, regulations, restrictions, and red tape which makes it very difficult to determine real production costs. So if government subsidies are paid on the basis of land farmed, the value of land rises to reflect not only its productive potential, but also its economic potential as a means of accessing government assistance. From the consumer's perspective, the real price of subsidized domestic agricultural products includes both the amount charged at supermarkets and the portion of his tax money that went to producers and the agricultural bureaucracy.

Regulated and distorted markets reinforce the political powers of beneficiary groups such as subsidized commodity producers, prevent or hinder the reallocation of scarce resources from less efficient producers to more efficient ones, generally discourage innovative behavior, and encourage the wasteful use of subsidized inputs while protecting polluters from sanctions. As such, they can never—in contrast to liberalized markets—simultaneously deliver greater output, lower prices, and reduced environmental impact. The road to food insecurity, higher prices, and greater environmental damage is paved with well-meaning policies.

CONCLUSION

Let Them Eat Global Cake!

Nations are no longer independent. We have become dependent on a great fabric of trade; when it is destroyed, we die.

—JOSEPH RUSSELL SMITH. 1919.
The World's Food Resources. H. Holt & Company, p. 3

To a locavore, food in the future should be created pretty much like it was in the not-so-distant past: Produce and animals raised lovingly in urban backyards, turning domestic waste into hearty dishes. Farmers' markets in every small town and city neighborhood, where people rediscover the joys of real food and get reacquainted with one another. The rebuilding of small-scale slaughterhouses and canning factories to serve area producers and foster the preservation of local food items for consumption in the off-season.

Ideally, this local system would also be built on seeds saved from the previous harvest rather than purchased from giant corporate seed producers; ancient "heirloom" cultivars developed before synthetic fertilizers and pesticides became available and that, as a result, are better able to seek nutrients in the soil, don't require any chemicals, and are naturally resilient to drought and pests ("If it's old seed, it's good seed!"); and "heritage" animal breeds better able to withstand diseases and harsh environments and grow fat and happy on pastureland alone. Pest control would be achieved through traditional "natural" products based on plants and minerals; manual labor, such as crushing or picking bugs and larvae off foliage or removing weeds by hands; and biological control methods, such as introducing exotic animals, insects, and bacteria that feed on invasive pests. Finally, factory-made fertilizers would be replaced by animal manure and rotating fodder crops, such as clover and alfalfa.

This scenario, however, begs an obvious question, the one we raised at the beginning of this book: If our agricultural past was so great, why were modern animal and plant breeds, long distance trade in food, and modern production and processing technologies developed in the first place? As discussed in these pages, the simple answer is that, to the people who lived through them, the "good old days" were more akin to "trying times." In a market economy, people do not bother tinkering with advances unless they are facing pressing problems. True, no innovative solution is ever perfect, but the essence of progress is to create less significant problems than those that existed before. Unfortunately, many activists endorse the so-called "precautionary principle," which in its purest form prevents technological changes in the absence of full scientific certainty as to their potential negative consequences. Yet, those who promote this stance ignore the harm that this worldview creates. Had resistance to innovation and change been more significant in the last two centuries, real income, life expectancy, and food consumption would undoubtedly be much lower than they currently are, while infant mortality, food prices, and hours worked, among other things, would have been much higher. Stagnation is fundamentally incompatible with any meaningful notion of sustainable development.

No one denies that our modern food system can be improved in various ways and for a long time to come —we personally look forward to the day when humans will be able to "grow" or clone cuts of meat without having to raise and kill animals—but critics should at least try to understand why we now produce food the way we do. Could it be, for instance, that some varieties of heirloom plants were abandoned *because* they not only had lower yields, but were also less resistant to diseases and bad weather or else displayed significant challenges, such as less regular ripening, shorter shelf lives, and lesser resistance to mechanical handling and transportation? That, for all their flaws in terms of taste, Iceberg lettuces and Elberta peaches provided the best fresh options in quality and price when alternatives were unavailable? Perhaps one hears comparatively little about heritage animal breeds not only because of their lower feed-to-meat conversion ratios (the amount of feed needed to produce a pound of meat), but also because they didn't taste that good and were more aggressive creatures? Finally, isn't it conceivable that those who espouse the notion that we should go back to "the sort of food our great grandmothers would recognize" are forgetting that our great grandmothers' great grandmothers would have heartily embraced the variety of new products available at the turn of the 20th century, from canned condensed milk and soups to breakfast cereals, frozen meat, and tropical offerings, such as fresh bananas?[1]

Isn't it possible that crushing bugs and removing weeds by hands were neither very effective nor the most productive use of one's time? That seeds purchased from commercial suppliers offered access to superior genetic material, were not mixed up with unwanted material and were readily available when needed? That "natural" manure has always been dirty, smelly, chock full of pathogens, and requires several months of composting? That the "slow release" of nutrients from green manures and organic compost could never be as adequately controlled to match crop demands with nutrient supply as is now possible with synthetic fertilizers? Further, that old mineral (including arsenic) and plant-based pesticides were less harmful to plant pests (and thereby more likely to promote insect resistance) and more problematic to human health than more recent offerings? That introducing nonnative insects, mammals, and bacteria in a new ecosystem often had unintended, broader, and longer-lasting negative consequences for non-targeted species?[2] And that, unlike chemical pesticides that typically do not persist in an ecosystem once application has ceased, exotic insects who have successfully adapted to a new environment are practically impossible to eradicate and do not remain confined to one geographical location? In the end, why are modern agricultural producers willing to purchase costly synthetic inputs, hormonal growth promoters, antibiotics, and genetically modified seeds when the methods agri-intellectuals prefer are either completely free (such as giving up on the use of these inputs and on equipment such as poultry housing) or seemingly much cheaper (such as feeding cattle entirely on pastureland and saving one's seeds instead of relying on those marketed by specialized producers)?

On the retail side, perhaps supermarkets and large chain stores displaced farmers' markets because of their more convenient hours, better parking conditions, greater mastery of logistics and inventory management, higher quality products, lower prices, and superior record in terms of food safety. On the latter topic, couldn't it be the case that the risk that large processing plants will spread pathogens over long distances is mitigated by the fact that they have better technologies to detect, control, and track such problems in the first place? And let's not forget that the long distance trade in food and agricultural inputs had the not inconsequential result of eradicating famine and malnutrition wherever it became significant.

Some locavores may continue to believe that our globalized food supply chain is the result of colonial and corporate agri-business raiders who crushed small farmers, packers, and retailers the world over simply because they could. But we contend that modern practices are but the latest in a long line of innovations, the ultimate goal of which has always been to increase the accessibility, quality, reliability, and affordability of humanity's food supply. And if we may be so blunt, how many activists still use locally manufactured electric typewriters and copper-wired rotary-dial phones to spread their message and set up "grassroots" links between food consumers and producers?[3] How many move around in horse-drawn tramways, Ford Model Ts, or even old-fashioned roller skates with parallel wheels? How many would trust doctors, meteorologists and computer engineers clinging to 1940s technology? If nonlocal modern technologies are good enough to serve the locavores' needs, why aren't they also desirable for agricultural producers?

We covered much historical material in this book in our attempt to look beyond the anti-corporate, romantic, and protectionist underpinnings of locavorism and to illustrate the rationale behind improvements in food production, processing, and transportation technologies, along with the benefits of an ever broader division of agricultural labor. To quote the historian Paul Johnson, the study of history "is a powerful antidote to contemporary arrogance," for it is always humbling "to discover how many of our glib assumptions, which seem to us novel and plausible, have been tested before, not once but many times, and in innumerable guises; and discovered to be, at great human cost, wholly false."[4] The available historical evidence tells us that locavorism, far from being a step forward, can only deliver the world our ancestors gladly escaped from,[s] and which subsistence farmers mired in similar circumstances around the world would also escape if given opportunities to trade. It would not only mean lower standards of living and shorter life expectancy, but also increased environmental damage and social turmoil.

Perhaps the most fitting conclusion to our book is in the words of the American lawyer and legislator William Bourke Cockran, made famous by Winston Churchill in his 1946 "iron curtain" speech: "There is enough for all. The earth is a generous mother; she will provide in plentiful abundance for all her children if they will but cultivate her soil in justice and peace."[5] And, we would add, if they will trade ever more with each other.

EPILOGUE

It was during the 2009–2010 academic year that Pierre and I packed our bags and hit the American interstate highway system en route from Toronto to Bozeman, Montana, where we would stay for several months before moving on to Durham, North Carolina, for a semester. This was my first time crossing "fly-over" country at ground level. Over the next several months we would travel more than 35,000 miles, and I would get to experience some of America's commercial landscapes, national parks, villages, small towns, and cities.

Life in a beautiful small college town in Montana was a completely new experience for me, a born and bred city girl. I enjoyed some juicy bison burgers at Ted's Montana Grill (a chain owned by media mogul Ted Turner) and a few other local delicacies, although for someone used to the diversity of Toronto's foodscape and a sushi purist, it proved a bit challenging at times. Fortunately, the globalized food supply chain had already worked its magic. Many once "exotic" food items were in ready supply at the local grocery store: tofu, good quality soy sauce, bean sprouts—I even discovered Vietnamese rice paper at Wal-Mart!

Traversing the middle part of the United States, I got the opportunity to visit once thriving Native American settlements (Mesa Verde, Chaco Canyon, and the Cahokia Mounds) where the local inhabitants had obviously belonged to wider trading and cultural networks. I experienced a wide array of agricultural landscapes: pasturelands in the Shenandoah Valley and Wyoming; apple orchards in Virginia; dairy farms in Wisconsin; wheat fields in Montana; cotton fields in Georgia; abandoned tobacco fields in North Carolina that had reverted to forests; and many other agricultural landscapes. Most impressive, though, was the sea of corn that surrounded us from Ohio to North Dakota. To locavores and food activists this is probably the most despicable part of America, but I couldn't help but think how much worse off we would all be without it—and be thoroughly impressed by how much of an agricultural powerhouse the United States is.

Americans seem to take their extraordinary agricultural sector for granted and, in my experience, are typically unable to imagine that sometimes things can go horribly wrong. I never experienced hunger myself, but my parents did. My father was born in Tokyo in 1936 and my mother in Kyushu in 1941. They both suffered through the deprivations of the Second World War and its aftermath. As a child, my father, like many others, was sent away to the Japanese countryside in order to escape the firebombing of his city. To this day he can't stand kabocha squashes and sweet potatoes, as these were the only foods available to him—and even then, he was not fed the sweet potato itself but the vines. My mother told me more times than I care to remember that one of her dreams as a child was to get the opportunity to eat a full bowl of rice. She was the youngest of ten children, only five of whom made it to the age of 20. One of my surviving aunts, severely malnourished as a child, suffered significant rheumatism and osteoporosis for the rest of her life as a result.

True, many other people have had it worse than the Japanese and the members of my family. Yet, it seems that one of the main lessons to be learned from my native country's experience over the last century and a half is that pushes towards autarkic food policies can only result in disaster. As we wrote in the book—and as many other people have said before us—if goods don't cross borders, armies eventually will. My parent's generation is living proof that what militaristic people thought they could only achieve by force can be accomplished much more effectively and successfully through free trade and peace. And, just as important, globalization affords people all kinds of possibilities. About half a century ago, my parents never imagined how abundant and affordable their future food supply would turn out to be (let alone that one of their children would marry a foreigner and move to Canada).

As the Harvard psychologist Steven Pinker observes in *The Better Angels of Our Nature*, we may be living in the most peaceful time in our species' existence. This blessed state of affairs, though, was a long time coming and was only made possible through the worldwide exchange of products, resources, ideas, and culture. Despite our current economic woes, we have almost vanquished famine. Most of us live longer, healthier, safer, and more enjoyable lives than previous generations. It seems incumbent upon us to put forward some constructive proposals to improve the global food supply chain rather than turn back the clock to some imagined era of pastoral bliss that most people escaped from when given the opportunity. Growing more and better quality food, and doing so ever more efficiently, healthily, safely, and sustainably is what we should aim for.

Food cosmopolitanism is in everybody's and the planet's best interest. It is my hope that "Buy Local" will soon be replaced by the more desirable slogan, "Buy Global—The Planet Is Our Garden!"

—Hiroko Shimizu

NOTES

Foreword

1. Beverly Bell. 2010. "Groups around the US Join Haitian Farmers in Protesting 'Donation' of Monsanto Seeds." *Other Worlds* (June 4) http://www.otherworldsarepossible.org/another-haiti-possible/groups-around-us-join-haitian-farmers-protesting-donation-monsanto-seeds.

2. Beverly Bell. 2010. "Haitian Farmers Commit to Burning Monsanto Hybrid Seeds." *Other Worlds* (May 17) http://www.otherworldsarepossible.org/another-haiti-possible/haitian-farmers-commit-burning-monsanto-hybrid-seeds.

3. Ingo Potrykus. 2010. "Regulation must be Revolutionized." *Nature* 466: 561.

4. Matthew Ridley. 2011. "Why Deny Biotech to a Hungry Africa?" *Wall Street Journal* (December 10) http://online.wsj.com/article/SB100014240529702 04770404577080264187783818.html.

Preface

1. According to a rough estimate, Japanese people suffered on average one year of famine out of seven between 600 AD and 1885. The last major famine to hit the islands occurred in the 1830s (see Osamu Saito. 2002. "The Frequency of Famines as Demographic Correctives in the Japanese Past." In Tim Dyson and Cormac Ó Gráda (eds). *Famine Demography: Perspectives from the Past and Present*. Oxford University Press, pp. 218–239). For readers fluent in Japanese, see the Japanese Ministry of Agriculture, Forestry and Fisheries discussion of what present day self-sufficiency would entail in terms of available food supply at http://www.maff.go.jp/j/zyukyu/index.html.

2. We discuss these issues in much greater detail in chapter 4.

3. See their "Enterprise Africa" initiative http://mercatus.org/enterprise-africa.

4. Pierre Desrochers and Hiroko Shimizu. 2008. *Yes, We Have No Bananas. A Critique of the "Food Miles" Perspective.* Mercatus Policy Series Primer no. 8, Mercatus Center (George Mason University) http://mercatus.org/publication/yes-we-have-no-bananas-critique-food-miles-perspective?id=24612.

5. On average, farmers in African countries use 8 kilograms of synthetic fertilizers per hectare as opposed to 107 kilograms in the developing world as a whole.

6. Bruce Gardner. 2003. "U.S. Agriculture in the Twentieth Century". In Robert Whaples (ed.) *EH.Net Encyclopedia* http://eh.net/encyclopedia/article /gardner.agriculture.us.

7. Malnutrition or undernutrition refers to either or both a calorie and micronutrient (vitamins and minerals) deficit. Stunting occurs when an individual's stature is too short relative to his or her age and wasting when his or her weight is too low. For a more detailed introduction to the topic and the latest statistics on world hunger, see the "Hunger Portal" of the Food and Agricultural Organization (FAO) of the United Nations at http://www.fao.org/hunger/en/.

Introduction

1. Columella's two millennia–old text is freely available at http://penelope .uchicago.edu/Thayer/E/Roman/Texts/Columella/de_Re_Rustica/Praefatio*.html #ref1.

2. Pépin has discussed his failed doctoral proposal in a few venues, such as in Grace Russo Bullaro. 2009. "Blue Collar, White Hat: The Working Class Origins of Celebrity Superstar Jacques Pepin." *The Columbia Journal of American Studies*, Volume 9 (Fall), pp. 28–47 http://www.columbia.edu/cu/cjas/Jacques _Pepin.html.

3. Pollan's website is at http://michaelpollan.com/ For an online synthesis of his policy thinking, see Michael Pollan. 2008. "Farmer in Chief." *New York Times Magazine* (October 9) http://www.nytimes.com/2008/10/12/magazine/12 policy-t.html.

4. As of this writing, less than 0.6% of the U.S. population was employed as full-time farmers while several others supplemented their farm production income with other off-farms sources of revenue. For a concise portrait of the evolution of this sector in the context of the overall U.S. economy, see Carolyn Dimitri, Anne Effland, and Neilson Conklin. 2005. *The 20th Century Transformation of U.S. Agriculture and Farm Policy.* Electronic Information Bulletin No. 3, USDA http://www.ers.usda.gov/publications/eib3/eib3.htm. The reference to lawyers is borrowed from Peter C. Timmer. 2009. *A World without Agriculture? The Historical Paradox of Agricultural Development.* Development Policy Outlook, Ameri-

can Enterprise Institute, May http://www.aei.org/docLib/01%20DPO%20 May%202009g.pdf.

5. In essence, vitalism is the belief that a molecule produced in a bird's or a cow's stomach is inherently superior to a chemically identical molecule produced through industrial processes.

6. Professor Tom Perrault, Department of Geography, Syracuse University, course syllabus for GEO 400: Food: A Critical Geography https://www.maxwell .syr.edu/uploadedFiles/faculty/geo/Food.pdf.

7. GRAIN (Genetic Resources Action International). 2008. "Making a Killing from Hunger" *Against the Grain* (April) http://www.grain.org/articles/?id=39.

8. Michael Pollan. 2008. "Farmer in Chief." *New York Times Magazine* (October 9) http://www.nytimes.com/2008/10/12/magazine/12policy-t.html.

9. The label "SOLE food" is usually traced back to a 2006 entry on the Ethicurean blog.

10. A typical statement to this effect is Bryan Walsh. 2009. "Getting Real about the High Price of Cheap Food," *Time* (August 21) http://www.time.com /time/health/article/0,8599,1917458,00.html See also John Ikerd. 2005. "Eating Local: A Matter of Integrity" Paper presented at the at *The Eat Local Challenge* (Eco Trust, Portland, OR), June 2, available at http://web.missouri.edu /~ikerdj/papers/Alabama-Eat%20Local.htm.

11. Of course, political problems still prevent nearly one individual in seven from eating a satisfactory diet, but political problems rather than food production per se are the real cause of this situation.

12. The terms "localvorism" and "localvores" are also used by some activists. Our choice of "locavore" was motivated by its more common usage and its selection as "word of the year" by the *New Oxford American Dictionary* in 2007.

13. Anonymous. 2009. "Tom Vilsack, The New Face Of Agriculture." *The Washington Post* (February 11) http://www.washingtonpost.com/wp-dyn/content /story/2009/02/10/ST2009021002624.html.

14. News Desk. 2011. "USDA Rule Encourages Local Food for School Meals." *Food Safety News* (April 29) http://www.foodsafetynews.com/2011/04 /usda-rule-to-encourage-local-food-for-school-meals/.

15. Sherrod Brown. 2011. "Brown Introduces Bill to Expand Markets for Farmers and Increase Access to Local Foods Legislation Would Boost Ohio's Rural Economy, Improve Consumer Access to Healthy, Fresh Foods." Press Release, Senator Sherrod Brown Office http://brown.senate.gov/newsroom/press _releases/release/?id=62ee64a8-f401-4387-9b2f-ab35ed0fbacc .

16. Danna Staaf. 2011. "West Coast Locavores Should Turn Teuthovore." *Science 2.0* (May 25) http://www.science20.com/squid_day/west_coast_locavores _should_turn_teuthovore-79384.

17. For a concise presentation of these alleged advantages from a proponent of this shopping lifestyle, see Molly Watson. *Eight Reasons to Eat Local Foods. Straight-Forward Benefits of Eating Local Foods. About.com Guide* http://local-foods.about.com/od/finduselocalfoods/tp/5-Reasons-to-Eat-Local-Foods.htm For a more detailed discussion of these arguments, see Steve Martinez, Michael Hand, Michelle Da Pra, Susan Pollack, Katherine Ralston, Travis Smith, Stephen Vogel, Shellye Clark, Luanne Lohr, Sarah Low and Constance Newman. 2010. *Local Food Systems: Concepts, Impacts, and Issues.* Economic Research Report #97. United States Department of Agriculture (USDA) Economic Research Service http://www.ers.usda.gov/Publications/ERR97/ERR97.pdf.

18. Blake Hurst. 2009. "The Omnivore's Delusion: Against the Agri-Intellectuals." *The American* (July 30) http://www.american.com/archive/2009/july/the-omnivore2019s-delusion-against-the-agri-intellectuals/.

19. Joe Pompeo. 2009 "The Foodiots." *New York Observer* (September 22) http://www.observer.com/2009/food-amp-drink/foodiots.

20. Stephen Budiansky. 2010. "Math Lessons for Locavores." *New York Times* (August 19) http://www.nytimes.com/2010/08/20/opinion/20budiansky.html.

21. Ronald Bailey. 2008. "The Food Miles Mistake: Saving the Planet by Eating New Zealand Apples." *Reason.com* (November 28) http://reason.com/archives/2008/11/04/the-food-miles-mistake.

22. Dave Lowry. "The Locavore's Dilemma: One Critic's Take." *StLMag.com,* September 20, 2010 http://www.stlmag.com/Blogs/Relish/September-2010/The-Locavore-039s-Dilemma/.

23. Greg Critser. 2001. "Mean Cuisine: Gone Is the Joy of Cooking. Today's Celebrity Chefs are Serving Up a Menu of Global Doom and Politically Twisted Snobbery." *Washington Monthly* (July/August) http://www.washingtonmonthly.com/features/2001/0107.critser.html .

24. Thomas R. DeGregori. 2004. "Julia Child's Legacy for the Future." *Health FactsandFears.com*, August 16 http://www.acsh.org/factsfears/newsID.436/news_detail.asp.

25. Art Carden. 2008. "Should we Only Buy Locally Grown Produce?" *Mises Daily* (July 15) http://mises.org/daily/3026 and "The Locavore's Dilemma: Local Food, Continued." *Mises Daily* (August 18) http://mises.org/daily/3059.

26. Steven Landsburg. 2010. "Loco-Vores." *The Big Questions* (August 23) http://www.thebigquestions.com/2010/08/23/loco-vores/.

27. Steven Sexton. 2009. "Does Local Production Improve Environment and Health Outcomes?" *ARE Updates* 13 (2): 5-8 http://giannini.ucop.edu/media/are-update/files/articles/v13n2_2.pdf.

28. Edward L. Glaeser. 2011. "The Locavore's Dilemma: Urban Farms Do More Harm than Good to the Environment." *Boston.com* (April 16) http://articles

.boston.com/2011-06-16/bostonglobe/29666344_1_greenhouse-gas-carbon-emissions-local-food.

29. Jayson L. Lusk and F. Bailey Norwood. 2011. "The Locavore's Dilemma: Why Pineapples Shouldn't be Grown in North Dakota." *Library of Economics and Liberty* (January 3) http://www.econlib.org/library/Columns/y2011/Lusk Norwoodlocavore.html.

30. Robert Paarlberg. 2010. "Attention Whole Food Shoppers." *Foreign Policy* May/June http://www.foreignpolicy.com/articles/2010/04/26/attention_whole _foods_shoppers?page=full.

31. Gary Blumenthal. 2011. "Creating False Markets." *World Perspectives, Inc.* (February), p. 1.

32. Robert Paarlberg. 2010. "Attention Whole Food Shoppers." *Foreign Policy*, May/June http://www.foreignpolicy.com/articles/2010/04/26/attention_whole _foods_shoppers?page=full.

33. The Polyface website is at http://www.polyfacefarms.com/ A typical uncritical piece on Salatin's approach is Bryan Walsh. 2011. "This Land is your Land." *Time* (October 24) http://www.time.com/time/magazine/article/0,9171 ,2096846-1,00.html Among other problems usually ignored by his supporters is that his grass-fed cattle requires about twice the lifespan and produces only about half of the meat of modern operations. Chicken are not raised in winter and the stock must be replenished each spring through purchases from conventional operations. Salatin also buys weaner pigs, turkey poults, and many cows from sale barns and lets them run outside together which not only exposes them to sometimes harsh weather conditions and predators, but also facilitates the transmissions of viruses such as influenza among them (to say nothing of the increased risk to the health of nearby humans). (We discuss health and safety issues on operations such as Polyface in more detail in chapter 6.) Of course, such old fashioned practices also mean that, like in the old days, Salatin's pigs eat a substantial amount of cow manure. According to the SpeakerMix website, Salatin charges between $15,000 and $20,000 per speech http://speakermix.com /joel-salatin. Critics of Salatin's approach include Nathan Fiala. 2009. "Recent Trip to Polyface Farms." *Post Conflicted* (May 27) http://postconflicted.blogspot. com/2009/05/recent-trip-to-polyface-farms.html and the "About Food, Inc." webpage of the agriculture industry website SafeFoodInc.com http://www.safe foodinc.org/index.php?option=com_content&view=article&id=3&Itemid=11.

34. Dave Lowry. 2010. "The Locavore's Dilemma: One Critic's Take." *StL-Mag.com* (September 20) http://www.stlmag.com/Blogs/Relish/September -2010/The-Locavore-039s-Dilemma/.

35. Greg Critser. 2001. "Mean Cuisine: Gone is the Joy of Cooking. Today's Celebrity Chefs are Serving Up a Menu of Global Doom and Politically Twisted

Snobbery." *Washington Monthly* (July/August) http://www.washingtonmonthly
.com/features/2001/0107.critser.html.

36. Dave Lowry. 2010. "The Locavore's Dilemma: One Critic's Take." *StL-Mag.com* (September 20) http://www.stlmag.com/Blogs/Relish/September
-2010/The-Locavore-039s-Dilemma/.

37. Gary Blumenthal. 2011. "Creating False Markets." *World Perspectives, Inc.* (February), p. 1.

38. Clara Jeffery and Monika Bauerlein. 2009. "Editors' Note: Want to Fix the Country? Fix Food." *Mother Jones* (March / April) http://motherjones.com
/toc/2009/03/editors-note.

39. The USDA program website can be found at http://www.usda.gov/wps
/portal/usda/knowyourfarmer?navid=KNOWYOURFARMER. The letter is available at http://www.farmpolicy.com/wp-content/uploads/2010/04/JM_SC
_PR_Know-Your-Farmers.pdf.

40. Quoted in Linda Baker. 2002. "The Not-so-sweet Success of Organic Farming." Salon.com (July 29). http://www.salon.com/technology/feature/2002
/07/29/organic/print.html.

41. See Corby Kummer. 2010. "The Great Grocery Smackdown." *The Atlantic* (March) http://www.theatlantic.com/magazine/archive/2010/03/the-great
-grocery-smackdown/7904/ Wal-Mart's *Heritage Agriculture* initiative is aimed at farms located within a day's drive of its warehouses and currently account for between 4 and 6% of its produce sales.

42. For a recent debate over this issue, see the commentary section of *Renewable Agriculture and Food Systems* 22 (4), 2007.

43. See, among others, Robert Paarlberg. 2010. *Food Politics. What Everyone Needs to Know*, Oxford University Press; Thomas de Gregori. 2002. *Bountiful Harvest: Technology, Food Safety and the Environment.* Cato Institute; Dennis Avery. 2000. *Saving the Planet with Pesticides and Plastics.* Hudson Institute; Alex Avery. 2006. *The Truth about Organic Foods.* Henderson Communications http://www.thetruthaboutorganicfoods.org/; and Nina V. Fedoroff and Nancy Marie Brown. 2004. *Mendel in the Kitchen: A Scientist's View of Genetically Modified Foods,* Joseph Henry Press. A recent re-statement of the main points made by such authors, but filtered through the eyes of a former food activist who still clings to a number of misconceptions and ultimately refuses to follow his argumentation to its logical conclusion, is James McWilliams. 2009 *Just Food. Where Locavores Get It Wrong and How We Can Truly Eat Responsibly.* Little, Brown and Company.

44. Molly Watson. *Eight Reasons to Eat Local Foods. Straight-Forward Benefits of Eating Local Foods. About.com Guide* http://localfoods.about.com/od/finduse
localfoods/tp/5-Reasons-to-Eat-Local-Foods.htm.

45. See, for instance, Michael Pollan. 2008. "Farmer in Chief." *New York Times Magazine* (October 9) http://www.nytimes.com/2008/10/12/magazine /12policy-t.html. A typical statement in this respect is by Ferd Hoefner, the policy director of the National Sustainable Agriculture Coalition, who mentioned in an interview that getting the "Department of Defense or the VA hospitals" to change their purchase would obviously be beneficial to his movement. Quoted by Paul Roberts. 2009. "Spoiled: Organic and Local Is so 2008: Our Industrial Food System Is Rotten to the Core. Heirloom Arugula Won't Save Us. Here's What Will." *Mother Jones* (March/April) http://motherjones.com/environment/2009 /02/spoiled-organic-and-local-so-2008 One of the few locavores (at least in season) and alternative food supporter we know who has written explicitly against mandatory purchases and taken an explicitly "live and let live" approach to the issue is Canadian libertarian lawyer—and personal friend—Karen Selick. See Karen Selick. 2008. "The Buy-Locally-Owned Fallacy." *Library of Economics and Liberty* (November 3) http://www.econlib.org/library/Columns/y2008/Selick local.html.

46. Thomas Hudson Middleton. 1923. *Food Production in War*. Clarendon Press. p. 324.

47. Katherine Kemp, Andrea Insch, David K. Holdsworth and John G. Knight. 2010. "Food Miles: Do U.K. Consumers Actually Care?" *Food Policy* 35 (6): 504–513.

Chapter 1

1. Russell Smith's classic text is available at http://www.archive.org/details /worldsfoodresour00smituoft.

2. Branden Born and Mark Purcell. 2006. "Avoiding the Local Trap: Scale and Food Systems in Planning Research." *Journal of Planning Education and Research* 26 (2): 195–207.

3. To give but one illustration, in a survey conducted at the request of North Carolina State University researchers, 74% of the polled public answered "no" and 17% "yes" when asked "If the U.S. could buy all its food from other countries cheaper than it can be produced and sold here, should we?" In Ronald C. Wimberley et al. 2003. *Food for our Changing World: The Globalization of Food and How Americans Feel about It* http://faculty.chass.ncsu.edu/wimberley/Global-Food /foodglobal.pdf .

4. For a broader overview of the various subjects discussed in this section and additional references, see among others Kenneth F. Kiple and Kriemhild Coneè Ornelas. 2000. *The Cambridge World History of Food*. Cambridge University Press; Maguelonne Toussaint-Samat. 1994/1987. *History of Food* (translated by Anthea

Bell). Blackwell Publishing; Vaclav Smil. 2010. *Prime Movers of Globalization. The History and Impact of Diesel Engines and Gas Turbines.* MIT Press; and Robert P. Clark. 2000. *Global Life Systems. Population, Food, and Disease in the Process of Globalization.* Rowman & Littlefield Publishers, Inc.

5. Adam Smith. 1776. *An Inquiry Into the Nature and Causes of the Wealth of Nations, Vol. 1, Book I, chapter II:* Of the Principle which gives occasion to the Division of Labour. Available at http://www.econlib.org/library/Smith/smWN 1.html#B.I, Ch.2, Of the Principle which gives Occasion to the Division of Labour.

6. Gisday Wa and Delgam Uukw. 1989 *The Spirit in the Land.* Reflections, p. 44.

7. For genus *Homo* as a whole, this would amount to 99% of its record.

8. In the last several decades, X-rays, gamma rays, fast neutrons and thermal neutrons were used to cause mutations in plants. Among other cases, the Rio Red grapefruit was created in 1968 by exposing grapefruit buds to thermal neutron radiation. Much pasta today is made from an irradiated variety of durum wheat. Golden Promise, a variety of barley popular among organic brewers, was created in an atomic reactor in the 1950s. Nasty chemicals such as ethyl methane sulfate and mustard gas were also used to cause mutations and to allow the hybridization of varieties that would not otherwise crossbreed. A case in point is triticale, a cross between wheat and rye that, without the use of the toxic natural product colchicine, could not naturally hybridize. It is now popular in "natural" health food stores because of its higher percentage of higher quality proteins than its parent seeds. See, among others, Nina Fedoroff and Nancy Marie Brown. 2004. *Mendel in the Kitchen: A Scientist's View of Genetically Modified Foods.* Joseph Henry Press.

9. See, among others, Adi B. Damania. 2008. "History, Achievements, and Current Status of Genetic Resources Conservation." *Agronomy Journal* 100: 9–21.

10. Alan W. Olmstead and Paul W. Rhode. 2008. *Creating Abundance. Biological Innovation and American Agricultural Development.* Cambridge University Press, pp. 3 and 140–141.

11. For a more detailed discussion of this issue, see Pierre Desrochers and Samuli Leppälä. 2010. "Industrial Symbiosis: Old Wine in Recycled Bottles? Some Perspective from the History of Economic and Geographical Thought." *International Regional Science Review* 33 (3): 338–361.

12. Xenophon. Early 4th C BCE. *Cyropaedia, The Education Of Cyrus.* 1914 edition, F. M. Stawell (translated by Henry Graham Dakyns) http://www .gutenberg.org/dirs/2/0/8/2085/2085.txt.

13. Edward Glaeser. 2011. *Triumph of the City. How our Greatest Invention Makes Us Richer, Smarter, Greener, Healthier, and Happier.* Penguin Press, p. 7. See

also Mario Polèse. 2010. *The Wealth and Poverty of Regions. Why Cities Matter.* University of Chicago Press.

14. For a more detailed discussion of the issue, see Pierre Desrochers. 2001. "Geographical Proximity and the Transmission of Tacit Knowledge." *Review of Austrian Economics* 14 (1): 25-46.

15. United Nations. 2008. *World Urbanization Prospects: The 2007 Revisions.* United Nations Department of Economic and Social Affairs, Population Division http://esa.un.org/unup/. For a concise overview of recent global trends, see Anonymous. 2008. "Cities and Growth: Lump Together and Like It." *The Economist* (November 6) http://www.economist.com/node/12552404 For a much more comprehensive historical perspective on the issue, see Paul Bairoch. 1988. *Cities and Economic Development: From the Dawn of History to the Present.* University of Chicago Press. A recent concise analytical discussion of the issue can be found in Mario Polèse. 2009. *The Wealth and Poverty of Regions. Why City Matters.* University of Chicago Press, chapter 5.

16. Jane Jacobs. 1969. *The Economy of Cities.* Random House, p. 7.

17. Plato. Around 360 BCE. *The Republic*, Book II http://classics.mit.edu/Plato/republic.3.ii.html.

18. For a popular history of these latter developments, see Susan Freidberg. 2009. *Fresh. A Perishable History.* Belknap Press (Harvard University Press). For a more concise discussion of these advances in the French context, see Pierre Desrochers and Hiroko Shimizu. 2010. *L'autosuffisance alimentaire n'est pas gage de développement durable.* Cahier de recherche de l'Institut économique Molinari http://www.institutmolinari.org/IMG/pdf/cahier1010_fr.pdf.

19. George Rogers Taylor. 1951. *The Transportation Revolution, 1815–1860 (Volume IV: The Economic History of the United States).* Harper Torchbooks, p. 160.

20. Oscar Diedrich von Engeln. 1920. "The World's Food Resources." *Geographical Journal* 9 (3): 174. For an introduction to the academic literature and debates on the subject along with further references, see, among others, C. Knick Harley. 1988. "Ocean Freight Rates and Productivity, 1740–1913: The Primacy of Mechanical Invention Reaffirmed." *Journal of Economic History* 48 (4): 851-876.

21. Stanley Jevons. 1905. *The Principles of Economics : A Fragment of a Treatise on the Industrial Mechanisms of Society and Other Papers*, MacMillan, p. 28 http://www.archive.org/details/principlesofecon00jevouoft .

22. Christian Wolmar. 2010. *Blood, Iron & Gold. How the Railroads Transformed the World.* PublicAffairs, p. 223.

23. In the middle of the 19th century, Parisian truck farmers worked between eighteen and twenty hours a day during the seven busiest months and between

fourteen and sixteen during the rest of the year. These long hours could be traced back to "normal" agricultural chores in light of the technologies of the time (for instance, controlling pests and weeds, irrigating crops and trucking produce to market and manure back to production grounds were much more labor intensive practices than they would later become), but also to the fact that because these producers were growing things in what was for most of the year an unsuitable climate, they made an extensive use of protective devices like cloches, cold frames and unheated greenhouses and had to ensure almost daily that plants would not overheat in the sun or freeze at night. For instance, because cloches and hotbeds could overheat on sunny days, growers would spend hours manually propping them open in the morning and closing them at night. See J. G. Moreau and J. J. Daverne. 1845. *Manuel pratique de la culture maraîchère de Paris*. V. Bouchard-Huzard, p. 84 http://books.google.ca/books?id=YclBAAAAIAAJ&source=gbs _navlinks_s.

24. For an introduction to the topic, see G. Stanhill. 1977. "An Urban Agro-Ecosystem. The Example of Nineteenth Century Paris." *Agro-Ecosystems* 3: 269–284.

25. J. G. Moreau and J. J. Daverne. 1845. *Manuel pratique de la culture maraîchère de Paris*. V. Bouchard-Huzard, p. 85 http://books.google.ca/books?id =YclBAAAAIAAJ&source=gbs_navlinks_s .

26. Avant l'introduction des cultures forcées dans les marais de Paris, la classe maraîchère... ne jouissait que d'une faible considération... aujourd'hui il n'en est plus ainsi » and « leur seule ambition... est de chercher les moyens d'arriver les premiers à porter des primeurs à la halle" J. G. Moreau and J. J. Daverne. 1845. *Manuel pratique de la culture maraîchère de Paris*. V. Bouchard-Huzard, pp. 85 and 83 http://books.google.ca/books?id=YclBAAAAIAAJ&source=gbs_navlinks_s.

27. Of course, these numbers are only rough estimates. See Alberto Zezza and Luca Tasciotti. 2010. "Urban Agriculture, Poverty and Food Security: Empirical Evidence from a Sample of Developing Countries." *Food Policy* 35 (4): 265-273.

28. Lorian P. Jefferson. 1926. "The Balance of Trade in Farm Products." *Journal of Farm Economics* 8 (4): 451–461, p. 451.

29. Edward Francis Adams and Louis Adalbert Clinton. 1899. *The Modern Farmer in his Business Relations: A study of some of the principles underlying the art of profitable farming and marketing, and of the interests of farmers as affected by modern social and economic conditions and forces.* N.J. Stone Company, p. 16 http://chla.library.cornell.edu/cgi/t/text/text-idx?c=chla;idno=2927196 .

30. The original quote is "la vapeur a supprimé les saisons" by Henri Hitier, 1901. "L'évolution de l'agriculture." *Annales de géographie* 10 (54): 385–400, p. 386 .

31. Jacques Redway, 1907. *Commercial Geography. A Book for High Schools, Commercial Courses, and Business Colleges*. Charles Scribner's Sons, pp. 1–2 http://www.gutenberg.org/files/24884/24884-h/24884-h.htm.

32. Susanne Freidberg. 2009. *Fresh. A Perishable History*. Belknap Press (Harvard University Press), p. 9.

33. Jacques W. Redway. 1923. *Geography. Commercial and Industrial*. Charles Scribner's Sons, pp. 82–83.

34. For a more detailed look at the issue, see Ndiame Diop and Steven M. Jaffee, 2005. "Fruits and Vegetables: Global Trade and Competition in Fresh and Processed Product Markets." In M. Ataman Aksoy and John C. Beghin (eds) *Global Agricultural Trade and Developing Countries*, World Bank, pp. 237–57. http://siteresources.worldbank.org/INTGAT/Resources/GATChapter13.pdf.

35. For a more detailed discussion of the issue, see Robert Tripp. 2002. *Seed Provision & Agricultural Development: The Institutions of Rural Change*. Overseas Development Institute; and Robert Tripp. 2003. "How to Cultivate a Commercial Seed Sector." Overseas Development Institute http://www.syngentafoundation.org/db/1/447.pdf.

36. Matt Ridley. 2010. *The Rational Optimist. How Prosperity Evolves*. Harper-Collins Publishers, p. 149.

37. For a detailed survey of these issues, see Indur M. Goklany. 2007. *The Improving State of the World*. Cato Institute. We will address health and safety concerns in more details in chapter 6. On food prices, suffice it to say that the average wheat price in the late 20th century was only 10% of the historical average in previous centuries. The same basket of agricultural goods bought in the United States in the early 21st century cost only about a third as much as it would have five decades earlier and in the United Kingdom about only one-thirteenth of what it would have cost 150 years earlier. On that last statistics, see BBC News UK. 2012. "Groceries 'Cheaper' Now than in 1862, *Grocer* Magazine Finds." (January 6) http://www.bbc.co.uk/news/business-16450526 .

38. David J. Spielman and Rajul Pandya-Lorch. 2009. *Millions Fed. Proven Success in Agricultural Development*. International Food Policy Research Institute. http://www.ifpri.org/book-5826/ourwork/programs/2020-vision-food-agriculture-and-environment/millions-fed-intiative .

39. Peter Garnsey. 1999. *Food and Society in Classical Antiquity*. Cambridge University Press, pp. 23–24.

40. See, among others, Kym Anderson. 2009. *Five Decades of Distortion to Agricultural Incentives*. Agricultural Distortion Working Paper No. 76. World Bank http://siteresources.worldbank.org/INTTRADERESEARCH/Resources/544824-1163022714097/Five_decades_of_distortions_0309rev.pdf.

41. Joseph Edward de Steiguer. 2006. *The Origins of Modern Environmental Thought*. University of Arizona Press, p. 6.

42. Basic information on these experiments can be found on the American Transcendentalism website http://www.vcu.edu/engweb/transcendentalism/index .html and on the Fruitlands Museum website http://www.fruitlands.org/. Louisa May Alcott's 1873 satire *Transcendental Wild Oats* is based on her family's experience at Fruitlands. It is available online in her collection of short stories *Silver Pitchers: and Independence* http://books.google.ca/books?id=-5m5obve7XUC&dq =transcendental+wild+oats&source=gbs_navlinks_s.

43. See Telfair Museum of Art. 2009. *Dutch Utopia: American Artists in Holland, 1880-1914*. University of Georgia Press.

44. For more details and additional references on this history, see "History of Urban Agriculture." *Sprouts in the Sidewalk* http://sidewalksprouts.wordpress .com/history/ A recent detailed case study of one such past experiment is Sarah Moore. 2006. "Forgotten Roots of the Green City: Subsistence Gardening in Columbus, Ohio, 1900-1940." *Urban Geography* 27 (2): 174–192.

45. USDA. War Era Food Posters from the Collection of the National Agricultural Library http://www.good-potato.com/beans_are_bullets/index.html .

46. Charles Lathrop Pack. 1917. "Urban and Suburban Food Production" *Annals of the American Academy of Political and Social Science* 74: 203–206, p. 203.

47. Charles Lathrop Pack. 1919. *The Victorious Garden*, National War Garden Commission, p. 1 http://books.google.ca/books?id=fLMo180ErtYC&dq=editions :x7pJ7CT6nigC&source=gbs_navlinks_s.

48. The Arthurdale Heritage website can be found at http://www.arthurdale heritage.org/. A recent book on this failed experiment is C. J. Maloney. 2011. *Back to the Land: Arthurdale, FDR's New Deal, and the Costs of Economic Planning*. Wiley.

49. Morriss Llewellyn Cooke. 1918. *Our Cities Awake. Notes on Municipal Activities and Administration*. Doubleday, Page & Company, p. 269 http:// www.archive.org/details/ourcitiesawakeno00cookrich.

50. Morriss Llewellyn Cooke. 1918. *Our Cities Awake. Notes on Municipal Activities and Administration*. Doubleday, Page & Company, p. 269 http://www .archive.org/details/ourcitiesawakeno00cookrich.

51. Anonymous. 1913. "Why Food is Dear. City Distribution Adds Usually 50 Per Cent. to Price Received by Farmers." *New York Times* (July 13) http:// query.nytimes.com/mem/archive-free/pdf?res=F40F13FB3E5B13738DDDA A0994DF405B838DF1D3.

52. Quoted by Joseph Russell Smith. 1919. *The World's Food Resources*. H. Holt & Company, p. 567 http://www.archive.org/details/worldsfoodresour00smituoft.

53. Quoted in Oscar Diedrich von Engeln. 1920. "The World's Food Resources." *Geographical Review* 9 (3): 170–190, pp. 185–186.

54. Michael Pollan. 2008. "Farmer in Chief." *New York Times Magazine* October 9 http://www.nytimes.com/2008/10/12/magazine/12policy-t.html.

55. Morriss Llewellyn Cooke. 1918. *Our Cities Awake. Notes on Municipal Activities and Administration*. Doubleday, Page & Company, pp. 269–270 http://www.archive.org/details/ourcitiesawakeno00cookrich.

56. Morriss Llewellyn Cooke. 1918. *Our Cities Awake. Notes on Municipal Activities and Administration*. Doubleday, Page & Company, p. 270 http://www.archive.org/details/ourcitiesawakeno00cookrich.

57. A. B. Ross. 1917. "The Point of Origin Plan for Marketing." *Annals of the American Academy of Political and Social Sciences* 74: 206–210, p. 206.

58. Idem, p. 207. The plan is also summarized in Joseph Russell Smith. 1919. *The World's Food Resources*. H. Holt & Company, pp. 567–571 http://www.archive.org/details/worldsfoodresour00smituoft.

59. Joseph Russell Smith. 1917. "Price Control Through Industrial Organization." *Annals of the American Academy of Political and Social Science* 74 (Special Thematic Issue: The World's Food): 280–287, p. 283.

60. Russell Smith, idem, pp. 285–286.

61. For a list of similar "local food" studies conducted in other locations between the First World War and the late 1920s, see Lorian P. Jefferson. 1926. "The Balance of Trade in Farm Products." *Journal of Farm Economics* 8 (4): 451–461 and Henry C. and Ann Dewees Taylor. 1952. *The Story of Agricultural Economics in the United States, 1840–1932*. Iowa State College Press. The context of such studies was a drastic decline in agricultural commodity prices in the 1920s.

62. See, among others, Michele VerPloeg et al. 2009. *Access to Affordable and Nutritious Food. Measuring and Understanding Food Deserts and Their Consequences*. United States Department of Agriculture http://www.ers.usda.gov/publications/ap/ap036/ap036.pdf.

63. We will discuss a few of these broader policies in chapter 5, but not the European equivalents of Victory Gardens, such as the "Dig for Victory" campaign in the United Kingdom. A recent book on the latter topic is Twigs Way and Mike Brown. 2010. *Digging for Victory: Gardens and Gardening in Wartime Britain*. Sabrestorm Publishing http://www.sabrestorm.com/digging.html .

64. Frederic Clemson Howe. 1915. *The Modern City and Its Problems*. Charles Scribner's Sons, pp. 5–6.

Chapter 2

1. Plato. Around 360 BCE. *The Republic*, Book II http://classics.mit.edu/Plato/republic.3.ii.html .

2. Frédéric Bastiat. 1862. « La peur d'un mot. » In *Oeuvres complètes, Tome Deuxième*, Guillemin, p. 397.

3. Thomas Hardy. 1891. *Tess of the d'Urbervilles: A Pure Woman Faithfully Presented* http://www.gutenberg.org/files/110/110-h/110-h.htm.

4. Ray Hughes Whitbeck. 1924. *Industrial Geography. Production, Manufacture, Commerce.* American Book Company, pp. 12–13.

5. Frédéric Bastiat. 1848. "What is Seen and What is Not Seen." In *Selected Essays on Political Economy* (nonpaginated) http://www.econlib.org/library /Bastiat/basEss1.html#Chapter%201,%20What%20Is%20Seen%20and%20 What%20Is%20Not%20Seen.

6. Thomas Robert Malthus. 1800. *An Investigation of the Cause of the Present High Price of Provisions.* Davis, Taylor, and Wilks. Nonpaginated version available at http://socserv.mcmaster.ca/econ/ugcm/3ll3/malthus/highpric.txt .

7. Jill Richardson. 2010. "Locavore Lessons for Curmudgeons." *Grist* (August 22) http://www.grist.org/article/food-fight-do-locavores-really-need-math -lessons/P4.

8. To give of sense of how much still needs to be accomplished though, according to a USDA report, direct sale to consumers, like farmers markets, only accounted for 0.4 percent of total agricultural sales in 2007 (excluding nonedible products only brought the total up to 0.8 percent). See Steve Martinez, Michael Hand, Michelle Da Pra, Susan Pollack, Katherine Ralston, Travis Smith, Stephen Vogel, Shellye Clark, Luanne Lohr, Sarah Low and Constance Newman. 2010. *Local Food Systems: Concepts, Impacts, and Issues.* Economic Research Report #97. United States Department of Agriculture (USDA) Economic Research Service http://www.ers.usda.gov/Publications/ERR97/ERR97 .pdf .

9. The issue is obviously trickier for processed products depending on the various rules of origins regulating them. For instance, "Canadian" pickled products are often grown in other countries, but if enough processing activities take place in Canada, they can earn a national designation.

10. Joseph Russell Smith. 1917. "Price Control through Industrial Organization." *Annals of the American Academy of Political and Social Science* 74 (The World's Food): 280–287, p. 285.

11. Joseph Russell Smith. 1917. "Price Control through Industrial Organization." *Annals of the American Academy of Political and Social Science* 74 (The World's Food): 280–287, p. 285.

12. USDA grading services http://www.ams.usda.gov/AMSv1.0/Grading and food standards http://www.ams.usda.gov/AMSv1.0/standards can be found on the agency's website.

13. John M. McKee. 1925. "The Relation of Local Farm Output to the Local Product." *Annals of the American Academy of Political and Social Science* 117: 278–284, p. 282.

14. Idem, p. 284.

15. For a recent discussion of the issue, see Bee Wilson. 2008. *Swindled: The Dark History of Food Fraud, from Poisoned Candy to Counterfeit Coffee.* Princeton University Press. For a more ancient and concise source, see « Adulteration. » 1911. *Encyclopedia Britannica* http://en.wikisource.org/wiki/1911_Encyclop %C3%A6dia_Britannica/Adulteration. For a concise history of food adulteration in the United States, along with regulatory attempts to address the problem, see Marc T. Law. 2010. "History of Food and Drug Regulation in the United States." In Robert Whaples (ed.) *EH.Net Encyclopedia* http://eh.net /encyclopedia/article/Law.Food.and.Drug.Regulation.

16. Friedrich Christian A. Accum. 1820. *A Treatise on Adulterations of Foods, and Culinary Poisons*, Longman, Hurst, Rees, Orme, and Brown http://books .google.ca/books?id=YWAUAAAAQAAJ&hl=fr&source=gbs_navlinks_s.

17. Quoted in Bertie Mandelblatt. 2007. "A Transatlantic Commodity: Irish Salt Beef in the French Atlantic World." *History Workshop Journal* 63 (1): 18–47, p. 29.

18. Adulteration. 1911. *Encyclopedia Britannica* http://en.wikisource.org/wiki /1911_Encyclop%C3%A6dia_Britannica/Adulteration.

19. See, among others, Lauren Etter. 2010. "Food for Thought: Do you Need Farmers for a Farmers Market?" *Wall Street Journal* (April 29) http://online .wsj.com/article/SB10001424052748703404004575198270918567074.html# articleTabs%3Darticle.

20. Colleen Vanderlinden. 2010. "Scammers at the Farmers' Market: How to Make Sure You're Supporting Local Farmers. Be educated, be vigilant, know what's in Season!" *PlanetGreen.com* (September 29) http://planetgreen.discovery .com/food-health/scammers-at-the-farmers-market—-and-how-to-make-sure -youre-supporting-local-farmers.html.

21. Linda Crago. "Growing Food in Niagara—How Things Change in 14 Years. Part 3: Local and Organic." *Tree and Twig Farm Blog* (April 17) http://tree-andtwigheirlooms.blogspot.com/2011/04/growing-food-in-niagara-how-things_17.html; See also Mischa Popoff. 2011. "Beware of Organic Crusaders." *The National Post*, March 11 http://fullcomment.nationalpost.com/2011/04 /11/mischa-popoff-beware-of-organic-crusaders/.

22. US House of Representatives. 2009. "Statement of Joel Salatin (April 17, 2008)." *After the Beef Recall: Exploring Greater Transparency in the Meat Industry.* Hearing before the Subcommittee on Domestic Policy of the Committee on Oversight and Government Reform http://www.gpo.gov/fdsys/pkg/CHRG -110hhrg51700/html/CHRG-110hhrg51700.htm.

23. Russ Parsons. 2008. "Food Fight Grows over the Cream of the Crop." *Los Angeles Times* (March 9) http://articles.latimes.com/2008/mar/09/local/me -market9.

24. Some farm-to-institution programs (such as farm-to-school http:// www.farmtoschool.org/) also operate on the same model and can be subjected to the same kind of criticism we raise for CSA initiatives.

25. Patti Ghezzi. 2009. "The Tasty Advantages of Community Supported Agriculture." *Divine Caroline* http://www.divinecaroline.com/22145/70730 -tasty-advantages-community-supported-agriculture.

26. Lynda Altman. 2001. "Pros and Cons of Community Supported Agriculture. CSAs are not for everyone" Associate Content from Yahoo.com (February 15) http://www.associatedcontent.com/article/7734092/pros_and_cons_of _consumer_supported.html?cat=6 .

27. Adapted from the Tucson Community Supported Agriculture initiative website http://www.tucsoncsa.org/about/why-you-should-join/.

28. Gary Blumenthal. 2011. "Creating False Markets." *World Perspectives, Inc.* (February), p. 1.

29. One estimate of the number of different physical products marked by a barcode in the greater New York City area is 10 billion. True, many of these are supplied by small businesses that cater to narrower niches, but the diversity and affordability of products offered by large supermarket chains and "Big Box" retail stores has become truly astounding, even by recent historical standards.

30. For a more detailed examination of this claim that isn't limited to food offerings, see Tyler Cowen. 2002. *Creative Destruction: How Globalization Is Changing the World's Cultures.* Princeton University Press.

31. For a more detailed discussion of the issue, see Susan Fleiss Lowenstein. 1965. "Urban Images of Roman Authors." *Comparative Studies in Society and History* 8 (1): 110–123.

32. Virgil. 37 BCE. *The Eclogues* http://classics.mit.edu/Virgil/eclogue.html.

33. Horace. Approx. 35 BCE. *Satires*, Book 2, Satire VI: The Country Mouse and the Town Mouse. http://www.poetryintranslation.com/PITBR/Latin/Horace SatiresBkIISatVI.htm#_Toc98155109 and Horace. 14 BCE *Epistles*, Book 2, Part 2: An Answer to Florus' Complaints http://www.poetryintranslation .com/PITBR/Latin/HoraceEpistlesBkIIEpII.htm.

34. For a more detailed treatment of the romantic and aristocratic roots of environmentalism in the English-speaking world, see Donald Gibson. 2002. *Environmentalism: Ideology and Power.* Nova Publishers.

35. Rob Harris. 2007. "Let's Ditch this 'Nostalgia for Mud,' *Spiked* (December 4) http://www.spiked-online.com/index.php?/site/article/4144.

36. Genesis 3: 17–19.

37. Henry David Thoreau. 1854. *Walden, or Life in the Woods* http://books
.google.ca/books?id=pbElaJ5zROUC&dq=thoreau+walden&source=gbs_nav
links_s.

38. Karl Kautsky. 1899 (1988). *The Agrarian Question in Two Volumes*. Zwan
Publications, p. 218. Kautsky further observed that the individuals most likely to
leave the countryside were "propertyless labourers, and of these the unmarried"
and that it was "not simply the physically strongest, but also the most energetic
and intelligent" that migrated (p. 224).

39. Mario Polèse. 2009. *The Wealth and Poverty of Regions. Why Cities Matter*.
University of Chicago Press, p. 139. See also Edward Glaeser. 2011. *Triumph of
the City. How our Greatest Invention Makes Us Richer, Smarter, Greener, Healthier,
and Happier*. Penguin Press, p. 7.

40. Mario Polèse. 2009. *The Wealth and Poverty of Regions. Why City Matters*.
University of Chicago Press, p. 140.

41. Edward Glaeser. 2011. *Triumph of the City. How our Greatest Invention
Makes Us Richer, Smarter, Greener, Healthier, and Happier*. Penguin Press, p. 70.

42. Ben Worthen. 2010. "A Dozen Eggs for $8? Michael Pollan Explains the
Math of Buying Local." *Wall Street Journal* (August 5) http://online.wsj.com
/article/SB10001424052748704271804575405521469248574.html For another
acknowledgement of this fact by an organic food supporter, see Jeffrey Kluger.
2010. "What's so Great about Organic Food?" *Time* (August 25) http://www
.time.com/time/specials/packages/article/0,28804,2011756_2011730_2011720,00
.html.

43. Gary Blumenthal. 2008. "Hand Building Automobiles (Food)." *World Perspectives, Inc.* (May), p. 2.

44. USDA website. *Food CPI, Prices and Expenditures: Expenditures on Food, by
Selected Countries* (various tables) http://www.ers.usda.gov/Briefing/CPIFood
AndExpenditures/.

Chapter 3

1. Quoted in Kaori O'Connor. 2009. "The King's Christmas Pudding: Globalization, Recipes and the Commodities of Empire." *Journal of Global History* 4 (1):
127–155, p. 143. The [British] Empire Marketing Board's (1926–1933) mission
was to encourage "local" Empire shopping campaigns. A collection of posters produced by this organization is available on the website of the Manchester Art
Gallery at http://www.manchestergalleries.org/the-collections/revealing-histories
/propaganda-pride-and-prejudice-posters-from-the-empire-marketing-board/.

2. Interview with Michael Pollan. 2008. *Bill Moyers Journal*. (November 28)
http://www.pbs.org/moyers/journal/11282008/transcript1.html.

3. Michael Pollan. 2008. "Farmer in Chief." *New York Times Magazine* (October 9) http://www.nytimes.com/2008/10/12/magazine/12policy-t.html.

4. Leah Bloom. 2010. "Comment on Steven Landsburg's 'Loco-Vores'." *The Big Questions* (August 23) http://www.thebigquestions.com/2010/08/23/loco-vores/.

5. Frédéric Bastiat. 1848. "What Is Seen and What Is Not Seen." In *Selected Essays on Political Economy* (nonpaginated) http://www.econlib.org/library/Bastiat/basEss1.html#Chapter%201,%20What%20Is%20Seen%20and%20What%20Is%20Not%20Seen.

6. Center for Consumer Freedom. 2009. "Come On Down to the Farmers Market (Bring Your Wallet and Your Food Orthodoxy), (September 17) http://www.consumerfreedom.com/news_detail.cfm/h/3992-come-on-down-to-the-farmers-market-bring-your-wallet-and-your-food-orthodoxy.

7. Alisa Smith and J.B. MacKinnon. 2005. "Living on the 100-mile Diet," *The Tyee* (June 28) http://thetyee.ca/Life/2005/06/28/HundredMileDiet and Alisa Smith and J.B. MacKinnon. 2007. *The 100-Mile Diet. A Year of Local Eating*. Random House Canada.

8. Adam Smith. 1776. *An Inquiry Into the Nature and Causes of the Wealth of Nations*, Vol. 1, Book IV, chapter II: Of Restraints upon the Importation from Foreign Countries of Such Goods as Can Be Produced at Home http://oll.libertyfund.org/?option=com_staticxt&staticfile=show.php%3Ftitle=237&chapter=212328&layout=html&Itemid=27.

9. See, among others, Tom Philpott. 2011. "Freakonomics Blog: Still Wrong on Local Food." *MotherJones.com* (November 18) http://motherjones.com/tom-philpott/2011/11/freakonomics-blog-still-wrong-local-food.

10. See Peter Garnsey. 1988. *Famine and Food Supply in the Graeco-Roman World: Responses to Risk and Crisis*. Cambridge University Press, pp. 54–55.

11. Michael Pollan. 2008. "Farmer in Chief." *New York Times Magazine* (October 9) http://www.nytimes.com/2008/10/12/magazine/12policy-t.html.

12. See, among others, Laura Miller. 2002. "Duck Power and a Tale of Success: From Six Acres to an Ecosystem." *Leopold Letter* (Spring). Leopold Center for Sustainable Agriculture. http://www.leopold.iastate.edu/news/leopold-letter/2002/spring/duck-power-and-tale-success-six-acres-ecosystem.

13. For a more detailed introduction to the topic, see the FAO webpages devoted to the topic at http://www.fao.org/sard/en/sard/754/946/index.html.

14. FAO. 2002. "Spotlight: Agricultural Heritage System." *FAO Magazine* (November) http://www.fao.org/ag/magazine/0211sp1.htm.

15. Peter Garnsey. 1988. *Famine and Food Supply in the Graeco-Roman World: Responses to Risk and Crisis*. Cambridge University Press, p. 49.

16. Paul Roberts. 2009. "Spoiled: Organic and Local Is so 2008: Our Industrial Food System Is Rotten to the Core. Heirloom Arugula Won't Save Us. Here's What Will." *Mother Jones* (March/April) http://motherjones.com/environment /2009/02/spoiled-organic-and-local-so-2008.

17. Idem.

18. Barbara Kingsolver (with Steven L. Hopp and Camille Kingsolver). 2007. *Animal, Vegetable, Miracle: A Year of Local Food.* HarperCollins, p. 3.

19. Blake McKelvey. 1940. "The Flower City: Center of Nurseries and Fruit Orchards." *The Rochester Historical Society Publications* 18: 121–169. Nonpaginated version available at http://www.history.rochester.edu/flowercity/frontier.htm.

20. George Richardson Porter. 1838. *The Progress of the Nation, in Its Various Social and Economical Relations from the Beginning of the Nineteenth Century to the Present Time: Sections III and IV: Interchange, and Revenue and Expenditure.* Charles Knight & Co., pp. 82-83 http://books.google.ca/books?id=908KAQAA MAAJ&source=gbs_navlinks_s.

21. Idem, p. 83.

22. John Page. 1880. "The Sources of Supply of the Manchester Fruit and Vegetable Markets." *Journal of the Royal Agricultural Society of England* 16 (2nd series), pp. 477-480 http://books.google.ca/books?id=epoEAAAAYAAJ&source =gbs_navlinks_s.

23. See, among others, G. Ronald White. 1932. "Live-Stock By-Products and By-Product Industries." *Journal of the Royal Statistical Society* 95 (3): 455–497, p. 466.

24. Barry Estabrook. 2011. "The Santa Barbara Syndrome: Evidence of a Broken Food System." *The Atlantic* (February 14) http://www.theatlantic.com/life /archive/2011/02/the-santa-barbara-syndrome-evidence-of-a-broken-food -system/71244/ .

25. David A. Cleveland, Corie N. Radka, Nora M. Müller, Tyler D. Watson, Nicole J. Rekstein, Hannah Van M. Wright, and Sydney E. Hollingshead. 2011. "Effect of Localizing Fruit and Vegetable Consumption on Greenhouse Gas Emissions and Nutrition, Santa Barbara County." *Environmental Science & Technology* (45): 4555–4562.

26. The meat-packing industry got its name from the practice of early settlers of curing, smoking and packing pork domestically, a practice that was later commercialized. Other past cases of external economies of scale are discussed in Pierre Desrochers and Samuli Leppälä. 2010. "Industrial Symbiosis: Old Wine in Recycled Bottles? Some Perspective from the History of Economic and Geographical Thought." *International Regional Science Review* 33 (3): 338–361.

27. As we further discuss in chapter 6, criticisms of the sanitary character of American meatpacking operations predated by at least three decades the

publication of Sinclair's fictional work. Besides, in his novel Sinclair also described (or rather indicted) the government inspectors who were already working on the premises at the turn of the twentieth century.

28. George Powell Perry. 1908. *Wealth from Waste, or Gathering Up the Fragments.* Fleming H. Revell Company, pp. 74–75.

29. There were also a number of "long drives," some of which came to be immortalized in famous Western movies, but many of these took place after the conclusion of the Civil War and ended up at a railroad terminal. Apart from its economic benefit, shipping cattle by rail also add the advantage of avoiding damages to farmland located between the pastureland and the slaughterhouses.

30. In business jargon, "forward integration" refers to a business strategy whereby activities are expanded to include control of the direct distribution of a firm's own products while "backward integration" involves the purchase of suppliers in order to reduce dependency.

31. David Ames Well. 1889. *Recent Economic Changes and their Effect on the Production and Distribution of Wealth and the Well-Being of Society.* D. Appleton and Company, p. 98 http://books.google.ca/books?id=LG2oz49UcykC&dq =Recent+Economic+Changes&source=gbs_navlinks_s An independent restatement of this position several decades later can be found in John Ise. 1950. *Economics*, revised edition. Harper & Brothers, p. 111.

32. Rudolf A. Clemen. 1927. *By-Products in the Packing Industry.* University of Chicago Press, pp. 2-3, 27 http://chla.library.cornell.edu/cgi/t/text/text-idx?c =chla;idno=3081287 .

33. William Cronon. 1991. *Nature's Metropolis: Chicago and the Great West.* W. W. Norton, p. 242.

34. See, among others, Janet Blackman. 1963. "The Food Supply of an Industrial Town: A Study of Sheffield's Public Markets, 1780–1900. *Business History* 5: 83–97, p. 89; Robert Scola. 1992. *Feeding the Victorian City.* Manchester University Press, Chapter IV: Dairy Products.

35. Donald Boudreaux and Thomas J. DiLorenzo. 1993. 'The Protectionist Roots of Antitrust,' *Review of Austrian Economics* 6(2): 81–96.

36. Fred A. Shannon. 1963. *The Economic History of the United States, Volume V: The Farmer's Last Frontier. Agriculture, 1860-1897.* Holt, Rinehart and Winston, p. 235.

37. For a concise overview of the validity of American agricultural producers' complaints against packers and railroad operators, see James Stewart. 2008. "The Economics of American Farm Unrest, 1865-1900". In Robert Whaples (ed.) *EH.Net Encyclopedia* http://eh.net/encyclopedia/article/stewart .farmers.

38. The Editors. 2010. "Making it Easier to Eat Local Food." *New York Times* (April 19) http://roomfordebate.blogs.nytimes.com/2010/04/19/making-it-easier -to-eat-local-food/.

39. Katie Zezima. 2010. "Push to Eat Local Food is Hampered by Shortage." *New York Times* (March 27) http://www.nytimes.com/2010/03/28/us/28slaughter .html?pagewanted=1&ref=style.

40. Michael Pollan. 2008. "Farmer in Chief." *New York Times Magazine* (October 9) http://www.nytimes.com/2008/10/12/magazine/12policy-t.html.

41. Steve Landsburg. 2010. "Loco-Vores." *The Big Questions* (August 23) http://www.thebigquestions.com/2010/08/23/loco-vores/; See also Steve Landsburg. 2011. "D'Oh—Second in a Series." *The Big Questions* (May 2) http://www .thebigquestions.com/2011/05/02/doh-second-in-a-series/.

42. American Farmland Trust. *Growing Local: Sustaining Farms and Farmland for the Future* http://www.farmland.org/programs/localfood/planningfor agriculture/Sustaining-Farms-Farmland-Future.asp.

43. For a more detailed presentation of his own work, see Despommiers's website at http://www.verticalfarm.com/ and Dickson Despommiers. 2011. "Vertical Farming." In Cutler J. Cleveland (editor). *Encyclopedia of the Earth* http://www.eoearth.org/article/Vertical_farming.

44. D.V Marino, Tilak Ram Mahato, John W. Druitt, Linda Leigh, Guanghui Lin, Robert M. Russell and Francesco N. Tubiello. 1999. "The Agricultural Biome of Biosphere 2: Structure, Composition and Function." *Ecological Engineering* 13: 199-234. To be fair, the designers of such schemes are more nuanced on this issue than their supporters. For instance, in his encyclopedia entry on vertical farming (ff 209), Despommier writes that his scheme promises to "eliminate external natural processes as confounding elements in the production of food," but he only claims that his proposal "reduces the risk of infection from agents transmitted at the agricultural interface," not that it would be pesticide-free. In other words, his proposal would deliver no additional benefits over conventional greenhouses.

45. For a concise description of the project, see Marc Lostracco. 2007. "Grow Up." *Torontoist.com* (June 15) http://torontoist.com/2007/06/is_toronto_a_fu.php.

46. Dennis Avery. 2010. "City Farming—Pigs in the Sky" *Center for Global Food Issues* (October 19) http://www.cgfi.org/2010/10/city-farming%e2%80% 94pigs-in-the-sky-by-dennis-t-avery/.

47. We discuss the issue in more detail in chapter 4.

48. The issue is particularly significant in the Greater Toronto area because of a massive 1.8 million "Green Belt" initiative on prime farmland, an area larger than Prince Edward Island. The case for it and descriptions of local food initiatives to support local producers can be found on the Friends of the Greenbelt's http:// www.greenbelt.ca/ and the Ontario Greenbelt Alliance's http://www.greenbelt

alliance.ca/ websites. The policy enjoyed much support from urban dwellers (who were not asked to pay for it) and environmentalist groups. The opposition was spearheaded by farmers whose property rights, most notably their ability to sell their land for development, were curtailed without fair and proper compensation. For a critical academic study of this particular policy, see B. James Deaton and Richard J. Vyn. 2010. "The Effect of Strict Land Zoning on Agricultural Land Values: The Case of Ontario's Green Belt." *American Journal of Agricultural Economics* 92 (4): 941–955.

49. Holly Hill. 2008. *Food Miles: Background and Marketing*. ATTRA—National Sustainable Agriculture Information Service, p. 9 http://attra.ncat.org /attra-pub/PDF/foodmiles.pdf.

50. Michael Pollan. 2008. "Farmer in Chief." *New York Times Magazine* (October 9) http://www.nytimes.com/2008/10/12/magazine/12policy-t.html.

51. Gove Hambidge. 1929. "This Age of Refrigeration." *Ladies' Home Journal* (August): 103.

52. Mario Polèse. 2009. *The Wealth and Poverty of Nations. Why Cities Matter*. University of Chicago Press, p. 134.

53. Rob Lyons. 2010. "The Tarantino of Food Writing." *Spiked* (September 3) http://www.spiked-online.com/index.php/site/article/9485/.

54. Jacques Redway. 1907. *Commercial Geography. A Book for High Schools, Commercial Courses, and Business Colleges*. Charles Scribner's Sons, p. 5. http:// www.gutenberg.org/files/24884/24884-h/24884-h.htm.

55. Bloomberg News. 2011. "China's Soybean Imports in 2011 May Decline, Shanghai JC Says." *Bloomberg.com* (November 24) http://www.bloomberg.com /news/2011-11-24/china-s-soybean-imports-in-2011-may-decline-shanghai-jc -says.html In 2010, the USA, Brazil, Argentina and China produced respectively 35, 27, 19 and 6% of the world's total production ("World Statistics" at soy stats.com http://www.soystats.com/2011/Default-frames.htm).

56. Quoted in Alan L. Olmstead and Paul W. Rhode. 2008. *Creating Abundance. Biological Innovation and American Agricultural Development*. Cambridge University Press, p. 381.

57. Adam Smith. 1776. *An Inquiry Into the Nature and Causes of the Wealth of Nations*, Vol. 1, Book I, chapter 8: On the Wages of Labour http://oll.libertyfund .org/?option=com_staticxt&staticfile=show.php%3Ftitle=220&chapter=217399 &layout=html&Itemid=27.

Chapter 4

1. See, among others, Dennis E. Jelinski. 2005. "There is no Mother Nature—There is no Balance of Nature: Culture, Ecology and Conservation." *Human Ecology* 33 (2): 271–288.

2. The ancestors of today's large African animals who had co-evolved with them, on the other hand, had long learned to be more careful around these seemingly puny creatures. Animals such as cats, rats and pigs whose arrival was directly linked to that of humans also proved significant in the disappearance of bird species in island environments.

3. In Australia, this practice has been labeled "firestick farming."

4. For a more elaborate discussions of these issues, see Michael Williams. 2003. *Deforesting the Earth. From Prehistory to Global Crisis*. University of Chicago Press. See also Erle C. Ellis. 2011. "Anthropogenic Transformation of the Terrestrial Biosphere." *Proceedings of the Royal Society A: Mathematical, Physical and Engineering Science* 369 (1938): 1010–1035.

5. Knut Faegri. 1988. "Preface." In Hilary H. Birks, H. J. Birks, Peter Emil Kaland and Dagfinn Moe (eds). *The Cultural Landscape. Past Present and Future*. Cambridge University Press, pp. 1–2.

6. For a popular treatment of the issue, see Charles C. Mann. 2002. "1491." *The Atlantic* (March) http://www.theatlantic.com/magazine/archive/2002/03/1491/2445/ and his book of the same title, Charles C. Mann. 2005. *1491*. Alfred A. Knopf http://www.charlesmann.org/Book-index.htm. For a relatively accessible survey of the academic literature, see Michael Heckenberger and Eduardo Góes Neves. 2009. "Amazonian Archeology." *Annual Review of Anthropology* 38 (October): 251-266 http://www.annualreviews.org/doi/abs/10.1146/annurev-anthro-091908-164310?prevSearch=%28amazon%29+AND+[journal%3A+anthro]&searchHistoryKey.

7. A vascular plant possesses a well-developed system of conducting tissue to transport mineral salts, water, and sugars.

8. Ronald Bailey. 2010. "Invasion of the Invasive Species! Local Biodiversity is Increasing because of Man, Not Despite Him." *Reason* (November) http://reason.com/archives/2010/09/19/invasion-of-the-invasive-speci.

9. Mark Davis et al. 2011. "Don't Judge Species by their Origins." *Nature* 474 (7350): 153–154.

10. Paul J. Heald and Susannah Chapman. 2011. *Veggie Tales: Pernicious Myths About Patents, Innovation, and Crop Diversity In The Twentieth Century*. Illinois Program in Law, Behavior and Social Science Paper No. LBSS11-34 http://papers.ssrn.com/sol3/papers.cfm?abstract_id=1928920.

11. Mark Davis et al. 2011. "Don't Judge Species by their Origins." *Nature* 474: 153–154.

12. Nina V. Fedoroff and Nancy Marie Brown. 2004. *Mendel in the Kitchen: A Scientist's View of Genetically Modified Foods*, Joseph Henry Press, p. 315.

13. While the debate between proponents of less productive but more diverse agricultural production systems and defenders of large-scale monocultures is

long-standing, our reading of the available evidence suggests that it was won by the latter group. See Pamela Matson and Peter Vitousek, 2006. "Agricultural Intensification: Will Land Spared from Farming Be Land Spared for Nature?" *Conservation Biology* 20 (3): 709–710.

14. For more detailed discussions of these issues and additional references, see Paul E. Waggoner. 1996. "How Much Land Can Ten Billion People Spare for Nature?" *Daedalus* 125 (3): 73-93; and Pierre Desrochers. 2010. "The Environmental Responsibility of Business is to Increase its Profits (By Creating Value within the Bounds of Private Property Rights)" *Industrial and Corporate Change* 19 (1): 161-204.

15. Plato. 360 BCE. *Critias* (translated by Benjamin Jowett) http://classics .mit.edu/Plato/critias.html .

16. See Michael Williams. 2003. *Deforesting the Earth. From Prehistory to Global Crisis.* University of Chicago Press, p. 96.

17. G. V. Jacks and R. O. Whyte. 1939. *The Rape of the Earth. A World Survey of Soil Erosion.* Faber and Faber Ltd. The title of the American edition was the more prudish *Vanishing Lands: A World Survey of Soil Erosion.* The notion of the Earth (a female entity) being raped by industry (a male entity) is now a mainstay of so-called ecofeminism.

18. G. V. Jacks and R. O. Whyte. 1939. *The Rape of the Earth. A World Survey of Soil Erosion.* Faber and Faber Ltd, p. 21.

19. G. V. Jacks and R. O. Whyte. 1939. *The Rape of the Earth. A World Survey of Soil Erosion.* Faber and Faber Ltd, p. 26.

20. Dennis Avery. 2000. *Saving the Planet with Pesticides and Plastics.* Hudson Institute, pp. 7 and 201–202.

21. Several 19th and early 20th-century French writers who made such comments are discussed in Pierre Desrochers and Hiroko Shimizu. 2010. *L'autosuffisance alimentaire n'est pas gage de développement durable.* Cahier de recherche de l'Institut économique Molinari http://www.institutmolinari.org/IMG/pdf /cahier1010_fr.pdf.

22. Karl Kautsky. 1899 (1988). *The Agrarian Question in Two Volumes.* Zwan Publications, p. 254.

23. A. Y. Hoekstra (ed.). 2003. "Virtual Water Trade: Proceedings of the International Expert Meeting on Virtual Water Trade." Value of Water Research Report Series No.12, UNESCO-IHE http://www.waterfootprint.org/Reports /Report12.pdf.

24. Michael Williams. 2003. *Deforesting the Earth: From Prehistory to Global Crisis.* University of Chicago Press.

25. Pekka E. Kauppi, Jesse H. Ausubel, Jingyun Fang, Alexander S. Mather, Roger A. Sedjo and Paul E. Waggoner. (2006). 'Returning Forests Analyzed with

the Forest Identity', *Proceedings of the National Academy of Sciences* 103 (46): 17574-17579 http://www.pnas.org/content/103/46/17574.full.pdf+html The term *forest transition* as used in this essay is based on the Scottish geographer Alexander Mather's concept of a reversal or turnaround in land-use trends for a given territory from net deforestation to net reforestation in times of economic and population growth. As such, it differs from the notion of forest transition commonly used by landscape biologists and physical geographers that describes landscape changes between different ecosystems such as grassland or tundra and forest.

26. In places with stable or growing populations and little ability to import forest products, continued declines in forest cover spur increases in prices of forest products, causing landowners to plant trees instead of crops or pasture grasses. Significant erosion problems and disastrous floods in deforested watersheds have also motivated government officials in developing countries to implement reforestation programs.

27. For more detailed discussions of these issues and additional references, see Paul E. Waggoner. 1996. "How Much Land Can Ten Billion People Spare for Nature?" *Daedalus* 125 (3): 73–93; Indur M. Goklany. 2007. *The Improving State of the World*. Cato Institute; Pierre Desrochers. 2010. "The Environmental Responsibility of Business is to Increase its Profits (By Creating Value within the Bounds of Private Property Rights)"*Industrial and Corporate Change* 19 (1): 161–204; and Pierre Desrochers. 2008. "Bringing Inter-Regional Linkages Back In: Industrial Symbiosis, International Trade and the Emergence of the Synthetic Dyes Industry in the Late 19th Century."*Progress in Industrial Ecology* 5 (5–6): 465–481.

28. For a broad and accessible introduction to the purpose, scope and limits of LCA, see, among others, the webpage of the US Environmental Protection Agency on this research methodology at http://www.epa.gov/nrmrl/lcaccess/. We reviewed this literature in more detail in Pierre Desrochers and Hiroko Shimizu. 2008. *Yes, We have no Bananas. A Critique of the 'Food Miles' Perspective*.Mercatus Policy Series Primer no. 8, Mercatus Center (George Mason University) http://mercatus.org/publication/yes-we-have-no-bananas-critique-food -miles-perspective?id=24612.

29. Caroline Saunders and Peter Hayes. 2007. *Air Freight Transport of Fresh Fruit and Vegetables– Report for the International Trade Centre (ITC), Geneva, Switzerland*. Research Report No. 299. New Zealand: AERU, Lincoln University) http://researcharchive.lincoln.ac.nz/dspace/bitstream/10182/248/1/aeru_rr _299.pdf.

30. DEFRA. 2005. *Validity of Food Miles as an Indicator of Sustainable Development*, ED50254 Issue 7 (July) http://www.defra.gov.uk.

31. Christopher L. Weber and H. Scott Matthews. 2008. "Food Miles and the Relative Climate Impacts of Food Choices in the United States," *Environmental Science & Technology* 42 (10): 3508-3513.

32. DEFRA. 2005 *Validity of Food Miles as an Indicator of Sustainable Development*, ED50254 Issue 7(July). http://www.defra.gov.uk. A ton is a metric measurement of 1000 kilograms (kg), where 1 kg. = 2.2 lbs.

33. Caroline Saunders, Andrew Barber, and Greg Taylor. 2006. *Food miles—Comparative Energy/Emissions Performance of New Zealand's Agriculture Industry*. Research Report No.285, New Zealand: AERU, Lincoln University http://www.lincoln.ac.nz/documents/2328_rr285_s13389.pdf Apples and similar fruits are frequently kept in storage with higher than normal CO2 concentrations. Temperature control involves either maintaining lower than ambient temperatures to inhibit spoilage or maintaining higher than ambient temperatures to prevent freezing, depending on the location.

34. LlorençMilà i Canals, Sarah J. Cowell, Sarah Sim, and Lauren Basson. 2007. "Comparing Domestic versus Imported Apples: A Focus on Energy Use," *Environmental Science and Pollution Research* 14 (5): 338-344.

35. Jenny Gustavson; Christel Cederberg, Ulf Sonesson, Robert van Otterdijk, Robert and Alexandre Meybeck. 2011. *Global Food Losses and Food Waste*. FAO. The number is based on 2007 data. http://www.fao.org/fileadmin/user_upload /ags/publications/GFL_web.pdf. See also Amanda D. Cuéllar and Michael E. Webber. 2010. "Wasted Food, Wasted Energy: The Embedded Energy in Food Waste in the United States." *Environmental Science & Technology* 44 (6): 6464–6469. For recent discussions of these issues, see H. Charles J. Godfray et al. 2010. "The Future of the Global Food System." *Philosophical Transactions of the Royal Society B* 365 (3554): 2769–2777 http://rstb.royalsocietypublishing.org/content /365/1554/2769.abstract; John D. Floros et al. 2010. "Feeding the World Today and Tomorrow: The Importance of Food Science and Technology." *Comprehensive Reviews in Food Science and Technology* 9 (5): 572–599 http://onlinelibrary .wiley.com/doi/10.1111/j.1541-4337.2010.00127.x/abstract.

36. Lorrayne Ventour. 2008. "The Food We Waste" WRAP http://wrap.s3 .amazonaws.com/the-food-we-waste.pdf See also Tara Garnett. 2006. "*Fruit and Vegetables & UK Greenhouse Gas Emissions: Exploring the Relationship.*" FCRN Working paper 06-01, rev. A, Food Climate Research Network http://www.fcrn .org.uk/sites/default/files/fruitveg_paper_final.pdf.

37. Kenneth Marsh and Betty Bugusu. 2007. "Food Packaging: Roles, Materials and Environmental Issues." *Journal of Food Science* 72 (3): R39–R55 http:// www.ift.org/knowledge-center/read-ift-publications/science-reports/scientific -status-summaries/~/media/Knowledge%20Center/Science%20Reports/Scientific %20Status%20Summaries/FoodPackagingEnviron_0407.pdf.

38. Quoted in Paul Monaghan. 2008. "Why the Co-Op Is Wary of Food Miles Labeling." *The Guardian* (Green Living Blog) April 24 http://www .guardian.co.uk/environment/ethicallivingblog/2008/apr/24/soilassociation-vcoop?INTCMP=ILCNETTXT3487 .

39. For a more detailed discussion of this issue, see Kelly Rae Chi, James Mc-Gregor and Richard King. 2009. *Fair Miles: Recharting the Food Miles Map*. International Institute for Environment and Development (IIED) and Oxfam http://pubs.iied.org/pdfs/15516IIED.pdf.

40. Tracy Miles. 2006. "Concern Mounts over UK Soil Association Food Miles Plan." *Organic Pathways* http://www.organicpathways.co.nz/business /story/567.html.

41. International Trade Statistics http://www.intracen.org/tradsat and Trade Competitive Map http://www.intracen.org/appli1/TradeCom.

42. Catherine Riungu. 2005. "Why Kenya Dominates Export of Flowers to the EU market," *The East African* (February 21) http://www.theeastafrican.co .ke/business/-/2560/245890/-/7oem2tz/-/index.html.

43. James MacGregor and Bill Vorley. 2006. "Fair Miles?: The Concept of "Food Miles" through a Sustainable Development Lens." *Fresh Perspectives* No.1 (IIED) http://pubs.iied.org/11064IIED.html.

44. Freshinfo. 2008. "Airfreight Proposals Vilified by Industry." (April 8) http://www.agrifoodstandards.net/en/news/global/airfreight_proposals_vilified _by_industry.html.

45. James MacGregor and Bill Vorley. 2006. "Fair Miles?: The Concept of "Food Miles" through a Sustainable Development Lens." *Fresh Perspectives* No.1 (IIED) http://pubs.iied.org/11064IIED.html.

46. James MacGregor and MuyeyeChambwara. 2007. "Room to Move: 'Eco-logicalSpace" and Emissions Equity," *Fresh Perspective* No.14 (IIED) http:// pubs.iied.org/17023IIED.html.

47. Adrian Williams. 2007. *Comparative Study of Cut Roses for the British Market Produced in Kenya and the Netherlands*, Précis Report for World Flowers (Cranfield University) http://wwww.fairflowers.de/fileadmin/flp.de/Redaktion /Dokumente/Studien/Comparative_Study_of_Cut_Roses_Feb_2007.pdf.

48. Adrian Williams. 2007. *Comparative Study of Cut Roses for the British Market Produced in Kenya and the Netherlands*, Précis Report for World Flowers (Cranfield University http://wwww.fairflowers.de/fileadmin/flp.de/Redaktion /Dokumente/Studien/Comparative_Study_of_Cut_Roses_Feb_2007.pdf.

49. Peter W. Huber and Mark P. Mills. 2000. "How Cities Green the Planet." *City Journal* (Winter) http://www.city-journal.org/html/10_1_how_cities.html.

50. Ed Glaeser. 2011. *Triumph of the City. How our Greatest Invention Makes Us Richer, Smarter, Greener, Healthier, and Happier*. Penguin Press, p. 201.

51. David Owen. 2009. "Is Locavorism Good for the Environment?" http://*www.davidowen.net* (September 9) www.davidowen.nethttp://www.davidowen.net/david_owen/2009/09/is-locavorism-good-for-the-environment.html His more detailed argument can be found in David Owen. 2009. *Green Cities. Why Living Smaller, Living Closer, and Driving Less are the Keys to Sustainability.* Riverhead Books.

52. For a more detailed discussion of these issues, see Ed Glaeser. 2011. *Triumph of the City. How our Greatest Invention Makes Us Richer, Smarter, Greener, Healthier, and Happier.* Penguin Press.

53. That they are now denigrated as "sprawl" doesn't change the fact that they are as old as the first cities and, as such, much more ancient than racial problems, modern tax policies and the automobile.

54. For a more detailed examination of these issues, see Robert Bruegmann. 2006. *Sprawl, A Compact History.* University of Chicago Press.

55. Eric Jaffe. 2011. "If the World Lived Like New Yorkers, We'd All Fit Into Texas." *The Infrastructurist* July 22. http://www.infrastructurist.com/2011/07 /22/if-the-world-lived-like-new-yorkers-wed-all-fit-into-texas/.

Chapter 5

1. World Health Organization, *Glossary*—Food Security http://www.who .int/trade/glossary/story028/en/ For a broader discussion of the concept since its emergence in the early 1980s, see Simon Maxwell and Rachel Slater. 2003. "Food Policy Old and New." *Development Policy Review* 21 (5-6): 531–553. Much relevant and freely accessible material on the topic can be found on the Global Food Security website (U.K. Biotechnology and Biological Sciences Research Council) http://www.foodsecurity.ac.uk/.

2. Peter Garnsey. 1988. *Famine and Food Supply in the Graeco-Roman World: Responses to Risk and Crisis.* Cambridge University Press, p. 6 defines food shortages as a "short-term reduction in the amount of available foodstuffs, as indicated by rising food prices, popular discontent, hunger, in the worst cases bordering on starvation" and a famine as a "critical shortage of essential foodstuffs leading through hunger to starvation and a substantially increased mortality rate." More general treatments of the issue include Robert W. Fogel. 2004. *The Escape from Hunger and Premature Death, 1700–2100: Europe, America, and the Third World.* Cambridge University Press; Brian Murton. 2000. "Famine." In Kenneth F. Kiple and Kriemhild Coneè Ornelas. *The Cambridge World History of Food.* Cambridge University Press, pp. 1411–1427; and Cormac Ó Gráda. 2009. *Famine. A Short History.* Princeton University Press.

3. For a more detailed portrait of current hunger in underdeveloped economies, see the Global Hunger Index of the International Food Policy Research Institute http://www.ifpri.org/publication/2010-global-hunger-index.

4. For a concise survey of the issue, see Jere. R. Berhman, Harold Alderman and John Hoddinott. "Malnutrition and Hunger." In BjørnLomborg (ed.) 2004.*Global Crises, Global Solutions*. Cambridge University Press, pp. 363-420. The worldwide number of undernourished people is based on diverse statistical aggregates and, unavoidably, the underlying methodology has been the subject of various criticisms. For a discussion of some of these problems, see Derek Headey. 2011. "Was the Global Food Crisis Really a Crisis? Simulation Vs Self-Reporting." *Vox* (June 6) http://www.voxeu.org/index.php?q=node/6615.

5. As of this writing, major food price spikes occurred in 2008 and late 2010. It is probably fair to say that the former was primarily driven by very high oil prices that were made worse by policy decisions such as food export bans and the latter by high fuel prices and bad weather in the U.S., Australia, Russia and China. The *New York Times* now devotes a portion of its website to the issue http://topics.nytimes.com/top/reference/timestopics/subjects/f/food_prices/index.html?inline=nyt-classifier.

6. See, among others the *Declaration NGO Forum Rome Summit* +5 http://www.viacampesina.org/main_en/index2.php?option=com_content&do_pdf=1&id=418; Josh Brem-Wilson. 2010 The Reformed Committee on World Food Security. A Briefing Paper for Civil Society (Section 1) http://www.foodsovereignty.org/Portals/0/documenti%20sito/Home/News/reformed%20CFS_english.pdf; and the websites of organizations such as *La Via Campesina* http://viacampesina.org/en/ and the *International Planning Committee for Food Sovereignty* http://www.foodsovereignty.org/.

7. See, among others, Peter Rosset. 2008. "Food Sovereignty and the Contemporary Food Crisis." *Development* 51 (4): 460–463.

8. Standard statements to this effect are found in Oakland Institute. 2008. *The Food Crisis and Latin America*, Policy Brief http://media.oaklandinstitute.org/content/food-crisis-and-latin-america; and Frederic Mousseau. 2010. *The High Food Price Challenge: A Review of Responses to Combat Hunger*. Oakland Institute http://media.oaklandinstitute.org/sites/oaklandinstitute.org/files/high_food_prices_web_final.pdf.

9. Brian Murton. 2000. "Famine." In Kenneth F. Kiple and Kriemhild Coneè Ornelas. *The Cambridge World History of Food*. Cambridge University Press, p. 1412.

10 Of these factors, drought is generally thought to have been the most significant historically. See Cormac Ó Gráda. 2009. *Famine. A Short History*. Princeton University Press, pp.14–15.

11. Vaclav Smil. 2002. *China's Past, China's Future.* Routledge, p.72.

12. Frank Dikköter. 2010. *Mao's Great Famine: The History of China's Most Devastating Catastrophe, 1958–62.* Bloomsbury Publishing.

13. One such instance is described in chapter 5 of the Hebrew Bible's *Book of Nehemiah.* Various translations of the book can be found at http://www.early-jewishwritings.com/nehemiah.html.

14. George Dodd. 1856. *The Food of London: A sketch of the chief varieties, sources of supply, probable quantities, modes of arrival, processes of manufacture, suspected adulteration, and machinery of distribution, of the food for a community of two millions and a half*. Longman, Brown, Green and Longmans, p. 27. http://books .google.ca/books?id=wlUZAAAAYAAJ&source=gbs_navlinks_s.

15. William Wilson Hunter. 1871. *The Annals of Rural Bengal, fourth edition.* Smith, Elder and Co http://books.google.ca/books?id=yEoOAAAAQAAJ& dq=related:OCLC19227940&source=gbs_navlinks_s; .

16. Cormac Ó Gráda. 2009. *Famine. A Short History.* Princeton University Press, pp. 157 and 219.

17. Global Food Markets Group. 2010. *The 2007/08 Agricultural Price Spikes: Causes and Policy Implications.* DEFRA, pp. 14 and 90 http://archive.defra .gov.uk/foodfarm/food/pdf/ag-price100105.pdf.

18. Accounts of such migrations can be found in, among other places, William Wilson Hunter. 1871. *The Annals of Rural Bengal, fourth edition.* Smith, Elder and Co, p. 55 http://books.google.ca/books?id=yEoOAAAAQAAJ&dq=related :OCLC19227940&source=gbs_navlinks_s; and Peter Garnsey. 1988. *Famine and Food Supply in the Graeco-Roman World: Responses to Risk and Crisis.* Cambridge University Press.

19. Louis Torfs. 1839. *Fastes des calamités publiques survenues dans les Pays-Bas et particulièrement en Belgique, depuis les temps les plus reculés jusqu'à nos jours.* Casterman, p. 209 http://books.google.com/books?id=W1ZbAAAAQAAJ&hl=fr &source=gbs_navlinks_s.

20. Aristotle. 350 BCE. *Meteorology* Book II, Part 4 http://classics.mit.edu /Aristotle/meteorology.2.ii.html.

21. Saint Gregory of Nazianzus App. 382 AD. "On St. Basil the Great, Bishop of Caesarea" (translated by Leo P. McCauley, SJ), pp. 27-99. Reprint in 2004/1953 *The Fathers of the Church: Saint Gregory of Nazianzus and Saint-Ambrose, Funeral Orations.* The Catholic University Press of America, p. 57.

22. Benjamin Franklin. 1774. "Principles of Trade."Reprint in Jared Sparks (ed.) 1836. *The Works of Benjamin Franklin, volume 2.* Hilliard, Gray and Company: 383-409, p. 407 http://books.google.ca/books?id=IvE_AAAAYAAJ &source=gbs_navlinks_s.

23. Christian Wolmar. 2010. *Blood, Iron & Gold. How the Railroads Transformed the World.* PublicAffairs, p. 224.

24. For a complementary discussion of some of the issues raised in this section, see Thomas R. DeGregori. 2003. "The Anti-Monoculture Mania." *Butterflies and Wheels* (July 12) http://www.butterfliesandwheels.org/2003/the-anti-monoculture-mania/.

25. George W. Norton, Jeffrey Alwang and William A. Masters. 2010. *Economics of Agricultural Development. World Food Systems and Resource Use, Second Edition.* Routledge, p. 139.

26. Rachel Carson. 2002/1962. *Silent Spring (40th anniversary edition).* Houghton Mifflin Company, p. 10.

27. William A. Haviland and Gary Crawford. 2009. *Human Evolution and Prehistory,* Second Canadian edition, Nelson Education Ltd, pp. 315–316.

28. James Whorton. 1974. *Before Silent Spring. Pesticides and Public Health in Pre-DDT America.* Princeton University Press, p. 6.

29. Thomas R. DeGregori. 2003. "The Anti-Monoculture Mania." *Butterflies and Wheels* (July 12) http://www.butterfliesandwheels.org/2003/the-anti-monoculture-mania/.

30. Randy C. Ploetz. 2005. "Panama Disease: An Old Nemesis Rears Its Ugly Head. Part 1. The Beginnings of the Banana Export Trades." *APS-Plant Health Progress* (August) http://www.apsnet.org/publications/apsnetfeatures/Pages/PanamaDiseasePart1.aspx; and Adi B. Damania. 2008. "History, Achievements, and Current Status of Genetic Resources Conservation." *Agronomy Journal* 100: 9–21. Whether or not the taste of Gros Michel was incomparably superior to Cavendish as if often claimed by opponents of monocultures is not something we are able to ascertain. .

31. Jock Galloway. 2000. "Sugar." In Kenneth F. Kiple and Kriemhild Coneè Ornelas. 2000. *The Cambridge World History of Food.* Cambridge University Press http://www.cambridge.org/us/books/kiple/sugar.htm; and Adi B. Damania. 2008. "History, Achievements, and Current Status of Genetic Resources Conservation." *Agronomy Journal* 100: 9–21.

32. Jeffrey Granett, M. Andrew Walker, Laszlo Kocsis and Amir D. Omer. 2001. "Biology and Management of Grape Phylloxera." *Annual Review of Entomology* 41: 387–412.

33. For a personal account of the research that resulted in this solution, see Charlie Martinson. 2008 "Looking Back at Nearly Fifty Years at Iowa State." *Essays on the College of Agriculture's History,* Iowa State University http://www.ag.iastate.edu/coa150/martinson.php .

34. Adi B. Damania. 2008. "History, Achievements, and Current Status of Genetic Resources Conservation." *Agronomy Journal* 100: 9–21.

35. Adi B. Damania. 2008. "History, Achievements, and Current Status of Genetic Resources Conservation." *Agronomy Journal* 100: 9–21.

36. For an overview that illustrates in much detail how severe these diseases were a century ago, see United States Department of Agriculture (USDA, Bureau of Animal Industry). 1916. *Special Report on Diseases of Cattle, revised edition.* Government Printing Office http://www.archive.org/details/specialreporton d04unit.

37. See, among others, Joint FAO/IAEA. 2005. *History of Battle against Rinderpest* http://www-naweb.iaea.org/nafa/aph/stories/2005-rinderpest-history .html and the *FAO Global Rinderpest Eradication Programme* http://www.fao .org/ag/againfo/programmes/en/grep/home.html.

38. Alonzo Dorus Melvin and John R. Mohler. 1915. "Foot and Mouth Disease." *Bulletin of the United States Live Stock Sanitary Association* Live Stock World http://www.archive.org/details/footandmouthdise00melv .

39. Thomas Robert Malthus. 1798. *An Essay on the Principle of Population as It Affects the Future Improvement of Society, with Remarks on the Speculations of Mr. Godwin, M. Condorcet, and Other Writers.* J. Johnson http://www.econlib .org/library/Malthus/malPop.html.

40. Malthus is often unfairly portrayed in social science textbooks as essentially absolving economic systems, political structures and wealthy elites for the faith of the poor. See, for instance, Paul Robbins, John Hintz and Sarah A. Moore. 2010. *Environment and Society: A Critical Introduction.* Wiley-Blackwell, p. 15. For a more nuanced yet accessible discussion of the issue, see Morgan D. Rose. 2002. "In Defense of Malthus." *Library of Economics and Liberty—Teacher's Corner* http://www.econlib.org/library/Columns/Teachers/defendmalthus.html.

41. Kenneth Smith. 1952. "Some Observations on Modern Malthusianism." *Population Studies* 6 (1): 92–105.

42. Alfred Marshall. 1920/1890. Principles of Economics, McMillan & Co., Ltd, Book IV, Chapter 10 http://www.econlib.org/library/Marshall/marP24 .html#Bk.IV,Ch.X.

43. K. M. de Silva. 1981. *A History of Sri Lanka, Volume 1.* C Hurst & Company, chapter 21 http://books.google.ca/books?id=dByI_qil26YC&source=gbs _navlinks_s.

44. Frederic Mousseau. 2010. *The High Food Price Challenge: A Review of Responses to Combat Hunger.* Oakland Institute, p. 11 http://media.oaklandinsti-tute.org/sites/oaklandinstitute.org/files/high_food_prices_web_final.pdf.

45. One of us even wrote an academic paper on the absurdity of doing so. See Samuli Leppälä and Pierre Desrochers. 2010. "The Division of Labor Needs Not Imply Regional Specialization." *Journal of Economic Behavior and Organization* 74 (1–2): 137–147.

46. We visited the site in 2010. The Cahokia Mounds State Historic Site's website can be found at http://cahokiamounds.org/ .

47. Because our aim in the following paragraphs is limited to the importance of transportation and economic development as they relate to food security, we limit ourselves to generally agreed upon facts rather than more controversial political debates (e.g., the impact of the land tenure system on peasant behavior, British trade policy and the nature and the actual scope and impact of public relief efforts). Concise discussions and further references on the subject can be found in Ellen Messer. 2000. "Potatoes (White)." In Kenneth F. Kipple and Kriemhild Coneè Ornelas (eds). *The Cambridge World History of Food*. Cambridge University Presshttp://www.cambridge.org/us/books/kiple/potatoes.htm; and Cormac Ó Gráda. 2009. "Irish Famine" in Cutler J. Cleveland. *Encyclopedia of the Earth* http://www.eoearth.org/article/Irish_famine?topic=49465. For a more sophisticated analysis of the subjects dealt with in the following paragraphs, including the impact of the potato blight in other European countries, see Cormac Ó Gráda, Richard Paping and Eric Vanhaute. 2007. *When the Potato Failed: Causes and Effects of the 'Last' European Subsistence Crisis*. Brepols.

48. Joseph T. Leydon. 1995. "The Irish Provision Trade to the Caribbean, c. 1650–1780: An Historical Geography." PhD Thesis, University of Toronto; Bertie Mandelblatt. 2007. "A Transatlantic Commodity: Irish Salt Beef in the French Atlantic World." *History Workshop Journal* 63 (1): 18–47.

49. Alan L. Olmstead and Paul W. Rhode. 2008. *Creating Abundance. Biological Innovation and American Agricultural Development*. Cambridge University Press, p. 264.

50. Joseph Russell Smith. 1919. *The World's Food Resources*. H. Holt & Company, pp. 3–4 http://www.archive.org/details/worldsfoodresour00smituoft.

51. Denis Mack Smith. 1981. *Mussolini* . Alfred Knopf, p. 122. For a more detailed account of the "Battaglia del grano," see also Alexander Nützenadel. 2006. "Dictating Food: Autarchy, Food Provision, and Consumer Politics in Fascist Italy, 1922-1943." In Frank Trentmann and Flemming Just. 2006. *Food and Conflict in the Age of the Two World Wars*. Palgrave MacMillan, pp. 88–108.

52. Thomas Wieland. 2009. "Autarky and *Lebensraum*: The Political Agenda of Plant Breeding in Nazi Germany." *HOST: Journal of the History of Science and Technology* 3 http://johost.eu/?oid=3&act=&area=3&ri=1 .

53. Ludwig von Mises. 1949. *Human Action: A Treatise on Economics* Chapter 34: The Economics of War: War and Autarky http://mises.org/humanaction /chap34sec3.asp .

54. Adam Smith. 1776. *An Inquiry Into the Nature and Causes of the Wealth of Nations* Vol. 1, Book 4, Chapter 2: Of Restraints Upon the Importation from Foreign Countries of Such Goods as Can Be Produced at Home. http://oll

.libertyfund.org/?option=com_staticxt&staticfile=show.php%3Ftitle=237&chapter=212333&layout=html&Itemid=27 .

55. For much evidence in this respect, see Steven Pinker. 2011. *The Better Angels of our Nature*. Viking.

56. Dennis T. Avery. 2000. *Saving the Planet with Pesticides and Platics,* 2nd edition. Hudson Institute, pp. 383–384.

57. We are not concerned here with rationing schemes, price controls, regulations and subsidies. This list was mainly derived from Karl Brandt (with Otto Schiller and Franz Ahlgrimm). 1953. *Management of Agriculture and Food in the German-Occupied and Other Areas of Fortress Europe. A Study in Military Government)*. Stanford University Press; and Mancur Olson. 1963. *The Economics of the Wartime Shortage: A History of British Food Supplies in the Napoleonic War and in World Wars I and II*. Duke University Press.

58. This summary account is based on Karl Brandt. 1945. *The Reconstruction of World Agriculture*. W.W. Norton & Company, chapter 1; C. Paul Vincent. 1985. *The Politics of Hunger. The Allied Blockade of Germany, 1915–1919*. Ohio University Press, chapter 5; and Ernest H. Starling. 1920. "The Food Supply of Germany during the War." *Journal of the Royal Statistical Society* 83 (2): 225–254. Detailed figures as to the actual performance of German agriculture at the time are available in the latter reference.

59. Karl Brandt. 1945. *The Reconstruction of World Agriculture*. W.W. Norton & Company, p. 10.

60. Ernest H. Starling. 1920. "The Food Supply of Germany during the War." *Journal of the Royal Statistical Society* 83 (2): 225–254, p. 230.

61. Arturo Bruttini. 1923. *Uses of Waste Materials*. P. S. King & Son Ltd, pp. 36–37.

62. Ernest H. Starling. 1920. "The Food Supply of Germany during the War." *Journal of the Royal Statistical Society* 83 (2): 225–254, p. 233.

63. Ernest H. Starling. 1920. "The Food Supply of Germany during the War." *Journal of the Royal Statistical Society* 83 (2): 225–254, p. 244.

64. This section is based for the most part on Karl Brandt (with Otto Schiller and Franz Ahlgrimm). 1953. *Management of Agriculture and Food in the German-Occupied and Other Areas of Fortress Europe. A Study in Military Government* (Volume II of *Germany's Agricultural and Food Policies in World War II)*. Stanford University Press, chapter 20: Denmark, pp. 299–311.

65. Karl Brandt (with Otto Schiller and Franz Ahlgrimm). 1953. *Management of Agriculture and Food in the German-Occupied and Other Areas of Fortress Europe. A Study in Military Government* (Volume II of *Germany's Agricultural and Food Policies in World War II)*.Stanford University Press, pp. 300 and 310.

66. Based on Ingrid Henrikscn. 2006. "An Economic History of Denmark." In Robert Whaples (ed) *EH.Net Encyclopedia* http://eh.net/encyclopedia/article /henriksen.denmark and Karl Brandt. 1945. *The Reconstruction of World Agriculture.* W. W. Norton & Company Inc, p. 11.

67. Karl Brandt. 1945. *The Reconstruction of World Agriculture.* W.W. Norton & Company, pp. 271–273.

68. Karl Brandt (with Otto Schiller and Franz Ahlgrimm). 1953. *Management of Agriculture and Food in the German-Occupied and Other Areas of Fortress Europe. A Study in Military Government* (Volume II of *Germany's Agricultural and Food Policies in World War II).* Stanford University Press, p. 303.

69. Karl Brandt (Otto Schiller and Franz Ahlgrimm). 1953. *Management of Agriculture and Food in the German-Occupied and Other Areas of Fortress Europe. A Study in Military Government* (Volume II of *Germany's Agricultural and Food Policies in World War II).* Stanford University Press, p. 310.

70. For more detailed introductions to energy issues that expand on the themes developed in this section, see Robert L. Bradley and Richard W. Fulmer. 2004. *Energy: The Master Resource.* Kendall Hunt Publishing Company http:// www.instituteforenergyresearch.org/2008/07/18/energy-the-master-resource/ and Vaclav Smil. 2010. *Energy Myths and Realities: Bringing Science to the Energy Policy Debate.* AEI (American Enterprise Institute) Press.

71. See, for instance, World Energy Council. 2010. *2010 Survey of Energy Resources.* World Energy Council http://www.worldenergy.org/documents/ser _2010_report_1.pdf .

72. In short, bunker fuel is what is left once more valuable products such as jet fuel, gasoline and diesel have been extracted from petroleum. The only things denser than this fraction of petroleum are carbon black feedstock and bituminous residue used for paving roads and sealing roofs. Because of the high sulfur content of bunker fuel, container ships are often mandated to switch to less polluting "marine diesel" as they get closer to coastlines.

73. See, among others, Edward D. Porter. 1995. "Are We Running Out of Oil?" *Discussion Paper* #81, American Petroleum Institute http://www.gisceu .com/epdf_files/U30.PDF .

74. Amy Myers Jaffe. 2011. "The Americas, Not the Middle East, Will Be the World Capital of Energy." *Foreign Policy* (September–October) http://www.foreign policy.com/articles/2011/08/15/the_americas_not_the_middle_east_will_be _the_world_capital_of_energy?page=0,0 .

75. For an accessible survey of the technical literature on the role of international trade in mitigating the effects of climate change, see Gerald Nelson, Amanda Palazzo, Claudia Ringler, Timothy Sulser and MiroslavBatka. 2009. *The Role of International Trade in Climate Change Adaptation.* Issue Brief #4.

ICTSD (International Center for Trade and Sustainable Development) and IF&ATPC (International Food and Agricultural Policy Trade Council) http://www.agritrade.org/events/documents/IssueBrief4_web.pdf .

76. Discussions of previous generations' fears of human-induced climate change are found in Hans Von Storch and Nico Stehr. 2006. "Anthropogenic Climate Change: A Reason for Concern since the 18th Century and Earlier." *Geografiska Annaler: Series A, Physical Geography* 88(2): 107-113; and Mike Hulme. 2008. "The Conquering of Climate: Discourse of Fear and Their Dissolution." *Geographical Journal* 174 (1): 5–16. Human-produced carbon dioxide is about 3% of greenhouse gas concentrations if one exclude water vapor, and insignificant if water vapor is included as a greenhouse gas.

77. Dennis Avery. 2011. "Are Climate Models Lying about Food Too?" *Center for Global Food Issues—Latest News* (May 24) http://www.cgfi.org/2011/05/are-climate-models-lying-about-food-too-by-dennis-t-avery/ .

78. Food and Agriculture Organization of the United Nations (FAO). 2010. *The State of Food Insecurity in the World: Addressing Food Insecurity in Protracted Crises*. FAO http://www.fao.org/docrep/013/i1683e/i1683e.pdf On a global level, the rural poor are more than three times more numerous than urban poor and rural poverty is twice as prevalent as urban poverty.

79. FAO. 2009. *How to Feed the World in 2050*. FAO, p. 3 http://www.fao.org/fileadmin/templates/wsfs/docs/expert_paper/How_to_Feed_the_World _in_2050.pdf.

80. For a concise discussion of the issue in the context of recent agricultural trade liberalization negotiations, see Charlotte Hebebrand and Kristin Wedding. 2010. *The Role of Markets and Trade in Food Security*. Center for Strategic and International Studies http://csis.org/files/publication/100622_Hebebrand_Role-OfMarkets_WEB.pdf.

Chapter 6

1. "Sophistication" in this context refers to making impure and adulterating.

2. Benjamin Franklin. 1786. "The Art of Procuring Pleasant Dreams." Reprint in Jared Sparks (ed.) 1836. *The Works of Benjamin Franklin, volume 2*. Hilliard, Gray and Company: 171-176, p. 172 http://books.google.ca/books?id=IvE _AAAAYAAJ&source=gbs_navlinks_s.

3. For a much more elaborate discussion of the evolution of the size, shape and capability of the human body in the last three centuries, see Roderick Floud, Robert W. Fogel, Bernard Harris and Sok Chu Hong. 2011. *The Changing Body: Health, Nutrition and Human Development in the Western World since 1700*. Cambridge University Press and National Bureau of Economic Re-

search; and Timothy Cuff. 2004. "Historical Anthropometrics." In Robert Whaples (ed.) *EH.Net Encyclopedia* http://eh.net/encyclopedia/article/cuff .anthropometric.

4. Clifford Cook Furnas and Sparkle Moore Furnas. 1937. *Man, Bread and Destiny.* The Williams & Wilkins Company, p. xiii.

5. Frances and Joseph Gies. *Life in a Medieval Village.* Harper and Row, Publishers, pp. 96–98.

6. Brian Murton. 2000. "Famine." In Kenneth F. Kiple and Kriemhild-ConeèOrnelas. *The Cambridge World History of Food.* Cambridge University Press, pp. 1411–1427, p. 1412.

7. Lizzie Collingham. 2011. *The Taste of War. World War II and the Battle for Food.* Allen Lane, p. 18.

8. Gregory Clark. 2007. *A Farewell to Alms.* Princeton University Press, pp. 38–41.

9. Thomas R. DeGregori. 2002. *Bountiful Harvest: Technology, Food Safety and the Environment.* Cato Institute, p. 93.

10. Roderick Floud, Robert W. Fogel, Bernard Harris and Sok Chu Hong. 2011. *The Changing Body: Health, Nutrition and Human Development in the Western World since 1700.* Cambridge University Press and National Bureau of Economic Research, p. 1.

11. Matt Ridley. 2010. *The Rational Optimist. How Prosperity Evolves.* Harper-Collins Publishers, p. 18.

12. Jeffrey M. Pilcher. 2006. *Food in World History.* Routledge, p. 20.

13. Jeffrey M. Pilcher. 2006. *Food in World History.* Routledge, p. 55.

14. Roderick Floud, Robert W. Fogel, Bernard Harris and Sok Chu Hong. 2011. *The Changing Body: Health, Nutrition and Human Development in the Western World since 1700.* Cambridge University Press and National Bureau of Economic Research, p. 5.

15. Based on Patricia Cohen. 2011. "Technology Advances; Human Supersize." *New York Times* (April 26) http://www.nytimes.com/2011/04/27/books /robert-w-fogel-investigates-human-evolution.html?_r=1; and Gina Kolata. 2006. "So Big and Healthy Granpa Wouldn't Even Know You." *New York Times* (July 30) http://www.nytimes.com/2006/07/30/health/30age.html?ex=115500 9600&en=6342cb47f342cde2&ei=5070&emc=eta1.

16. Robert Rector and Rachel Sheffield. 2011. *Air Conditioning, Cable TV, and an Xbox: What Is Poverty in the United States Today?* Backgrounder #2575, Heritage Foundation http://www.heritage.org/Research/Reports/2011/07/What -is-Poverty.

17. Stephen L. Morgan. 2000. "Richer and Taller: Stature and Living Standards in China, 1979–1995." *China Journal* 44: 1–39.

18. Daniel Schwekendiek. 2009. "Height and Weight Differences between North and South Korea." *Journal of Biosocial Science* 41 (1): 51-55. For nearly three decades, the North Korean regime has been pursuing an autarkic policy known as Juche with disastrous results. For a concise introduction to the issue, see Jordan Weissmann. 2012. "How Kim Jong Il Starved North Korea." *The Atlantic* (December 20) http://www.theatlantic.com/business/archive/2011/12/how-kim-jong-il-starved-north-korea/250244/.

19. For the latest statistics and a more detailed discussion of the issue, see the "Obesity" webpage of the World Health Organization http://www.who.int/topics/obesity/en/.

20. Greg Easterbrook. 2004. *The Progress Paradox*, Random House, p. xiv.

21. John Page. 1880. "The Sources of Supply of the Manchester Fruit and Vegetable Markets." *Journal of the Royal Agricultural Society of England* 16 (2nd series), p. 482 http://books.google.ca/books?id=epoEAAAAYAAJ&source=gbs_navlinks_s.

22. Robert Paarlberg. 2010. *Food Politics: What Everyone Needs to Know*. Oxford University Press, p. 86.

23. Extracted from the pyrethrum flower, it was first used to kill body lice on people in the early nineteenth century and then household pests. It is very similar in its chemical composition to military nerve weapons.

24. For a more detailed discussion of the true nature and real shortcomings of organic agriculture, see Alex Avery. 2006. *The Truth about Organic Foods*. Henderson Communications.

25. Gary Blumenthal. 2011. "Creating False Markets." *World Perspectives, Inc* (February), p. 2. Blumenthal observes that the National Organic Act "was required in the U.S. because government regulators lacked a science-based rationale" for organic foods. Furthermore, unlike conventional food products which are regulated by USDA, EPA and FDA scientists, organic products are regulated by marketing specialists at the Agricultural Marketing Service and overseen by a National Organic Standards Board comprised predominantly of organic growers, handlers, organic certifiers, consumer representatives and environmentalists. The sole scientist on the committee makes her living by giving advice to an organic foods marketer.

26. From the U.K. Food Standards Agency press release for the study (July 29, 2009) available at http://www.food.gov.uk/news/newsarchive/2009/jul/organic The study is Alan D. Dangour, Sakhi K. Dodhia, Arabella Hayter, Elizabeth Allen, Karen Lock and Ricardo Uauy. 2009. "Nutrional Quality of Organic Foods: A Systematic Review." *American Journal of Clinical Nutrition* 93 (6): 680–685 http://www.ajcn.org/content/early/2009/07/29/ajcn.2009.28041.full.pdf +html .

27. For several quotes to this effect see Alex Avery. 2006. *The Truth about Organic Foods*. Henderson Communications, chapter 12. To give but one illustration taken from Avery's book, the Organic Trade Association stated over a decade ago that "Whenever you buy organic products, [you are telling] farmers, producers and retailers that you care about the earth, too, and that you want them to continue with their efforts to save the planet.".

28. OECD, 2010. *Obesity and the Economics of Prevention: Fit not Fat*. OECD http://www.oecd.org/document/31/0,3746,en_2649_37407_45999775_1_1_1_37407,00.html .

29. For more elaborate introductions to food safety issues in the American context, see the respective webpages of the USDA Food Safety and Inspection Service on "Food Safety Education" http://www.fsis.usda.gov/Food_Safety_Education/index.asp; the US Centers for Disease Control and Prevention on "Food Safety" http://www.cdc.gov/foodsafety/; the Partnership for Food Safety Education http://www.fightbac.org/; and the US FDA on "Food Safety" http://www.fda.gov/Food/FoodSafety/default.htm.

30. This is not to say that some herbal remedies were not effective in some cases, if only as painkillers or for their narcotic properties. It is also worth noting that some chimpanzees in Tanzania have been observed to consume more than a dozen different kinds of plants for their curative rather than nutritional properties.

31. Heather Pringle, 1998. "The Sickness of the Mummies." *Discover* 19 (12) (December), pp. 74–83.

32. The scientist is Dr. Tim Sly of the School of Occupational and Public Health, Ryerson University (Toronto, Canada).

33. Thomas R. DeGregori. 2001. *Bountiful Harvest: Technology, Food Safety and the Environment*. Cato Institute, p. 90. The molehill and mountain metaphor is borrowed from journalist William Kay's review of an earlier version of DeGregori's book on his personal website. William Kay. 2007. Review of Thomas R. DeGregori's *Agriculture and Modern Technology: A Defense* (Iowa State University Press, 2001) http://www.ecofascism.com/review10.html .

34. See Bruce N. Ames and Lois Swirsky Gold. 1993. "Environmental Pollution and Cancer: Some Misconceptions." In Kenneth R. Foster, David E. Bernstein, and Peter W. Huber. *Phantom Risk: Scientific Inference and the Law*. MIT Press, p. 157.

35. Most (58%) illnesses with known agents were caused by norovirus, followed by nontyphoidal *Salmonella* spp. (11%), *Clostridium perfringens* (10%), and *Campylobacter* spp. (9%). Leading causes of hospitalization were nontyphoidal *Salmonella* spp. (35%), norovirus (26%), *Campylobacter* spp. (15%), and *Toxoplasma gondii* (8%). Leading causes of death were nontyphoidal *Salmonella* spp.

(28%), *T. gondii* (24%), *Listeria monocytogenes* (19%), and norovirus (11%). 80% of foodborne illness are attributed to unspecified agents, but again these have very little to do with herbicide and pesticide residues. For more detail, see Centers for Disease Control and Prevention. "Estimates of Foodborne Illness In the United States: 2011 Estimate Findings" http://www.cdc.gov/foodborne burden/2011-foodborne-estimates.html; Elaine Scallan, Robert M. Hoekstra, Frederick J. Angulo, Robert V. Tauxe, Marc-Alain Widdowson, Sharon L. Roy, Jeffery L. Jones, and Patricia M. Griffin. 2011. "Foodborne Illness Acquired in the United States—Major Pathogens» *Emerging Infectious Diseases* 17 (1) http://www.cdc.gov/eid/content/17/1/7.htm#1; Elaine Scallan, Patricia M. Griffin, Frederick J. Angulo, Robert V. Tauxe, and Robert M. Hoekstra. 2011. "Foodborne Illness Acquired in the United States—Unspecified Agents." *Emerging Infectious Diseases* 17 (1) http://www.cdc.gov/eid/content/17/1/16 .htm.

36. Thomas R. DeGregori. 2001. *Bountiful Harvest: Technology, Food Safety and the Environment*. Cato Institute, chapters 3 and 4.

37. For a brief introduction to the issue, see the CDC entry on raw milk at http://www.cdc.gov/foodsafety/rawmilk/raw-milk-index.html.

38. For a brief history of advances in this respect in the United States in the 20th century, see EPA et al. 1999. "Achievements in Public Health, 1900-1999: Safer and Healthier Foods." *Morbidity and Mortality Weekly Reports* (Centers for Disease Control and Prevention) 48 (40): 905–913 http://www.cdc.gov /mmwr/preview/mmwrhtml/mm4840a1.htm.

39. Steve Ettlinger. 2007. *Twinkie, Deconstructed*. Hudson Street Press, pp. 129–130.

40. The main approach in this respect is known as Hazard Analysis and Critical Control Points (HACCP) See the U.S. FDA webpage on this approach at http://www.fda.gov/food/foodsafety/hazardanalysiscriticalcontrolpointshaccp /default.htm.

41. Dennis Avery. 2010. "Why Tolerate Deadly Food Bacteria?" Hudson Institute (October 5) http://www.hudson.org/index.cfm?fuseaction=publication _details&id=7398&pubType=FoodPolicy.

42. Richard Williams, Robert L. Scharff, and David Bieler. 2010. "Food Safety in the 21st Century." *Mercatus on Policy* no. 71 (February) http://mercatus .org/sites/default/files/publication/MOP71_Food%20Safety_web.pdf.

43. From the Jensen Farms website at http://www.jensenfarms.com/index .cfm/pages/view/id/8/page/ROCKY-FORD-CANTALOUPE .

44 Source: US FDA. 2011. Information on the Recalled Jensen Farms Whole Cantaloupes, (October 21) http://www.fda.gov/Food/FoodSafety/CORENet-work/ucm272372.htm .

45. Jim Prevor. 2011. "The Cantaloupe Crisis: The Truth that Dares not Speak Its Name. The Priority can be Safe or the Priority can be Local, but It cannot be Both." *Perishable Pundit* (October 4) http://www.perishablepundit.com/index.php?article=2664.

46. Leigh Goessl. 2011. "Organic Shell Eggs Recalled Due to Salmonella." *Digital Journal* (October 24) http://digitaljournal.com/article/313273.

47. This paragraph was adapted from Rod Smith. 2010. "Cage Housing Tie to Egg Recall Shorts Truth." *Feedstuffs* (August 26). http://www.feedstuffs.com/ME2/Segments/NewsHeadlines/Print.asp?Module=News&id=769A8979 B98349AE8CEAB44119D8E3FF .

48. D. Worsfold, P.M Worsfold and C.J. Griffith. 2004. "An Assessment of Food Safety and Hygiene at Farmers' Markets." *International Journal of Environmental Health Research* 14 (2): 109-119, p. 109.

49. Uwe Spiekermann. 2010. "Dangerous Meat? German-American Quarrels over Pork and Beef, 1870-1900." *Bulletin of the German Historical Institute* 46 (Spring): 93–110 p. 99.

50. *Gardener's Chronicle, Horticultural Trade Journal*, Volume 78, October 17, 1925. The *Garderner's Chronicle* was a British publication that has since been incorporated in *Horticulture Week*. Quoted in Ruth deForest Lamb. 1936. *American Chamber of Horrors. The Truth about Food and Drugs.* Farrar & Rinehart, p. 207.

51. Ronald Bailey. 2006. "Don't Panic over Spinach." *Reason.com* (September 29) http://reason.com/archives/2006/09/29/dont-panic-over-spinach .

52. Robert Paalberg. 2010. "Attention Whole Food Shoppers." *Foreign Policy* (May/June) http://www.foreignpolicy.com/articles/2010/04/26/attention_whole _foods_shoppers?page=full.

Chapter 7

1. See, among others, Thomas Hudson Middleton. 1923. *Food Production in War.* Clarendon Press, p. 324.

2. Katherine Kemp, Andrea Insch, David K. Holdsworth and John G. Knight. 2010. "Food Miles: Do UK Consumers Actually Care?" *Food Policy* 35 (6): 504-513.

3. See, among others, Chantal Blouin, Jean-Frédéric Lemay, Kausar Ashraf, Jane Imai and Lazar Konforti. 2009. *Local Food Systems and Public Policy: A Review of the Literature.* Équiterre and The Center for Trade Policy and Law (Carleton University) http://www.ctpl.ca/publications/occasional-papers/local-food -systems-and-public-policy-review-literature; American Planning Association. 2007. *Policy Guide on Community and Regional Food Planning.* American Planning Association http://www.planning.org/policy/guides/adopted/food.htm; and

Wayne Caldwell, AnnelizaCollett, Therese Ludlow, Ian Sinclair and Jenny Whitehead. 2011. *Planning and Food Security within the Commonwealth: Discussion Paper.* Commonwealth Association of Planners http://www.commonwealth-planners.org/papers/food.pdf.

4. For a brief introduction to this issue, see Robert L. Schuettinger and Eamonn F. Butler. 1979. *Forty Centuries of Wage and Price Controls: How Not to Fight Inflation.* The Heritage Foundation http://mises.org/books/fortycenturies.pdf Unless otherwise specified, the illustrations discussed in this sub-section were taken from this source.

5. For a more detailed discussion of these measures from a sympathetic perspective, see Frederic Mousseau. 2010. *The High Food Price Challenge: A Review of Responses to Combat Hunger.* Oakland Institute http://media.oaklandinstitute.org/sites/oaklandinstitute.org/files/high_food_prices_web_final.pdf See also FAO (Trade and Markets Division). 2009. *The State of Agricultural Commodity Markets. High Food Prices and the Food Crisis—Experiences and Lessons Learned.* FAO http://www.fao.org/docrep/012/i0854e/i0854e00.htm.

6. OECD. 2010. Agricultural Policies in OECD Countries at a Glance. OECD. http://www.oecd.org/dataoecd/17/0/45539870.pdf For a much more elaborate discussion of the issue, see Kym Anderson (editor). 2009. *Distortions to Agricultural Incentives: A Global Perspective, 1955-2007.* Palgrave Macmillan and World Bank.

7. E. C. Pasour, Jr.'s and Randall R. Rucker. 2005. *Plowshares and Pork Barrels: The Political Economy of Agriculture.* The Independent Institute, p. 308.

8. Robert Paarlberg. 2010. *Food Politics. What Everyone Needs to Know.* Oxford University Press, p. 86.

9. For the European Union's official stance on the CAP and description of recent reforms, see http://ec.europa.eu/agriculture/capexplained/index_en .htm.

10. Caroline Boin. 2008. "Free Trade can Stop World Food Crisis turning into Tragedy." *The Scotsman* (April 19) http://thescotsman.scotsman.com/top-stories/Free-trade-can-stop-world.3999431.jp.

11. Michael Pollan. 2008. "Farmer in Chief." *New York Times Magazine* (October 9) http://www.nytimes.com/2008/10/12/magazine/12policy-t.html.

12. For a discussion of the recent evolution of national food reserves, see Global Food Markets Group. 2010. *The 2007/08 Agricultural Price Spikes: Causes and Policy Implications.* DEFRA http://archive.defra.gov.uk/foodfarm/food/pdf /ag-price100105.pdf.

13. See, among others, Robert Bailey. 2011. *Growing a Better Future: Food Justice in a Resource-Constrained World.* Oxfam International, p. 46 http://www .oxfam.org/en/grow/reports/growing-better-future.

14. IRIN (UN Office for the Coordination of Humanitarian Affairs). 2008. "Niger: Are Cereal Banks the Best Option to Fight Hunger?" *IRIN Humanitarian News and Analysis* (October 16) http://www.irinnews.org/Report.aspx?ReportId=80953.

15. For a discussion of strategic grain reserves between the early 1970s and mid-1990s, see John Lynton-Evans. 1997. *Strategic Grain Reserves - Guidelines for their establishment, management and operation.* FAO Agricultural Services Bulletin—126 http://www.fao.org/docrep/w4979e/w4979e00.htm.

16. Evan D. G. Fraser and Andrew Rimas. 2010. *Empires of Food. Feast, Famine, and the Rise and Fall of Civilizations.* Free Press, pp. 66–67.

17. The Food Corporation of India is a government entity charged with providing effective price support to farmers, distributing foodgrains to the public and maintaining buffer stocks of food grains to ensure food security. See its website at http://fciweb.nic.in/.

18. Rupashree Nanda. 2010. "One-Third of India's Food Reserves Left to Rot." *CNN-IBN Live* (July 25) http://ibnlive.in.com/news/onethird-of-indias-food-reserves-left-to-rot/127434-3.html.

19. See, among others, William Harte. 1764. *Essays on Husbandry.* W. Frederick, p. 116 http://books.google.com/books?id=DaI1AAAAMAAJ&source=gbs_navlinks_s; Anne Robert Jacques Turgot. 1770. "Seventh Letter [on the Grain Trade]." In David Gordon (editor). 2011. *The Turgot Collection. Writings, Letters and Speeches of Anne Robert Jacques Turgot, Baron de Laune.* Ludwig von Mises Institute, p. 240 http://mises.org/books/turgot_collection_turgot.pdf; and Edmund Burke. 1840/1795. *Thoughts and Details on Scarcity.* F. and C. Rivington, p. 28 http://books.google.com/books?id=DUgJA AAAQAAJ&hl=fr&output=text&source=gbs_navlinks_s For a more recent overview, see Cormac Ó Gráda. 2009. *Famine. A Short History.* Princeton University Press.

20. Louis Torfs. 1839. *Fastes des calamités publiques survenues dans les Pays-Bas et particulièrement en Belgique, depuis les temps les plus reculés jusqu'à nos jours.* Casterman, pp. 238–239 http://books.google.com/books?id=W1ZbAAA AQAAJ&hl=fr&source=gbs_navlinks_s For recent historical scholarship on the effectiveness of some past European and Chinese granaries, see, among others, Olivier Zeller. 1989. "Politique frumentaire et rapports sociaux à Lyon, 1772-1776." *Histoire, Économie et Société* 8 (2): 249–286 http://www.persee.fr/web/revues/home/prescript/article/hes_0752-5702_1989_num_8_2_2368; and Carol H. Shiue. 2004. "Local Granaries and Central Government Disaster Relief: Moral Hazard and Intergovernmental Finance in Eighteenth and Nineteenth Century China." *Journal of Economic History* 64 (1): 100–124.

21. William Harte. 1764. *Essays on Husbandry*. W. Frederick, p. 51 (adapted to modern English by the writers) http://books.google.com/books?id=DaI1A AAAMAAJ&source=gbs_navlinks_s.

22. Joachim von Braun and Maximo Torero. 2009. *Implementing Physical and Virtual Food Reserves to Protect the Poor and Prevent Market Failure*. IFPRI Policy Brief 10 http://www.ifpri.org/sites/default/files/publications/bp010.pdf.

23. See the IATP's Global Observatory on Food Reserves http://www .tradeobservatory.org/issue_foodSecurity.cfm.

24. STWR Brief. 2009. *Global Food Reserves—Framing the Context for a New Multilateralism* (October) http://www.stwr.org/food-security-agriculture/global -food-reserves-a-key-step-towards-ending-hunger.html.

25. Grassroots International and National Family Farm Coalition. 2008. *An Open Letter to Congress on the Need for Strategic Grain Reserves* (April 28) http://www.grassrootsonline.org/news/articles/open-letter-congress-need -strategic-grain-reserves.

26. For a more detailed introduction and criticism of these various forms of government-sponsored food reserves, see Brian Wright. 2009. *International Grain Reserves and Other Instruments to Address Volatility in Grain Markets*. World Bank Policy Research Working Paper 5028, World Bank http://econ.world bank.org/external/default/main?pagePK=64165259&theSitePK=477916&piPK =64165421&menuPK=64166093&entityID=000158349_20090825154655; and Global Food Markets Group. 2010. *The 2007/08 Agricultural Price Spikes: Causes and Policy Implications*. DEFRA http://archive.defra.gov.uk/foodfarm/food /pdf/ag-price100105.pdf.

27. FAO (Trade and Markets Division). 2009. *The State of Agricultural Commodity Markets. High Food Prices and the Food Crisis—Experiences and Lessons Learned*. FAO http://www.fao.org/docrep/012/i0854e/i0854e00.htm; See also, among others, Siddharta Mitra and Tim Josling. 2009. *Agricultural Export Restrictions: Welfare Implications and Trade Disciplines*. IPC Position Paper Agricultural and Rural Development Policy Series. International Food and Agricultural Trade Policy Council http://www.agritrade.org/documents/ExportRestrictions_final.pdf.

28. Cormac Ó Gráda. 2009. *Famine. A Short History*.Princeton University Press, p. 138.

29. William Harte. 1764. *Essays on Husbandry*. W. Frederick, p. 52 (adapted to modern English by the writers) http://books.google.com/books?id=DaI1AA AAMAAJ&source=gbs_navlinks_s According to the historian Peter Garnsey, Athens and Rome were the exception rather the rule in the Ancient World, at least inasmuch as the rulers of other cities did not object to food exports in good times as it brought them increased revenues. Peter Garnsey. 1988. *Famine and*

Food Supply in the Graeco-Roman World: Responses to Risk and Crisis. Cambridge University Press, chapter 5.

30. Arthur Young. 1792. *Travels in France during the Years 1787,1788, 1789.* George Bell and Sons, chapter 2 (unpaginated version available at http://www.econlib.org/library/YPDBooks/Young/yngTFCover.html).

31. Benjamin Franklin. 1774. "Principles of Trade." Reprint in Jared Sparks (ed.) 1836. *The Works of Benjamin Franklin, volume 2.* Hilliard, Gray and Company: 383-409, pp. 407-409 http://books.google.ca/books?id=IvE_AAAAYAAJ &source=gbs_navlinks_s.

32. See, among others, Siddharta Mitra and Tim Josling. 2009. *Agricultural Export Restrictions: Welfare Implications and Trade Disciplines.* IPC Position Paper Agricultural and Rural Development Policy Series. International Food and Agricultural Trade Policy Council http://www.agritrade.org/documents/Export Restrictions_final.pdf .

33. Quoted in Bernard Lugongo. 2010. "Debate on Food Export Ban Continues." *The Citizen* (November 29) http://thecitizen.co.tz/business/13-local -business/5957-debate-on-food-export-ban-continues.html.

34. Global Food Markets Group. 2010. *The 2007/08 Agricultural Price Spikes: Causes and Policy Implications.* DEFRA, p.11 http://archive.defra.gov.uk/food farm/food/pdf/ag-price100105.pdf ; See also Derek Headey. 2011. "Rethinking the Global Food Crisis: The Role of Trade Shocks." *Food Policy* 36 (2): 136-146.

35. E-mail correspondence with Gary Blumenthal of World Perspectives, Inc., December 2011.

36. Similar schemes were also in existence for a long time in advanced economies ranging from Canada to New Zealand.

37. William O. Jones. 1987. "Food-Crop Marketing Boards in Africa." *The Journal of Modern African Studies* 25 (3): 375–402.

38. For a more detailed survey of the impact of commodity marketing boards on less developed economies, see Lee R. Martin. 1991. *A Survey of Agricultural Economics Literature, volume 4: Agriculture in Economic Development 1940s— 1990s.* University of Minnesota Press, especially pp. 44–48 .

39. Edward R. Cook, Kevin J. Anchukaitis, Brendan M. Buckley, Rosanne D. D'Arrigo, Gordon C. Jacoby and William E. Wright. 2010. "Asian Monsoon Failure and Megadrought during the Last Millennium." *Science* 328 (5977): 486–489.

40. Robert L. Schuettinger and Eamonn F. Butler. 1979. *Forty Centuries of Wage and Price Controls: How Not to Fight Inflation.* The Heritage Foundation, pp. 33-34 http://mises.org/books/fortycenturies.pdf.

41. William Wilson Hunter. 1871. *The Annals of Rural Bengal, fourth edition.* Smith, Elder and Co, pp. 43–46 http://books.google.ca/books?id=yEoOA AAAQAAJ&dq=related:OCLC19227940&source=gbs_navlinks_s.

42. Mark Bittman. 2011. "Don't End Agricultural Subsidies, Fix Them." *Opiniator (The New York Times)* (March 1) http://opinionator.blogs.nytimes.com /2011/03/01/dont-end-agricultural-subsidies-fix-them/ .

43. Adam Smith. 1776. *An Inquiry Into the Nature and Causes of the Wealth of Nations,* Volume II, Book 4, Chapter 8, Conclusion of the Mercantile System http://oll.libertyfund.org/?option=com_staticxt&staticfile=show.php%3Ftitle=200&chapter=217484&layout=html&Itemid=27 .

44. Fonterra's website can be found at http://www.fonterra.com/wps /wcm/connect/fonterracom/fonterra.com For assessments of the environmental impacts of agricultural trade liberalization in New Zealand, see OECD. 1996. *The Environmental Effect of Removing Agricultural Subsidies: Case Study of New Zealand.* OECD COM/AGR/CA/ENV/EPOC (96), p. 119 and Willie Smith and Hayden Montgomery. 2003. "Revolution or Evolution? New Zealand Agriculture since 1984." *GeoJournal* 59 (2): 107–118 for a somewhat more critical analysis.

45. Eutrophication is the process through which water bodies receive excess nutrients that stimulate excessive plant growth.

46. See, among others, Elinor Ostrom. 1999. "Coping with Tragedies of the Commons." *Annual Review of Political Science* 2: 493-535; and Elinor Ostrom. 2000. "Private and Common Property Rights." In Boudewijn Bouckaert and Gerrit De Geest (eds.). *Encyclopedia of Law and Economics.* Edward Elgar, pp. 332–379.

47. Peter M. Kjellingbro and Maria Skotte. 2005. *Environmentally Harmful Subsidies. Linkages between Subsidies, the Environment and the Economy.* Environmental Assessment Institute http://imv.net.dynamicweb.dk/ Admin/Public/ Download.aspx?file=files/filer/rapporter/diverse/harmful_subsidies.pdf; OECD (Organisation for Economic Co-operation and Development). 2006. *Subsidy Reform and Sustainable Development: Economic, Environmental and Social Aspects.* OECD. Partly available at http://www.oecd.org/document/1/0,2340,en 26493742 5365 6691311137425,00.html.

Conclusion

1. The "great grandmother" line was made most famous by Michael Pollan in his various writings, such as in his In Defense of Food http://michaelpollan .com/books/in-defense-of-food/ While neither of us has met any of our great grandmothers, one of our grandmothers was rather fond of processed foods and the availability of fresh produce in the middle of the Canadian winter.

2. To give but one case among a multitude of others, the mongooses once brought to Hawaii to control imported rats quickly developed a taste for native

birds. Of course, sometimes events played out the other way, with a local pest discovering a particular fondness for an imported crop. A case in point is the Colorado potato beetle, an insect native to the Rocky Mountains which had previously thrived on the leaves of local wild plants.

3. Software specifically designed to help manage organic Community Supported Agriculture (CSA) schemes have long been part of the food activist's toolkit while a new "locavore" iPhone application had become available as we were beginning to write this book.

4. Paul Johnson. 2007. *Intellectuals: From Marx and Tolstoy to Sartre and Chomsky*, HarperCollins, p. 391.

5. Winston Churchill. 1946. *Address to Westminster College* http://www.history place.com/speeches/ironcurtain.htm.

INDEX

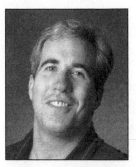

Pierre Desrochers is an associate professor of geography at the University of Toronto who writes frequently on economic development, globalization, energy, and transportation issues. He was a senior research fellow at the Center for the History of Political Economy at Duke University.

Hiroko Shimizu majored in history at Gakushin University and holds a master's of international public policy from Osaka University.

Desrochers and Shimizu have both been research fellows of the Property and Environment Research Center in Bozeman, Montana, and the Institute for Policy Studies at Johns Hopkins University.

PublicAffairs is a publishing house founded in 1997. It is a tribute to the standards, values, and flair of three persons who have served as mentors to countless reporters, writers, editors, and book people of all kinds, including me.

I.F. STONE, proprietor of *I. F. Stone's Weekly*, combined a commitment to the First Amendment with entrepreneurial zeal and reporting skill and became one of the great independent journalists in American history. At the age of eighty, Izzy published *The Trial of Socrates*, which was a national bestseller. He wrote the book after he taught himself ancient Greek.

BENJAMIN C. BRADLEE was for nearly thirty years the charismatic editorial leader of *The Washington Post*. It was Ben who gave the *Post* the range and courage to pursue such historic issues as Watergate. He supported his reporters with a tenacity that made them fearless and it is no accident that so many became authors of influential, best-selling books.

ROBERT L. BERNSTEIN, the chief executive of Random House for more than a quarter century, guided one of the nation's premier publishing houses. Bob was personally responsible for many books of political dissent and argument that challenged tyranny around the globe. He is also the founder and longtime chair of Human Rights Watch, one of the most respected human rights organizations in the world.

·   ·   ·

For fifty years, the banner of Public Affairs Press was carried by its owner Morris B. Schnapper, who published Gandhi, Nasser, Toynbee, Truman, and about 1,500 other authors. In 1983, Schnapper was described by *The Washington Post* as "a redoubtable gadfly." His legacy will endure in the books to come.

Peter Osnos, *Founder and Editor-at-Large*